# Archery, Projectiles, and Canoeing

# Archery, Projectiles, and Canoeing

## Secrets of the Forest: Volume 4

Written and illustrated by Mark Warren

 With more than 150 original hands-on activities

Guilford, Connecticut

An imprint of The Rowman & Littlefield Publishing Group, Inc.
4501 Forbes Blvd., Ste. 200
Lanham, MD 20706
www.rowman.com

Distributed by NATIONAL BOOK NETWORK

Photo credits: Betty Litsey, Dan McMahill, Bard Wrisley, Brad David, Hugh Norris, Vered Kleinberger, and Susan Warren

Illustrations by Mark Warren

British Library Cataloguing in Publication Information available

The first volume in this series was catalogued by the Library of Congress as follows:

Names: Warren, Mark, 1947- author, illustrator.
Title: Wild plants and survival lore : secrets of the forest, volume 1 /
written and illustrated by Mark Warren.
Other titles: Secrets of the forest, volume 1
Description: First Lyons Press edition. | Guilford, Connecticut : Lyons Press, 2020. | Includes bibliographical references and index. | Summary: "In this first volume of his Secrets of the Forest series, nature educator Mark Warren explains how to identify and use 100 wild plants as food, medicine, and craft. He also covers 'primitive' survival skills, from building a shelter, to purifying water, making tools, traps, and snares. Features over 200 hands-on activities."— Provided by publisher.
Identifiers: LCCN 2019044228 (print) | LCCN 2019044229 (ebook) | ISBN 9781493045556 (paperback) | ISBN 9781493045563 (epub)
Subjects: LCSH: Wilderness survival. | Plants, Edible.
Classification: LCC GV200.5 .W37 2020 (print) | LCC GV200.5 (ebook) | DDC 613.6/9—dc23
LC record available at https://lccn.loc.gov/2019044228
LC ebook record available at https://lccn.loc.gov/2019044229
ISBN 978-1-4930-4561-7 (paper : alk. paper)
ISBN 978-1-4930-4562-4 (electronic)

To Doug Berg who led so many young souls to the trails

and to the waters of the North Country


And to Betty Litsey who did the same in the South

# Contents

# Foreword

When I met Mark Warren almost a decade ago amongst the trees at Lookout Creek, I had no idea how his outdoor program would change not only my students' lives, but my own life in astounding ways. At our school, we support the idea of getting our students outside of their comfort zone to grow in ways that a traditional classroom cannot provide. Our monthly Trailwise outdoor education program with Mark invites students and teachers to walk in the shoes of the Native Americans before us and learn ways that we can respect and protect the natural world in which we live.

In Mark's classes, students are encouraged to slow down and use senses that are unique to being in nature, senses that require them to discover the quiet sounds and the abundance of life hidden within the forest. Mark encourages the students and teachers to focus on small signs in nature that can teach us so much about how Native Americans survived off of the land. Whether we are learning how to construct a shelter, find edible and medicinal plants, make rope, build a fire, stalk animals for observations, learn their tracks, or see the forest through their eyes, Mark is guiding our students and teachers in ways that will grow a passion for nature—a feat that cannot be accomplished within the walls of a classroom.

As a teacher and a parent, I feel that Mark Warren's nature and survival skills classes truly teach the "whole child." Not every student loves sports or excels in academics, but those students might just find their true passion and talents hidden in nature. I feel blessed that we have been given the amazing opportunity to learn primitive skills under the guidance of Mark. His engaging and meaningful lessons are ones that students and teachers will cherish and be eager to share with their own families.

—Randi Schlosser
Teacher/Curriculum Coordinator
St. Peter's Episcopal School, Chattanooga, Tennessee

# Introduction

There are two reasons that this last book of my *Secrets of the Forest* series is my favorite: Archery and canoeing have intertwined with my soul to become two of the most precious and defining parts of my life. So, in essence, I have saved the best for last.

Both arts originally came to me in the same arcane way. In each instance I was alone in the forest without a thought relating to either skill. One late afternoon—back in 1969—on a self-imposed "survival trip," I stood by the Chattooga River staring out over a dark emerald pool, a smooth tongue of water pouring into it from an upstream level three or four feet higher. The little falls made a steady rending sound as it broke into the lower pool's surface—a liquid song containing both treble and bass parts, a steady roar that filled the air in the gorge like a never-ending exhalation from deep in the Earth. Wafting from that breath, it seemed, was every secret of the forest that had existed since the beginning of time. I looked out at the moving water, and, unexpectedly, after days of not hearing my own voice, I spoke aloud.

"I should be in a canoe."

No truer words have I spoken. From that day on, I began a mission of riverine passion, exploring hundreds of streams by canoe from the Chattooga in Georgia, west to the Rio Grande and Colorado River, north to Minnesota's St. Croix and the Deerfield in Connecticut, and south to the mysterious blackwater rivers of northern Florida. Even in Georgia alone, one cannot cover all the creeks and rivers in one lifetime. But I tried.

A nearly identical revelation hit me one day as I walked a long open lane among the great white pines standing on the floodplain of Warwoman Creek. Again, without any premonition that I would do so, I spoke aloud.

"I should be shooting a bow," I said. And so it began.

# PART 1

# The Art of Archery and Other Projectiles

# Author's Note

The first simple projectiles were sticks and stones. Because the throwing stick is covered in Volume 1 of this series, we shall now address the latter. The compact heft of a rock must have quickly suggested its killing or maiming potential, but as a weapon it was most effective when affixed to the end of a handle. So attached it was a fearsome skull-cracker (the war-club), but to use it for hunting required one to stalk within reach of an animal. This proved to be, by and large, impractical. A "hunting" rock needed to travel through the air. And so, at first, man threw stones.

The first leap in stone-throwing technology came with the sling. From there the story evolved to modifying a stone to a sleek, sharp point and lashing it to a stick. Such a spear was originally a long-handled stabbing implement, until some unknown deft innovator(s) learned to send it sailing through the air javelin-style along a steady trajectory.

This tool was further improved by a mechanical advantage that might be said to emulate the architecture of a grasshopper's powerful rear leg. The atlatl—a wooden spear-launcher—had the effect of extending the length of the thrower's "arm" to provide more thrust. Eventually, a smaller spear came along to make a quantum leap, this one powered by the energy stored inside a stick that was bent out of shape by a taut string.

Surpassing the spear, the bow and arrow offered more distance and less chance for human error. However, as you will see, the delicate technique for releasing the string is the deciding factor in an archer's level of expertise and consistency. Archery epitomizes the marriage of strength and grace. Its proper technique is not innate. In fact, its secrets of operation seem so arcane as to elude all who pick up a bow for the first time without the benefit of instruction.

The blowgun is in a category of its own. It was not employed in warfare but used to hunt small animals like squirrels, rabbits, and birds. Invented in the southeastern corner of North America, it spread to Central and South America. Its uniqueness lies in its power source: a sudden expulsion of breath.

All but two of the weapons covered in this book held their glory days as "top-of-the-line" airborne implements of hunting and/or warfare, each in its own time. The exceptions are the knife and tomahawk. Both were highly valued tools and had their essential places in history—but not as projectiles . . . especially in warfare. (It was ill-advised to hand over one's weapon to an enemy, even if by a hostile throw.)

Part of this omission was due to the weapon's composition. What sane crafts-man would hurl his stone axe or knife at anything? Too much work went into the production of a fine edge. Even so, it is almost certain that men were sometimes forced to throw a knife or hand-axe out of desperation. If an enemy eyed you over the sights of a rifle, wouldn't you?

With the advent of knives and hawks forged from steel, it was inevitable that they would be thrown. Anyone who handles metal knives long enough will eventually yield to the compelling urge to throw one, trying to stick it in a stump. Once one has success at it, he will likely repeat it. In fact, it can become a passion. This I know, because I began my "knife-throwing career" when I was nine years old, secretly experimenting with all things with a sharp point from my mother's kitchen. More than six decades later I continue to feel that same craving to sink a blade into a target.

The novelty of throwing edged steel did emerge among the mountain men of the Rockies in the eighteenth and nineteenth centuries. At an annual rendezvous—the social event of their year—contests of knife- and hawk-throwing provided one more arena for taking bets and boosting reputations. Once it became a sport, I am inclined to bet that throwing these implements may have worked its way into practical application.

Whether or not that is true, these two sports are still alive today. The temptation to throw anything at a target is probably an atavistic itch—a carry-over from mankind's long history of hurling weapons toward prey. I see evidence of this every time a group of young students arrives at my school in my gravel parking lot. To their eyes, every stone is a projectile, every tree a target. Imagine their faces when I inform them that our agenda will include spears or knives or tomahawks. In an age of all things electronic and glittery, such enthusiasm is gratifying.

*Then he took his staff in his hands, chose five smooth stones from the stream, put them in the pouch of his shepherd's bag and, with his sling in his hand, approached the Philistine.*

—1 Samuel 17:40, *Revised Standard King James Version of the Bible*

## CHAPTER 1

# Rock and a Soft Place—The Sling

Think of it: A weapon capable of killing a giant and fearsome warrior can be folded up and carried nearly weightless in a pocket! Ammunition is free of charge and scattered across the landscape virtually everywhere one goes. When my childhood buddies and I learned the joys of whirling a rock over our heads in a sling and then letting go at some impromptu target, it's a wonder that none of us was clobbered by an unexpected release.

We roamed our neighborhood and slayed telephone poles, wheelbarrows, and trash cans. In the woods we slung rocks at stumps, bushes, creek banks, and, of course, hornets' nests. We were warriors in an idyllic era of harmless battles against imagined enemies . . . and then we discovered more dazzling ammo.

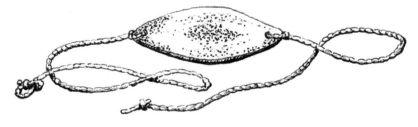

Dry dirt clods literally explode against a sunlit brick wall, creating a visual treat of "smoke and shrapnel." One summer afternoon I singled out a brick in a wall as a bull's-eye and laid siege to the enemy fortification. So rapt was I in my pretended war that I never stopped to consider the marring of the west side of my father's house.

When my parents made an unexpected early return from a friend's home, I was introduced to new chores around my house—one of those involving a ladder, a stiff brush, and a bucket of water. My sling was confiscated for a week for the welfare of all humankind. All further slinging of my childhood was confined to the forest.

## *The Sling*

The safest person in a sling scenario is the slinger—assuming his pouch is not too deep. It's the bystander who runs the greatest risk of injury. Therefore, using this hunter's tool is not recommended as a group activity. A sling should be used solo. It is included here for the individual who is keen on experiencing this ancient weapon.

In the hands of a beginner, a whirling, loaded sling is like a cocked gun spinning on a tabletop. Until a novice learns how to release a rock consistently at the "sweet spot," he must practice alone. A less dangerous method of slinging involves loading a soft projectile. A hacky-sack works well, but you'll need to add three-quarters of an inch to the width of the pouch detailed below in *Making a Sling*.

A sling is an easy tool to construct. The likeliest mistake might be to create a sack-like pouch instead of a flat, folded, temporary pocket that can easily open. (I once saw a boy from another neighborhood conk himself in the head with his loaded sling, because the rock would not release from his deep pouch.)

### Making a Sling

A sling requires only two materials: cordage and a swatch of leather. (Of course, other pocket materials are possible, including vinyl, nylon, and most kinds of cloth.) You can make both of the natural components—plant-fiber or animal-skin cordage and buckskin (see *Volumes 1 and 3* of this series).

For the pouch, cut out a long oval shape seven to eight inches long and three-and-a-half to four inches wide. (These are suggested dimensions. The size of the pouch is ultimately determined by the size stone you plan to hurl.) Make cordage or cut string half as long as your standing height. You'll need two of these strings.

Punch a small hole at each narrowed end of the leather oval a quarter-inch from the edge. Tie one end of each length of cordage to one hole in the pouch. At the free end of one string, tie a small loop to make a "lasso" to fit over the long finger of your throwing hand. With this finger so ringed, place a rock in the pouch and pinch the other string with the fingers of the throwing hand until you have gotten the two lengths equal to balance out the pouch.

Note where the second string meets your fingers. At that point you'll want to tie a simple overhand knot to give your fingers something to let go of during the release.

## Mechanics of the Sling

Stand facing your target then pivot your stance in a one-eighth turn toward your strong side. Turn your head toward your weak-side shoulder with your eyes on the target, your feet parted naturally, legs slightly bent for balance control.

There are several different throwing styles. My favorite is to whirl the sling above the head like a slanted helicopter blade—the plane of the whirl tilted downward on the strong side. Use a lot of shoulder rotation in the whirl while making only a small circle with the hand just above and away from the head. A single accelerating revolution will suffice. Performing multiple revolutions becomes nonproductive, as it becomes more difficult to time the release—that is, to let go at the proper point on the orbit.

### Throwing with the Sling

Load the sling with a hickory nut–sized stone and let the pouch hang down by your leg. Encourage the rock to swing back and forth in a small pendulum arc that grows to two feet. As the pouch reaches the farthest point of the backswing, begin your whirl by quickly bringing the sling up into the desired canted plane. If a right-hander were to look up at it (he shouldn't . . . a slinger keeps his eyes on the target) he would see a clockwise spin of the sling. Reverse all that for lefties.

Get the sling up to speed quickly, because on its next approach toward the target you are going to whip the sling forward and release. In other words, the rock does not quite complete one revolution while whirling in the slanted plane before launching. (After a little practice, two revolutions can be used, but more than two is not recommended.)

The instant before you whip the sling for an aggressive thrust forward (in the slanted orbit) for the release, take a controlled twelve-inch step forward with your leading foot (the left foot for a right-hander). When your weight comes down on that step, use your legs like shock absorbers for body control as you release.

Your first few throws will probably fly past the target, missing it on the weak side. In time you will get a feel for the "sweet spot"—the point on the orbit at which you should release the knotted string. You'll learn through trial and error that the time to release the stone is just after it has passed

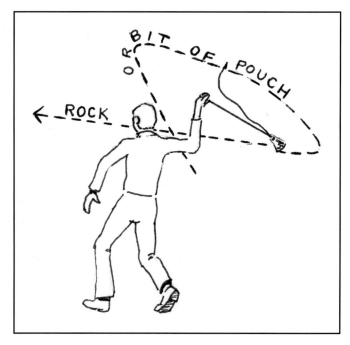

the point where the strings are perpendicular to the desired line of flight to the target.

Now and then check the knots of your sling—especially the ones attaching strings to pouch. Be prepared for some abrasion of the middle finger where the lasso is attached. A small padded sleeve of cloth or leather works well as a protective layer.

### Social Slinging

To practice with a friend, make or buy a few hacky-sacks (see *Volume 3, Making a Lacrosse Ball*) to use as projectiles. Only one slinger should throw at a time. The watcher should stand twenty yards behind the thrower.

For a target use a cardboard box or hang a bath towel from a low tree limb. Using the form just covered, stand back twenty feet and take at least six throws before taking turns. Each thrower can coach the other on orbit slant and form.

### Intermediate Slinging

Once you have become comfortable with the form and you are able to hit the box or towel four out of five times, you're ready to graduate to stones. Spherical to ovoid stones are best, but almost any reasonably sized rock will work. An ideal size ranges from hickory nut (without the husk) to hen's egg. It's the bulk and weight that count. You need to feel the stone's mass as you whirl it.

When using stones, a barrier is needed to protect any observer. While standing behind a tree, that person should be afforded a view of the target but not a view of the thrower. Such positioning makes an accident improbable. As you improve, increase your distance by stepping back to twenty-five and thirty feet and more.

### Sling Roving

You and your companion can roam the forest and, as a warmup, take turns selecting targets. Throw at boulders, dead tree trunks, shadows, stumps, etc. To make it a game: Whoever scores best on a target earns the right to choose the next one.

## CHAPTER 2

# A Pointed Stick—The Spear

"All things are decided by the spear!"

By the second day of summer camp I must have announced this declaration two dozen times. By the end of the session I had probably heard it over a hundred times from the campers, which means that I had witnessed that many "duels." It was the first year that I had chosen the spear as the focal point of my camp sessions.

On day one, each camper fashioned his own spear, personalizing it with a leather handle-wrapping, symbolic engravings, and runes painted with plant dyes. With so much care going into the making, they even gave names to their weapons, monikers like "Talon," "Wolf-eye," "Fire-bolt," and "Sting." Each person always kept his spear nearby, as if it were a newly acquired facet of his personality.

After all spears were crafted we began lessons in throwing—more for form than accuracy or distance. Without a target each spear-thrower attempted to hurl her weapon a mere ten yards. Top priority was given to the alignment of the spear in its own shallow arc of trajectory. In other words, wherever the spear point cut through the air, so followed the tail end. If done correctly such a throw resulted in an "in-line stick" or "impalement," which means that the spear pierced the earth cleanly, its tail pointed back at the arc through which it had just traveled. What we did not value were spears that veered off course, their tails pointed off to one side of the trajectory . . . or monster-throws that clattered and tumbled through the woods. In-line sticking was the mark of excellence.

Anytime the slightest disagreement or misunderstanding arose among campers (about any topic whatsoever), I was quick to herald the dramatic announcement that became the theme of our camp session: "All things are decided by the spear!" A throwing-line was established, and ten yards away a target circle was scratched into the earth. Then the world waited for a decision. Whoever had the better throw ruled. For the duration of the summer camp session, accountability for all things hinged upon the toss of a spear.

For example, if only one serving was left over at the end of the evening meal—and if three people wanted it—I (or one of the three) said, "All things are decided . . ."

We had a lot of fun with this novel law of life and never tired of it, especially as campers got better at throwing. Often, campers made impromptu challenges for personal gain: A loser of a duel might have to wash the winner's dishes at the next meal . . . or a winner might assign his firewood collecting duties to a loser. In the case of such a wager, both involved parties had to agree to the contest.

# Spear Design

My favorite spears have been slender hardwood trunks of dead saplings that were still standing and quite strong. Maple, dogwood, and sourwood provide excellent shafts. Simply carve away any rough places and whittle a point. Hardwood spears enter a target with heft and authority, but such wood might be too heavy for young spear-throwers. To benefit from a lighter spear, cut green or seasoned bamboo or rivercane.

### Harvesting a Spear

Whether searching for a dead hardwood shaft or live bamboo, look for a very straight section around which you can wrap your thumb and index at the shaft's midpoint so the tip of the thumb touches the outermost knuckle of the finger. Length should exceed the thrower's height by between six and thirty inches, this variation of measurement dictated by strength. The stronger the thrower, the longer the spear. Carve the shaft away from its root rather than break it. This way you can avoid a running crack that can later migrate deeper into the spear. Remove any limbs or nubs by carving toward the top of the plant.

Carve a point on the heavy end. A long-tapering point can break easily, so make the total length of a hardwood point two inches. This point should be carved as a perfect cone. For a bamboo shaft, locate the point just in front of one of the swollen, ringed nodes (a septum) where a dividing wall separates chambers. This will strengthen the point. Carve this point with a single stroke from one side at a slant, leaving a three-inch-long, 35-degree angle with the sharp tip off to one side.

Because all the spear training begins by throwing shallow arcs into the ground, the hollow interior of the bamboo point inevitably compacts with dirt. This added weight to the leading end of the spear is an asset.

### Fire-Hardening a Hardwood Point

From a creek's shoreline haul several bucketfuls of dry sand to your main campfire area. (Or build a fire on a high sandy beach.) Lay down a six-inch layer of sand in the fire pit and build a hardwood fire on top of the sand. After an hour or two, when your campfire has burned to a bed of glowing coals, insert your hardwood spear point into the sand under the coals and turn the shaft constantly, slowly. After an initial ten minutes check the point every few minutes to see its color and texture. Add hardwood fuel to the fire as needed. When the point is glassy black, the job is done.

### Wrapping the Spear Handle

Once the point has been established, nothing brings life to a spear like the handle wrap. You'll want the leading edge of your handle to be just behind the balance point. This way, when you throw, there will be slightly more spear weight in front of your hand than behind.

Wrap a six-inch handle with a two-foot by three-quarter-inch strip of leather. (You can get a lot of footage out of an oval or round scrap of old leather by cutting a spiral strip from the outside in.) Make one end of your strip tapered like a dagger point. Six inches back from the area you judged to be the leading edge of the handle, start wrapping the un-tapered end from the rear of the grip toward the forward part of the grip.

When you are three circular wraps from running out of strip, take a strong, thin cord one-and-a-half feet long and double it. Lay this on your handle with the loose ends toward the tail of the spear and with the loop beyond where the handle will eventually be wrapped to finish. Cover a section of the looped cord with the last two wraps, leaving the cord's loose ends exposed on one side and the loop exposed on the other. When only the long taper of the leather strip remains unwrapped, slip the tapered end into the loop and pull on the loose ends of string as one to force the tapered end of the leather to bury itself under your last coils of wrapping. Trim off any excess of the tapered end.

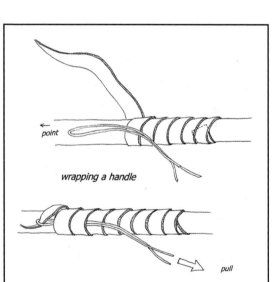

*point*

*wrapping a handle*

*pull*

## *A Hardwood Fore-Shaft for the Bamboo Spear*

When using a bamboo shaft, you can strengthen the point by inserting a piece of dead hardwood that extends from the spear shaft. The thickness of this fore-shaft should match the circumference of the leading end of the bamboo. The leading end of the fore-shaft of wood should be sharpened to a point, while the insert end should be carved as a solid cylinder to fit perfectly into the cylindrical cavity of the cane all the way to the first septum.

### Making the Fore-Shaft

With your knife, mark a perfect ring around the cane three inches in front of the first septum. Then grasp the main shaft of the spear and carve toward the thicker end, making small scallop-shaped cuts in repetitive strokes along the ring as you turn the shaft. Do this until the excess cane snaps off on its own. This technique prevents splitting in the cane.

Select a straight piece of dead hardwood with a thickness that matches the leading end of the bamboo spear. Before cutting the fore-shaft-to-be to a desired length, carve the insert plug of the fore-shaft to fit inside the cane to abut the first septum. The flange of the fore-shaft—in back of the point, in front of the insert plug—should contact the forward end of the cane to make a good seal. Then carve the spear point while gripping the fore-shaft by the plug.

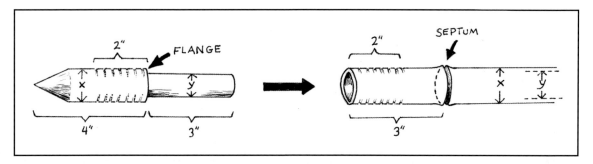

Using the point of a knife, score the front two inches of cane and the rear two inches of the exposed point, apply glue, and lash four inches of the combined fore-shaft and spear tightly with thin, strong cordage.

## *Seasoning and Straightening a Bamboo Spear*

As long as you don't harvest a cane too young in its first spring, you will find that green bamboo spears work nicely without seasoning. By the middle of summer you should be able to select any cane that suits you.

If you want a finely crafted spear—straighter, stronger, and lighter—trim the green cane of its branches, lash it to a stiff post or pole, and secure it somewhere off the ground and out of direct sunlight in a ventilated place. Under a porch works well if you prop the post up on blocks. Allow two months for drying. When you remove the spear from storage it will be ready for sanding any rough nubs left on after trimming.

To straighten the spear—both its zigzag alternating sections and each section's slight "banana curve," refer to Chapter 5 on arrow-straightening.

# *Gripping the Spear*

For a right-hander, hold your bent right arm to your side, elbow down, hand at the height of your ear, forearm vertical, wrist cocked back so your thumb is pointing directly behind you. In this position lay the spear handle in the palm over the heel of your thumb, the spear pointing the direction you are facing. This is less a grip than a balancing act.

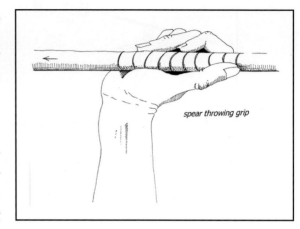

spear throwing grip

Without moving the wrist, grip the spear rather loosely with thumb, index, and longest finger—this latter finger being most important in the grip. The index fingertip touches the spear almost next to the "door-knocking knuckle" of the long finger. Without throwing, gently thrust the spear forward and back a few times to get the feel of the grip. As you do, pretend the spear is inside an invisible tube of fragile glass fixed in space. Don't "break the glass" as you move the spear back and forth.

## Throwing the Spear

Set up safety rules for practice: 1. All must stand behind a throwers' line; 2. all throwers must check in front and behind before throwing; and 3. always wait for the teacher's permission before throwing or retrieving. ("All clear to throw!" "All clear to retrieve!")

Begin throwing with form, not power . . . mastering the arced flight rather than a flat trajectory. Imagine the spear traveling through a series of rings, each with a diameter of twelve inches. Don't let the spear touch the rings! Using the grip just described, bring your right arm and hand directly in front of your right shoulder. The part of the spear just behind the handle is now directly over your shoulder. Now imagine the first ring of the arc is fixed in place over your shoulder.

Face your target, feet side by side and slightly spread, your free hand steadying the spear about a foot in front of the handle. Shift your body weight over your strong side and slightly bend both knees like shock absorbers. **Check behind you to make sure no one is going to be stabbed by the backward movement of your spear!**

Angle the spear upward 20 to 30 degrees for a ten- to fifteen-yard throw. As you cock the spear back as far as you can reach without touching a ring, let your free arm stretch forward into the air as a counterbalance. Keep your chest facing your target area throughout the throw. Smoothly take a step forward with your weak-side foot and throw, sending the spear through the imaginary arc of rings. Keep your torso erect; that is, don't lean away from your throwing arm. Do not let the spear touch a ring, and especially do not let the tail end veer off to one side to touch a ring.

You want the tail end of the spear to follow exactly where the point travels through the air. Keep the entire spear inside the rings.

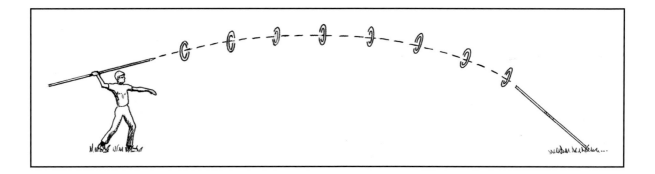

Ask observers to judge (from well behind the thrower) whether the tail veers out of the path of the point. Such a throw will usually result in the spear not sticking. A spear that does not stick is like a nail not hit squarely with a hammer. The front third of your spear is like the nail; the back two-thirds is its hammer. Keep throwing "through the rings" until you can make the spear stick in the earth every time.

Note: While the spear is in your hand during the throw, it should pass directly above your shoulder. Don't let the tail of the spear swing wide out to your strong side. This is the most common flaw made by beginner throwers. To remedy that problem, a teacher can remind the spear-thrower to keep his chest pointed at the target area. This eliminates body torque around the spine, which is often the source of veering. (As a spear-thrower advances his expertise, he can learn to use this torque to add power to his throw, as long as he learns to adjust his form to keep the spear inside the rings.)

**Safety Notes: The most common accident in spear throwing is stabbing someone with the tail of the spear! Throwers generally pay attention to what is in front of them but forget how far their spears extend behind them!**

**Establish a command: "Spears to the sky!" It is a signal to all people to hold their spears vertically. Use it when calling a group to the throwers' line, when retrieving, and when walking on a trail. While a group stands at the throwers' line, remind all to check behind them to ensure that the back lane is clear.**

### Throwing for Accuracy

On a gently rising bank of soft earth, lay down four sticks to make a two-foot-by-two-foot square. From level ground, throw at this from five, ten, and fifteen yards. Only spears that stick inside the square count as successful throws. Keep a running score for competition. Throwing across a gully works well, too. It is especially fun for young ones to throw from a higher point on one side with the target lower on the other side. Make the target smaller and try again. Concentrate on a graceful throw through the arc of rings—more like a free throw in basketball than a fastball from a baseball pitcher.

## In the Land of the Cyclops

Take your spear tribe into the "forbidden forest of the Cyclops," where you will encounter many hostile, one-eyed giants who must be slain in order for your group to continue passage. Sometimes these Cyclops look like root balls of fallen trees, sometimes a shadow on a bank, sometimes a hole in the ground. Use your imagination. Before you can travel past such a giant, someone must blind it from a safe distance. Define a throwing line and the exact boundaries of the eye. Let everyone have a throw at every giant during the day. (It's never a bad idea to send more than one spear into a Cyclops' eye.)

Roving through the forest and having fun with spears is the kind of experience that makes young people fall in love with and become comfortable in the forest.

## Live-Action Spears

Once your spear tribe has become adept at throwing, test them on their ability to spring into action with the poise necessary for accuracy. For this game you will need to make two grapevine hoops, each with a three-foot diameter. Both hoops should be held by the teacher. One hoop will be tossed to a surprise location to define the place from which the thrower launches her spear. The second hoop will serve as the target. Ask all students to lean their spears against a large tree. Then have all sit as a group ten yards from the tree and perpendicular to the proposed throwing lane.

When you call a student's name she must dash to the tree and retrieve her spear. As soon as you call her name, begin counting down from eight to zero. About the time she reaches her spear, toss one hoop (horizontally) so it falls flat to the ground somewhere near the tree. She must run to this hoop and jump into its circle.

Immediately after launching the first hoop, toss the second hoop (again, horizontally) where it will fall in a safe place (away from the spectating group) ten to fifteen yards from the first hoop. Before you reach zero, the thrower must launch her spear, attempting to stick it inside hoop #2.

If your students do well in this challenge, repeat it with a seven-second limit. Then six. And five. Find out how low the count can go. Students of all ages seem to love to meet this challenge of less and less time to perform an accurate throw, and you won't have to worry about a bored audience. The game is almost guaranteed to hold the group's attention. The anticipation is palpable as each awaits his turn.

## The Mightiest Throw

There will always be those who want to see who can throw a spear the farthest. But even more important is this: Who can throw for distance and still have the spear stick? Hold a javelin contest with a formal practice session that includes well-defined safety rules. When the competition begins, allow only one throw per person. The winner may be a surprise to everyone, because each thrower must weigh his ability to make a long-distance throw against his confidence and ability to make the spear stick. If the spear sticks for two seconds but then sags or collapses flat to the earth, the throw is considered good.

Sometimes this contest ends with a dozen spears littering the far end of the playing field like pick-up sticks but with one winning spear quite close to the throwing line sticking firmly into the ground. Such is the gamble inherent in this game.

### Chungkey

This popular game among the Cherokee (called "*gatayûstî*") was played in a field with two spear-throwers and a third person, who rolled a stone disk. A ten-inch-diameter, three-inch-thick disk sawed from a dead log can serve as the "chungkey."

Establish a "throwers' line" (a rope pegged at both ends) and a safe direction for throwing. Five yards back from the line, the chungkey-roller stands flanked on each side by a spear-thrower. For safety, the spear-throwers should stand four paces away from the roller, pitting the competitors eight paces apart.

When all are ready, the roller runs forward to the line and rolls the chungkey disk downfield away from the players. Just as he releases the disk, he turns and runs back behind the throwers, calling immediately "Chungkey! Three! Two! One! Zero!" At the first word the players run to the line where they must make their throws before "zero!" The object is to predict where the chungkey disk will come to rest and make the spear stick in the ground there. Whoever makes the throw that sticks closest to the resting chungkey wins.

Sometimes a thrower gambles that her competitor's spear will not successfully stick, and so she impales her spear into the ground just beyond the throwers' line to be sure that it sticks. Such strategies are all a part of the fun of the game.

### More Games

Virtually all the games listed in Chapter 11, *At Play in the Fields of the Archer*, can be played with spears but using variations on targets so the targets accommodate the cruder gouge made by spears.

*If you could jump as well as I do, two-legged human, you could leap the Chattahoochee River from bank to bank.*

—from a conversation with a very frank grasshopper

# CHAPTER 3

# The Super-Thrust Spear—The Atlatl

When a person first picks up an atlatl and attempts to use it, the performance might feel awkward and unnatural—certainly not as promising as that first spear thrown by hand. With practice, however, the atlatl practitioner can become deadly accurate.

What the sling is to the rock, the atlatl is to the spear. Both provide a mechanical advantage to improve the hurling of a projectile. Like the unlimbering of a grasshopper's bent rear legs, the atlatl, in effect, extends the length of the thrower's arm to provide a longer radius in the moving arc that provides propulsion. The sling enjoys a similar advantage, but the big difference in these two weapons lies in the plane in which the propelling action takes place.

As taught in Chapter 1, the sling's plane is tilted off the horizontal. Having a projectile come off that orbit and hit a target requires a great deal of practice. (It is true that a sling can be whirled in a vertical plane, but orbit-radius and power are sacrificed.)

Imagine sitting on a fast merry-go-round and trying to hurl a stone by hand at a target thirty feet away. This represents the difficulty of aiming with the near-horizontal motion of a sling. Now imagine sitting on a Ferris wheel and, as it takes you over and down in front of the wheel, you try to hit a target right in front of you thirty feet away. Your chances at success are much better in this vertical scenario, which is closer to the mechanics of the atlatl.

# The Atlatl Kit

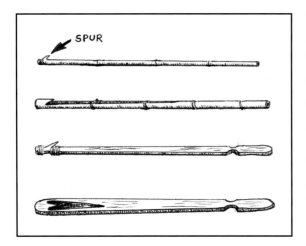

Take any arrow in your strong hand with the end-pad of the index finger hooked over the back of the arrow's nock. With the shaft resting on the flat of the palm, thrust the arrow forward. This toss demonstrates the dynamics of an atlatl. By using a stick with a spur (to replace forearm, palm, and index finger), the launching device is extended to add thrust. If this launcher is barely flexible, even more power is added. (A stone weight can be lashed to the launcher to encourage flexibility and "whip.") The handle notches shown in the lower two examples of the illustration are beveled out for thumb and index to reach through for stabilizing the spear on the launcher just before throwing. (Some designs call for the index and long finger to straddle the handle. We'll stay with the simpler technique using thumb and index, which feels more natural to the beginner.)

Like an arrow shaft, an atlatl spear should demonstrate the four Ls: linear, light, lithe, and ligneous (straight, lightweight, flexible, and yet woody-strong). A general rule for spear length is one to two feet longer than the thrower's height. The tail end of the spear needs a pocket to receive the spur of the launcher. Just in front of the pocket, feathers are attached to the spear for air-drag. This forces

POCKET FOR SPUR

the spear's tail end to follow last, keeping the spear aligned point-first during flight. The point should match the user's intent. (For practice: a hardwood or antler fore-shaft. For hunting in a survival scenario: sharpened stone or metal . . . or a finely edged bamboo fore-shaft.)

### A Starter Atlatl for the Young

Either bamboo or rivercane offer an easy construction method for a beginner atlatl kit. Consider a slow-tapering spear, its leading end as thick as the thrower's pinky, its length one foot longer than body height for youth and as much as two feet longer for strong adults. Simply trim the cane of all branching (always cutting toward the top of the cane with scalloped strokes) and carve a point from one side at an angle, leaving an off-center point. Don't expect to find perfectly straight cane. Grasses, like rivercane and bamboo, grow in zigzags from node to node. Furthermore, each section (between nodes) can be slightly curved. (For a starter kit simply find the straightest cane available and forego any straightening.) Lash several spear candidates to a board or post and allow to dry for two months. Such drying will lighten the spear, which will be a key ingredient for success. The spear should flex slightly when thrown, but if there is too much spring (you will discover this in launching),

off-center
cane point

you will see an erratic flight that does not feel controllable. In this case remove a section of the cane from the tail and make a new pocket at the next node.

The pocket is a natural feature of cane with hollow sections. Merely make the tail-cut of the spear just behind a node, leaving a quarter-inch-deep cavity where the spur will nestle into the tail.

The thickness of the launcher varies with throwers' strengths. Start with a thumb-thick (at base) piece of cane, its length equal to the forearm plus hand plus one more hand. (If the launcher flexes too much when throwing, graduate to a thicker cane.) Trim the launcher of all branching except for one at the thicker end to use as a spur. Whittle this one down to a quarter-inch to half-inch nub with a dull point. Smooth any rough spots on the launcher handle.

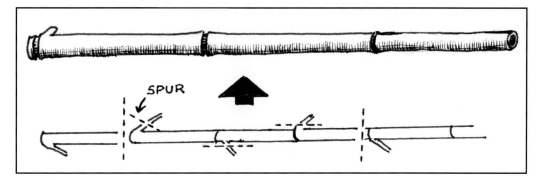

If you have seasoned hickory or yellow locust available, you can start right away to make a more sophisticated launcher. Otherwise, fashion a three-foot-long, de-barked section of hardwood that measures four inches wide and one inch thick. Store this blank off the ground under a shelter and out of direct sunlight for six months.

### Making a Finer Launcher

Using a sharp knife, carve the three-foot-long launcher blank down to a width of two inches and a thickness of a quarter-inch (except for the handle end . . . round off its corners but leave it thick for a reliable grip). At the handle end of the launcher (the area where thumb and index grip for throwing) carve a half-circle from each edge of the launcher—each notch large enough for a finger. These notches will accommodate the fingers that straddle the handle (thumb and index for beginner throwers), so you'll want to smooth the corners for comfort. Leave one inch of wood between the notches.

## *Finger Thongs*

Just above the two finger notches carve two more small notches to accommodate securing the finger thongs. These leather thongs will be looped over the straddling fingers to improve the thrower's grip on the launcher.

Test the bend of the launcher over your knee. You'll want the rear two-thirds of the launcher to bend a little when you throw . . . but not so much bend that the

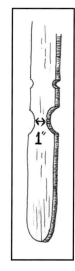

launcher doesn't fire the spear with authority. When used to hurl a spear, the launcher will move somewhat like the upper limb of an archer's bow. Shave the launcher sparingly from its underside (the side without the spur) to achieve such a bend when the spear is launched.

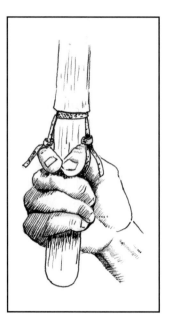

### Attaching Finger Thongs

Tie the midpoint of a supple eighteen-inch-long, three-eighths-inch-wide strip of leather to the thong notches. On each side of the handle fashion a leather loop for each finger to fill when grasping the handle. Experiment with the fit to get the loops positioned properly. When the loops are tied correctly, your fingers should exert pressure on the loops when you are holding the launcher for throwing.

### Fashioning the Spur

The spur can be made of anything hard enough to form a solid cone-shaped prong. Suggested materials are hardwood, bone, and antler. One of the easiest to make utilizes a natural branch nub from a dead hardwood limb. Part of the limb itself will be used as a base, as seen in the illustration.

Carve the spur base so it seats well on the launcher, where it will be lashed. Then carve the branch nub down to a quarter-inch- to half-inch-long cone tip that can fit into

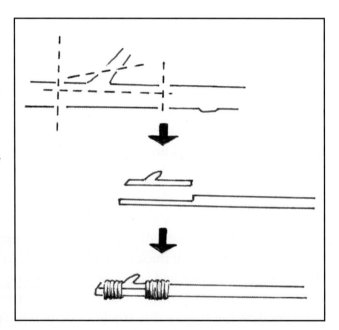

the pocket of the spear. Score a few small grooves into the sides of the launcher and the top of the base for the lashing. Wrap cordage around both the base of the spur and the launcher.

## The Stone Weight

The atlatl launcher is usable at this point, but there is one marked improvement that can be incorporated into its design. If a hefty, biscuit-sized stone is lashed to the launcher just below and on the opposite side of the spur, the spear travels decidedly faster by the increased whip of the launcher.

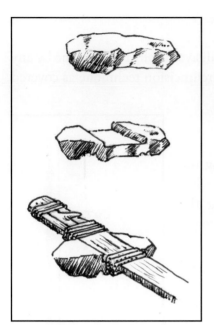

## Attaching the Stone Weight to the Launcher

There are various ways to attach the stone. Using any piece of scrap, rusted metal (an old file), scrape a wide groove on one side of the stone to accommodate its fit against the launcher. Then groove the stone on its other side for cross-tying cordage. Lash it tightly to the underside of the launcher.

Iron-rich stones, which oxidize and are responsible for the red clay of the South, can be easily scraped by harder stones or by metal tools. (See *Volume 2*, Chapter 3.)

## Crafting the Spear

Of course, cane can be used as a spear immediately after harvesting, but when seasoned for a few months it will lose much of its weight, fly faster and farther, and supply more spring in casting the spear forward. The instructions for making a hardwood insert as a fore-shaft are covered in Chapter 2, but a point cut into the cane itself (by a single, angled stroke of a knife made just in front of a node) makes a fine temporary "self-point." But a self-point will eventually split, forcing you to cut a new one, and thereby shortening your spear. After you have lopped off a spear once, when the point splits again you'll want to discard that spear and make another. Shorter spears show less flex and, therefore, don't fly as well.

## Trimming, Seasoning, and Straightening the Cane

Choose a length of cane one to two feet longer than your body height and as thick as your pinky or ring finger at its point-end. It is easiest to trim cane while it is green. To remove any branching start with your blade below the branch and cut in small scalloped arcs toward the top of the cane. Reduce the nubs and finally smooth these spots by scraping with a smooth stone.

If you prepare a number of cane spears, after smoothing their branch nubs, bundle all the shafts together tightly, alternating their directions (half the canes pointed one way and half the other in a mixed-up fashion). This orientation will help to make the shape of the bundle a more nearly perfect cylinder and allow the canes to dry straighter than if they were all pointing the same way. Lash the canes tightly to one another with spirals of rope and then lash the bundle to a board to prevent warping. Store on several supports off the ground in a place sheltered from rain and direct sunlight.

After two to three months the canes are ready for a final sanding of any rough places. The next step is straightening by fire. This process is described in Chapter 5 of this volume in the section on heat-straightening arrow shafts.

## *Finishing the Spear*

Even with the cane drier and woodier, you must still avoid splitting the cane by any hasty lopping off of unwanted material. Use the circumcision technique as covered in *Making the Fore-shaft* in Chapter 2.

### Making the Pocket

Cut the tail end of the spear squarely (again using the circumcision method) a quarter-inch behind the last trailing node. The resulting concavity (including the septum itself) will serve as the pocket, which receives the spur of the launcher.

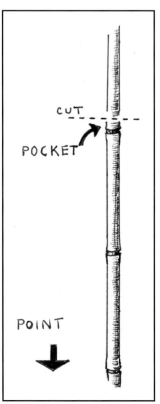

To reinforce the pocket, score its outside walls and continue three-quarters of an inch into the next section of the cane. Lash this tightly, starting at the tail end, continuing over the joint, and into the next section, all to bind the pocket to prevent its splitting. (This same lashing can extend forward on the spear to include securing the trailing end of the fletching, which will be covered soon.)

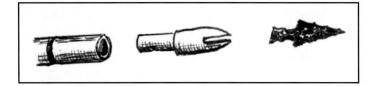

### Finishing the Point

Choose a self-point or a hardwood insert for your spear's penetrating end. For a serious hunter's point (in a survival scenario), cut a notch into the forward end of a hardwood fore-shaft to receive the base of the stone, metal, or bamboo point. Insert the point into the notch and lash it tightly.

Finally, lash the rear inch of the exposed fore-shaft to the leading inch of the cane.

Feathers will help to smooth the flight of a trouble-some spear by adding drag to the tail end. Turkey or vulture feathers work nicely.

## Attaching the Feathers

Using a knife, slice away an underside strip from the thick end of each quill so it can lie flat on the spear. You'll need only one inch of bare quill for lashing with sinew or other cordage to the cane. Position these two whole feathers (concave sides facing one another) opposite one another in front of the pocket.

Cut away each feather's vanes from the narrow ends of the quills, leaving one inch of quill to lash to the spear. If you so desire, you can lash the midpoint of the feathers also by cutting away a small section of vane filaments there.

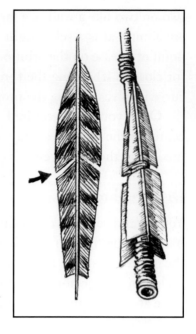

## Throwing with the Atlatl

Take a grip on the handle with thumb and index finger harnessed in the finger loops, other fingers gripped on the launcher. Secure the spear's pocket to the spur and raise the launcher to a horizontal position by your strong shoulder. Let the spear lie on top of the launcher nestled between the thong fingers. Keep the spear in place with your free hand as you set up to throw.

Stand facing your target (or slightly turned to your strong side) with your strong-side leg a half-step forward. Begin stepping forward with your weak-side leg, let go of the spear with your free hand, and hurl the spear forward using all the form you learned as a spear-thrower in Chapter 2.

As you get better at throwing, you may want to begin the throw with your body turned more to your strong side so you can utilize the torque of your shoulders to add to the thrust. Accuracy might be sacrificed by going too far with this. If so, reduce the torqueing motion to find the perfect blend of strength and accuracy.

## Accuracy Throw

Tighten four hay bales by adding an eighth-inch-thick lasso over each loop of baling twine. Cinch the lassos as tightly as possible and tie them off. Stack these bales

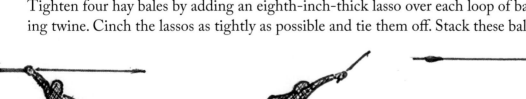

two on two like a wall as a target and throw from thirty feet away. To hit what you are aiming at is a self-taught process—much like throwing a rock or learning the point of release on the orbit of a sling. If the elbow and hand pass over the shoulder (or close to it) during the throw, the spear will not stray left or right. The learning curve involves finding the proper elevation angle of the spear for a given distance.

Once you have acquired some throwing skill, pin a smaller bull's-eye at the center of the hay bales. Stay at the prescribed thirty feet for a time and then start mixing up the distances.

### Distance Throw

Young ones seem to relish this mighty throw. All you need is a field and plenty of markers. The throwers will have to find the angle of release (45 degrees) that yields the greatest distance for a throw. This challenge presents an opportunity for a physics lesson in trajectory, showing how flights of a projectile launched with a constant force at varying angles will differ not only in arcs but in distances. When the angle of optimal-distance (45 degrees) is increased, distance begins to decrease.

Once the throwers have warmed up, have them perform three mighty throws from behind a line, hurling each as far as possible. Take an average distance for each thrower and mark it in the field. Without yet disclosing it to your students, you can use these marks to establish a handicap system that will put a keen edge on the competition to come.

Whoever has the longest average mark will continue to throw from the original throwers' line. Each of the other throwers will be given a handicap throwers' line that is measured from the original line and laid down closer to the downrange area. A thrower's handicap distance is measured from his average marker to the best thrower's average marker. Now hold a contest where each participant throws from behind his or her personalized throwing line and attempts to hurl a spear farthest downfield.

The teacher has the option of accepting graceless throws that do not stick or only those that do stick. If the former, the landing spot should be marked at the spot where the spear first touches ground. (If the spear lands flat, mark the location of its leading end when it lands.)

### Atlatl Games

Refer back to Chapter 2 and forward to Chapters 7 and 8. Every game with spears and bow and arrow outlined in those chapters can be modified for your class of atlatl throwers. For those archery games that require a traditional archery target, substitute a bank of a road-cut or a steep hillside with squares of sticks laid out as targets. The spear is too destructive to use on expensive foam or woven hay targets commonly used in archery.

*I gripped the tree's trunk and felt its cold winter sleep creep into my hand. Inside this wood, I knew, lay my bow . . . like a buried treasure I was about to unearth. All I had to do was remove every fiber of wood in which my bow was encased.*

—Stoney St. Ney, *A Copperhead Summer*

## CHAPTER 4

# A Bent Stick and a String— Bow-Making

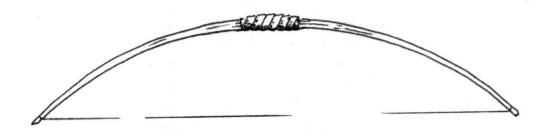

I walked quietly through a shaded forest of giant white pines by Warwoman Creek, my favorite stalking-ground. I had no purpose for being there but to see whatever I might see. My mind was relaxed. My eyes roved freely. My hands were empty. The only sounds were the creek and birdsong. I had no idea that a life-changing event was about to descend upon me. It revealed itself in such an ineffable way that I still wonder about its origin.

I stepped into a long open space between the thick trunks of the grandfather trees, and the orderliness and emptiness inside that colonnade of living wood stilled me. I stopped and gazed down the lane at nothing in particular, simply taking in the unobstructed distance. Then something clicked, as if a key had turned inside me, tripping a series of silent tumblers, unlocking a door that I had not known existed.

I had come alone to this forest, camped here, and had not uttered a word for days. Now, unexpectedly, I spoke aloud and heard my voice carry over the sound of the creek and down the shaded corridor. Six words tumbled out, like birds flying from a cage.

"I should be shooting a bow," I said.

And so began my life as an archer.

There is more to a bow than tying a stick to a string, though that is probably exactly how the prototype began. It is easy to imagine a paleo-child playing with a length of cordage, snapping it around like a whip. Next came the natural, aimless experimentation to which all children are prone. When tied to a stick, the cord swished through the air with even more authority. It was only a matter of time before that child bent that stick and shaped it into an arc by securing the cord at both ends.

At this point the new toy might have been intriguing simply for its musical potential, for, when plucked, the string made an interesting sound. Eventually the child may have figured out how to use the tension in the string to send something flying. Perhaps it was nothing more than a broken "wishbone" from a bird's skeleton. Upon seeing that flight, the boy's father might have taken over the project on an adult scale and tested the "toy" and its potential to launch serious projectiles.

Such stories are pure conjecture, of course, but the truth might be close to this version, especially concerning the child's part in it.

Refining the bow to a long-lasting tool must have taken generations. Certain species of wood performed better than others. And the technique of shaving the wood down to a proper size was all-important, making the building of a bow much more complicated than tying a string to a stick.

I have seen young summer campers randomly pick up a tree's discarded branch, bend it with taut string, and have a fairly serviceable bow for a time. In fact, I encourage eager young archers to experiment just like that. What better way to feel part of the forest than to accept its gifts and try them out?

Researchers do not trace the bow back to a single individual or location. It seems to have spontaneously combusted into use on each continent, as though the concept of the bow and arrow—like fire, cordage, and the wheel—was waiting for each civilization to mature to the point of recognizing it. Some people, of course, gained the knowledge of archery from their neighbors; but by whatever means the bow developed in any given area, the people quickly recognized its stellar advances over projectiles that were hurled by an arm. In terms of the history of humankind and the quest to hunt and wage war, the bow represents a major leap in firepower.

In the early days of human history, to see a bow cast an arrow with such speed (surpassing the stooping velocity of a peregrine falcon) must have been comparable to a later time when people saw what a firearm could do. To many modern-day experts on weaponry, the comparison of a bow to a rifle might be laughable. But in the early days of conflict between white intruders with firearms and native people with bows, this was not so.

Early pioneers using muzzle-loaders had to reload in a painstaking chain of actions before a second shot could be fired: pouring a measured amount of gunpowder into the barrel, adding a wadding and metal ball, and tamping it down with a ramrod. Then a finer gunpowder was poured into the firing pan. After cocking the hammer, he aimed and pulled the trigger, creating a spark to ignite the pan powder, which in turn ignited the powder inside the barrel.

Meanwhile a native archer might get off seven to ten shots. Of course, with the evolving technology of firearms—the self-contained cartridge, the lever action, then semi- and fully-automatic guns—a gunpowder-driven bullet has completely eclipsed the potential of an arrow delivered by a bow.

Or has it?

Thinking in terms of long-term survival, only one of these weapons has replaceable parts in the wild. Most people of the twenty-first century do not know how to make bullets, casings, firing caps, and gunpowder. And even if they did know, could they make these ingredients in a primitive setting? Yet, as you read these words, every part of the bow and arrow is waiting in a forest near you.

And let's not forget another characteristic of the bow—an asset that fairly shames the best of firearms. A bow is quiet. Furthermore, an archer reveals no muzzle flash or telltale odor.

Throughout its evolutionary history, the bow has been improved and protected from breakage by the addition of glued laminations to make it stronger, snappier, and more durable. Such a composite bow might be layered with wood, horn, bone, animal skin, sinew, or inner bark from certain trees. But the original bow was surely a self-bow—a single piece of dead wood (or in some areas, bone). From their experiences in breaking up firewood, early bowyers probably would have instinctively known which trees would serve well as a bow . . . and which would not. Anyone who has ever snapped a dead limb of tulip magnolia or pine, for example, would hardly waste time crafting a long-term bow of those materials. (An exception within the pine family is hemlock, which makes a serviceable bow.)

On the other hand, woods that crackle like a string of tiny fireworks when broken over the knee . . . and then stubbornly hold together (with what I call "chewy" tenacity) as the two broken halves are bent and twisted apart . . . that wood demonstrates a better composition for making a good bow.

| **Superior Bow Woods of the Eastern United States** | | | |
|---|---|---|---|
| ash, white | elm | locust, black | sassafras |
| birch | hickory | maple | walnut, black |
| butternut | hophornbeam | mulberry, white | yaupon holly |
| dogwood | juniper | oak, white | |

In Southern Appalachia the Cherokees' native bowwood of preference was yellow locust, called "black locust" today. When eastern tribes were forced west, the Cherokee moved into the range of a superior bow-wood tree. Osage orange is considered by most bowyers to be the premier native self-bow material in America. Like yellow locust, its golden-hued interior wood is aesthetically pleasing and remarkably functional for strength and speed in recovering its shape after being bent. Osage (also called "bois d'arc" and "bo-dark") can now be found in Southern Appalachia where it has been planted, but we will start with a more user-friendly wood for a first bow.

hickory

black locust (once called "Yellow Locust")

So many extant museum bows are made of hickory that it is tempting to call it the historically preferred bow wood. Whether or not that is true, hickory is an excellent choice because it is forgiving. Why? As most hickories mature you see the tough outer bark develop short fissures that eventually define diamond shapes with raised cross-hatchings of bark. (See photos.) The raised bark takes on the appearance of fabric that has been magnified so many times that the diamond "pores" between "threads" are visible.

This trademark fabric-like feature of hickory's outer bark is a symptom of its inner bark, which produces the outer bark. If the inner bark is like fabric, it has strength in many different directions.

The inner bark of most trees is comprised of fibers that run parallel and linearly along the trunk or branch. Hickory is more complicated. Because the inner bark makes not only outer bark but also the wood inside the trunk and branches, hickory's wood fibers are also "woven" like a fabric, which makes it difficult to break. (Anyone who has ever tried to split dried hickory for firewood knows this.) This woven feature is an asset for a bow, just as it is for all the tool handles that are made from hickory.

Diamond-shaped bark can be found on hickory, ash, yellow locust, butternut, black walnut, and on older sassafras and tulip trees. Of that list only the tulip tree is an exception to the rule. It does not make a lasting bow.

hickory bark, close up

One drawback to a hickory bow is that, in time, it will "follow the string." This is an archery term that means the bow will yield somewhat to the string tension and not fully straighten out to its original shape when unstrung. Such a bend does not doom a hickory bow. It simply renders the bow less strong than it had been. The bow tends to stabilize after losing some of its rigidity and does not continue to weaken.

My first handmade bow was hickory, which I made with no benefit of instruction. My only sculpting tool was a hatchet. This bow barely "followed the string," but with no significant loss in its power. That bow looked crude and completely unpolished, but it shot as accurately as any bow I have used since. It shot with authority and never broke. I suspect it might have lasted to this day had it not burned up in a house fire.

There is a meticulous procedure for more refined bow-making that involves a lot more work than hacking with a hatchet. The result will be a superior bow. We will get to such a project soon, constructing a Cherokee-style bow, but first . . . let's start primitive.

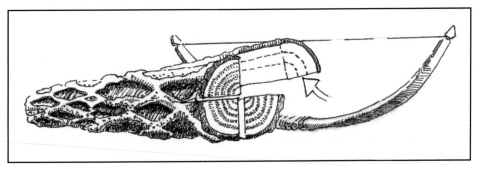

## Harvesting Wood for a Bow

In winter, when the sap is down, harvest a live hickory tree with a six-inch to seven-inch diameter and a straight six-foot section that is free of knots. A lot of tree has come down for the sake of the few bows you can make from it. Take advantage of the rest of the tree's inner bark for crafts requiring tough rope. (There may be additional sections of the tree that can be used for bows, atlatl launchers, lacrosse rackets, and basket rims.)

From the six-foot section remove both the outer and inner barks with a draw-knife. (If you don't remove the bark layers, insects will invade the inner bark and leave their larvae, which will riddle the wood with tunnels and render the wood inferior for a bow.) Try to leave the outermost layer of sapwood unscarred by your drawknife work. Soon after harvesting, split the log lengthwise down the center (start at the wider end with the splitting wedge; this will give you better accuracy in truly bisecting the log) and then do the same with each of those halves, giving you four quarters for four bow staves. (If you wait too long to do this splitting, the

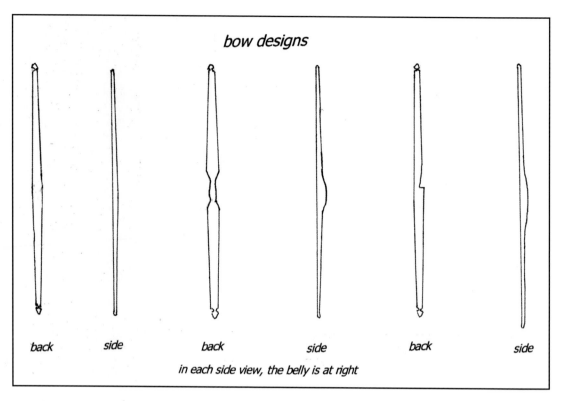

**bow designs**

back          side          back          side          back          side

*in each side view, the belly is at right*

drying of the wood makes this splitting a Herculean task.) All this splitting will require multiple wedges and a sledgehammer.

### Seasoning the Stave

Now it's time to season or dry the stave. This drying process slowly removes moisture from the wood. If the drying occurs too fast, the wood will check or crack. To slow down the drying rate and thereby prevent cracking, dip each stave end (four inches of each end) into a container of white pine glue. (See *Volume 1*, Chapter 6 on glue-making.) Commercial glue works fine, too. Then store the staves above ground under shelter for one year.

# One Year Later

Choose one of the bow designs illustrated above. Consider making this first bow one foot shorter than your height, and then saw the stave accordingly by cutting away any ends with knots or irregularities.

### Planning a Very Primitive Hickory Self-Bow

Mark the bow's midpoint. Three inches on either side of this point will make up a six-inch handle. The hand that grips this midpoint will serve as the arrow-rest, which means that the arrow will be shot from just above the midpoint.

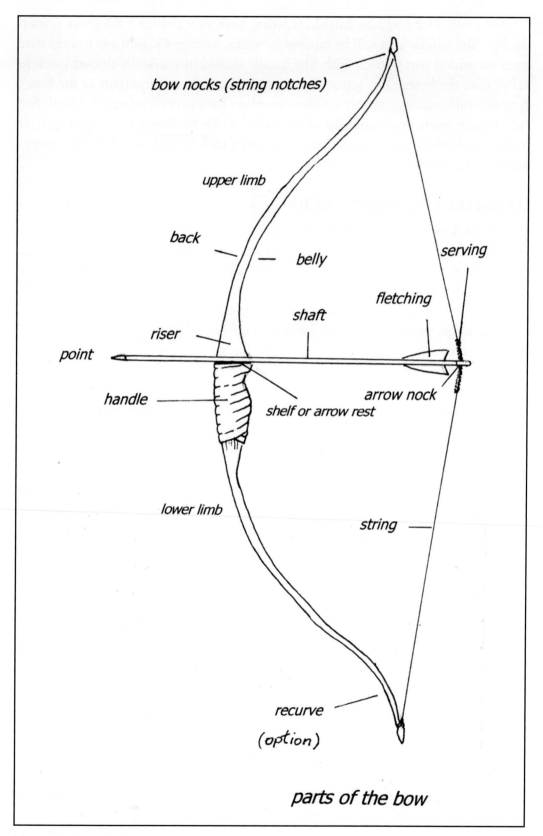

bow nocks (string notches)

upper limb

back

belly

serving

fletching

shaft

riser

point

handle

shelf or arrow rest

arrow nock

lower limb

string

recurve

(option)

**parts of the bow**

The vocabulary of archery

The bow's limbs will be flattish, tapering both in width and thickness toward the tips. The handle area will be tapered in width, leaving a reasonable inward flare from the widest part of each limb. The handle should be markedly thicker (back to belly) than the limbs. The actual measurements are not as important as the bow's symmetrical bending, but here are some numbers for a general reference: length five feet; handle width seven-eighths of an inch; handle thickness one-and-a-quarter inches; limb width near handle one-and-a-half inches; limb width at tips three-quarters of an inch.

### Hacking Out a *Very* Primitive Self-Bow

Let the back of the bow (side facing away from an archer while shooting) come from the outermost part of the tree—that smooth surface of sapwood left on the exterior of the stave after bark removal. The belly of the bow will come from the inner part of the tree. Place either end of the upright stave on a firm surface, like a boulder or tree stump. (Do not use the ground or a wobbly rock as a workbench. Such an insubstantial or unsteady work surface can cause you to make unwanted splits deep into the wood.) Working with a hatchet, progress patiently to remove wood from the sides and belly as you reduce the hickory stave to the finer dimensions of a working bow.

As you taper the limbs, as soon as the bow will yield to your strength, test the evenness of the bend from time to time by sitting or lying down, grasping each end of the bow, and bending it with the midpoint on the front of a knee. When you achieve a symmetrical bend with the desired bow-strength, carve notches at each end for a string, and you are done. Once the hatchet work begins, the final product can be reached in an hour or so.

A note on all self-bows: Do not overdraw! Do not hold at full-draw for an extended time! Self-bows are meant to be shot more quickly than more modern composite bows.

### Another *Very* Primitive Self-Bow

Find a two-inch-thick, dead and dry limb attached to one of the species from the list of better bow-making trees. Look for a straight (or slightly curved in one plane only) five-foot-long section. This section needs to be knot-free. Test the branch by breaking a part of it outside the bow-section. It should demonstrate a strong bending quality before breaking. If it proves brittle, find another tree. There should be no "green" scent or color at the break, nor should there be cracks or insect damage under the bark.

The outside of the limb will serve as the back of the bow. No carving will be done there. You may even leave the bark intact on the back. All carving will be done on the belly, which will be exposed by splitting the branch lengthwise with a sheath knife and mallet. (If the branch is curved, split with the curve . . . not perpendicular to it.)

Establish the width of the bow by trimming the sides to one-and-a-half inches at the midsection and one inch at the tips. Next begin carving a flat plane on the belly and reduce the thickness of the wood fairly evenly, leaving the midsection only slightly thicker than the limbs and their tips. Constantly test the bend over your knee to keep the bowing symmetrical. If the bend appears asymmetrical, carve the stiffer limb to match the more flexible limb. Once a desired stiffness and symmetry is achieved, take care to carve and smooth the tips to a rounded shape to prevent splitting.

Once all the knife-work is done, burnish the surface of the sides as if trying to round the squared edges. This can be done by rubbing firmly with a smooth and rounded section of bone or a small glass bottle. Cut and smooth notches in the sides of the tips (a half-inch from the end), then tie on a strong, non-elastic string to make the bow bend until the brace height (distance from string to belly on a strung bow at rest) measures six to seven inches.

bamboo cane

## The Bam-Bow

An easy-to-make bow can be constructed of two strips of bamboo, one of these one foot longer than the other, each concave side facing the other and lashed tightly together. Wood pegs keep the two pieces from sliding upon one another, and rawhide lashing binds the two laminations. This lightweight bow could serve well for hunting small animals (up to raccoon-size) in a survival situation.

## Building a Bam-Bow

Select a hard, mature bamboo cane with a minimum diameter of three inches. (This size should have a cane-wall-thickness of about three-eighths of an inch.) Saw the ends square on a straight four-and-a-half-foot section. Both strips that comprise the body of the bow will be carved from this blank. Using your knife as a wedge, split the cane down its center by hammering the back of the blade with a mallet.

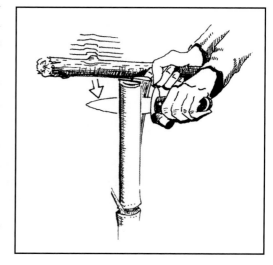

Use one strip four feet six inches long and saw the other to three feet six inches. Pare down the width of each strip from its outside edges, leaving the midpoint one-and-a-half inches wide on the longer strip, one-and-a-quarter inches wide on the shorter strip. Taper both in straight lines to an end-width of one inch. In this way the concave face of the shorter strip will nestle slightly inside the concavity of the longer strip.

With a gritty stone (or sandpaper) smooth all corners, edges, tips, and nodes inside and out. (Smoothed nodes can

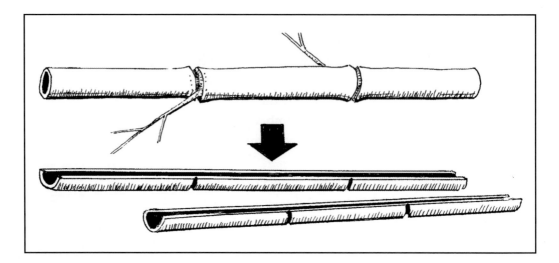

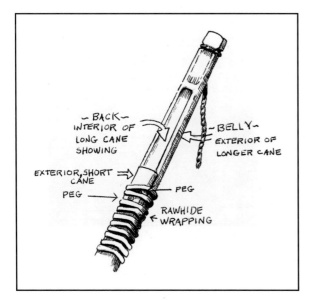

retain a subtle bump on the outside and a noticeable—but smooth—bump on the inside.) When sanding is complete, there should be no roughly textured spots remaining on any part of the strips.

Find the midpoint of each piece and make a mark on each concave side. Putting these marks together, lay the shorter piece on the longer, concave sides facing one another, and temporarily lash the two together in three places: at the midpoint and six inches inside each end of the shorter strip.

Drill pairs of three-eighths-inch holes offset diagonally (a quarter-inch apart) through both strips at the following locations: two-and-a-half inches from the ends of the shorter piece and three inches on either side of the midpoint. Carve eight hardwood dowels to size and fit a peg snugly into each hole.

Wrap each pair of pegs tightly with wet, flat strips of rawhide (see *Volume 3*), each lashing covering three inches of bow. Finish off the wrapping using the technique used in Chapter 2 for a spear handle. When the rawhide dries, remove the temporary lashing and cut (and sand smooth) string notches into the longer strip three-quarters of an inch from each end. The longer strip defines the belly of the bow, while the shorter strip defines most of the back.

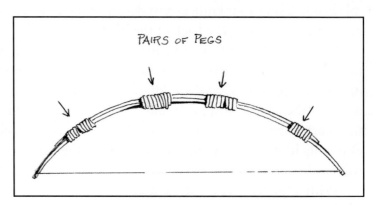

## *A More Sophisticated Self-Bow*

Follow the same hickory harvesting, debarking, splitting, and drying instructions found in the earlier project, *Harvesting Wood for a Bow*. Once your stave has seasoned, you will be ready to mark dimensions on the wood. How long should your bow be? There is no law dictating length. You may follow your preference. But for those wanting such a recipe, there is a general formula. This mathematical method is designed to reduce the chances of breaking the bow while shooting.

## *Determining Your Bow's Length*

Take a long arrow and make calibrated inch-marks along the shaft, measuring from the valley of the nock (where the string fits into the arrow's end-groove) to the point. You needn't mark the whole shaft. Start at twenty-two inches and make a mark for each inch up to thirty-three inches. This will give you a measuring arrow that determines the draw-length for all sizes of people.

Load the gauged arrow on any manageable bow and pull to full-draw. Have someone take note of the inch mark where the arrow just reaches the back of the bow. If you are new to archery, you'll find the proper spot (anchor point) to which you should pull the back of the arrow to your face in Chapter 9 under *The Direct Shot*.

Let's say that your draw-length is thirty inches. This means that your minimum length of arrow is thirty inches. (Practically speaking, you'll want shafts slightly longer for the sake of better aiming. An arrow that protrudes from the bow at full-draw is more visible in peripheral vision as your focus is riveted to the target.) Multiply your draw-length by two and add 10 percent to 20 percent of the draw-length. In this example, two by thirty inches equals sixty. Now add three inches to six inches, which equals sixty-three to sixty-six inches. Within these parameters lies your preferred bow-length. This formula and other calibrations for a Cherokee bow were taught to me by Al Herrin, a Cherokee bowyer with whom I corresponded over the years. His book, *Cherokee Bows and Arrows,* is a rich resource that I recommend (see Suggested Reading, page 269).

## *Wood Composition and the Bow*

The outer layer of the stave revealed after removing the inner bark is the tree's most recent layer of woody tissue in the sapwood. Deeper in the tree is heartwood. The two can be differentiated by the eye. One is lighter or darker than the other. With most bow trees, either sapwood or heartwood can be used for the self-bow. With hickory, we'll use the sapwood.

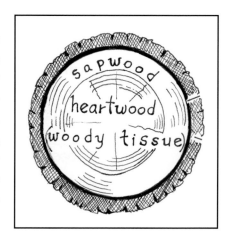

Sometimes bows are made at the juncture of the two wood types, using sapwood for the back of the bow and heartwood for the belly—the former bending and stretching with spreading tension and the latter compressing at full-draw. (The Cherokees, for example, used this combination for yellow locust.)

Each year a tree adds a layer of wood like a multi-appendaged sock slipped over every limb, branch, twig, and the trunk. This is what constitutes a tree ring, as seen on a cross-section cut of a tree. These concentric rings are countable because two colors are laid down each year. Spring growth is more porous and, therefore, lighter in tone. Summer growth is denser and darker, providing a contrast. For determining age, count either light or dark rings, not both.

Ideally, a bow should have just one growth ring exposed for its back. (In this case, from the sapwood.) This requirement is the single most tedious work of fine self-bow-making. Since the bow will taper in thickness from handle to tips, you will necessarily cut through several growth rings on its belly. (In this case, also sapwood.) This sloping graduation through various rings on the belly creates a visible parabolic pattern called "feathering."

yellow locust

The most demanding aspect of bow-making is maintaining the integrity of that single ring-layer on the back of the bow. It is this continuous and homogenous sheet of wood that gives the bow its best chance not to break. An accidental scrape or gouge through that layer with the drawknife calls for the bowyer to scrap that ring, scrape it away, and strive for the next ring as the back of the bow. (This is why we begin the scraping work on the back of the bow.) If such an error were made late in the scraping phase after the belly of the bow was established, a lot of time and work would have been for naught. Such a flawed bow might break at that too-deep scrape mark. More times than not, however, hickory will forgive you this transgression and not break at the flaw, making hickory a good choice for a first bow.

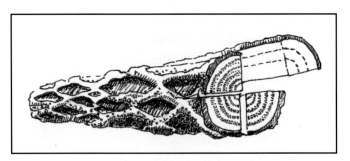

## Seasoning or Curing

The stave needs to be dried out for two reasons: 1. So wood can be carved or scraped away cleanly rather than pulled or gouged away. 2. So the wood will snap back into place briskly after being bent (when the bow is shot).

Very young would-be bowyers (curious children with busy hands), who fashion a bow from a green limb and string, are familiar with the transitory stiffness of an uncured bow. Such a bow soon becomes limp and barely able to launch an arrow, as it continues to "follow the string" to the point of being no longer able to cast an arrow with any authority.

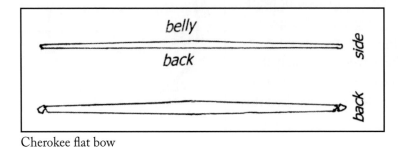

Cherokee flat bow

## Laying Out a Bow Design

Early Cherokee bows used a simple flattened design without a significant handle. This flat-bow bent fairly evenly throughout its length. (Bows with bulked-up handles—like the previous bow hacked out by a hatchet—bend mostly, if not exclusively, in the outer two-thirds of the limbs.)

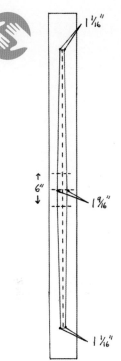

## Marking the Stave

After establishing the custom length of your bow, draw a long centerline right on the wood with a fine piece of charcoal from your fire pit (or with a soft pencil). If there is a knot on the stave, if at all possible, sketch the design so the knot is excluded. If the knot cannot be avoided, try to have that knot fall at the handle. If neither option is possible, ignore the knot. We will make allowances for it later.

Mark the midpoint on the centerline and measure three inches from it in both directions along the length of the bow (toward each limb). Mark this handle area, a rectangle that measures six inches long and one and nine-sixteenths inches wide. (This handle will eventually measure nine-sixteenths of an inch to five-eighths of an inch thick from back to belly.) Now mark the limbs by tapering the bow-width lines to one and one-sixteenth inches wide at the limb tips. (These limb tips will eventually measure five-sixteenths to seven-sixteenths of an inch thick from back to belly.) Note: These numerical measurements are not absolute but general. Different draw-weights require different thicknesses. You will find your correct thickness measurements in the actual making of the bow by patiently removing wood and testing the bend until the desired bow weight is achieved.

## Sculpting a Roughed-Out Bow

Use a hatchet to trim the stave down to within a half-inch of the marked width and thickness lines. (Later with a drawknife you'll shave down to within an eighth of an inch, then rasp to the mark.) Flatten the belly of the limbs so the stave will seat better on the vise we will soon use.

For all hatchet work be sure that your stave is propped on a solid "workbench," such as a log into which you have cut a divot for holding the bottom of the stave in place. Take care in this work. It is better to leave too much wood in an area than to remove too much.

## *Work Site Preparation*

Make a bow vise to use as a workstation that will hold the stave securely while you scrape. There are some clever designs for this, but I have stayed with the first apparatus I rigged up for my first scraped bow. This workbench looks like primitive uneven parallel bars lashed to two neighboring trees.

## Making a Bow Vise

Lash a sturdy dead log (three-and-a-half inches to four-and-a-half inches in diameter) horizontally three-and-a-half feet off the ground by securing it to two neighboring trees of equal thickness (one foot or more) that stand no more than six feet apart. At each tree, prop an end of this crossbar on a strong, Y-shaped support. On the other side of the standing trees, lash a second horizontal log three-and-a-half inches higher than the first. This crossbar needs Y-supports also.

Position the bow stave under the higher crossbar and over the lower one (belly-side down) with six inches of stave extending outward from the lower bar. Lash it tightly using slip knots, as you will be unlashing from time to time to reposition the stave. All the work

*bow vise in the forest*

that remains will be performed by carving with a drawknife, scraping with a wood rasp, or sanding with a stone or sandpaper.

### Following One Ring on the Back of the Stave

Begin work on the end of the stave extending from the lower bar. Shave with a drawknife on the back of the bow with this goal: to expose one growth ring for the entire length of the back of the bow. For bows made exclusively of sapwood, use the first full layer available. For bows using both sapwood and heartwood, leave one-eighth to three-sixteenths of an inch of sapwood on the bow. Achieving an intact, unscarred ring layer is the most meticulous phase of bow-making. It is best to expose a dark tough summer ring for the back of the finished bow; however, it is recommended first to shave to a thicker, paler spring ring and then rasp and sand to the darker layer so you won't make an error by cutting too deeply with the drawknife. Always adjust the stave on the vise so the spot you are shaving is no more than three inches from the vise's lower crossbar. (This placement will eliminate stave vibration and, therefore, an error.)

### Knots

If a woody knot lies within your design outline, don't slice through it. The ring layers contour over the knot, so you must guide your drawknife up and over the rise with each pass. But rather than revealing the desired ring layer on the knot, leave an extra layer to strengthen this area. The result will resemble a circular Band-Aid on a bump.

## *The Belly of the Bow*

Once you have revealed a single ring layer for the length of the bow's back, all the rest of the wood removal will be done to the sides and the belly. Sharpen your drawknife regularly with a file to make your work precise. (The Native Americans initially used stone scrapers for this work until they were introduced to metal blades from the white man's forge.) When working on the belly, take your time. You can always remove more wood later to decrease bow-poundage, but if you take off too much early in the craft, the only way to strengthen your bow is to laminate or "back" the bow with sinew or to cut the bow shorter. One inch taken off each end increases the draw-weight (bow-poundage) by about five pounds. However, keep in mind that making a bow shorter and shorter eventually decreases its shooting stability and accuracy.

### Removing Wood from the Belly

Lash the stave to the vise belly-side-up. Because these limbs must taper, you cannot, of course, follow one ring. Shave the belly down to a smooth taper within the suggested parameters stated earlier. When you get close to these measurements, remove the bow from the vise from time to time and test the bow's flexibility over your knee. Your first bend-tests will undoubtedly prove to be premature, and the bow will be much too strong to bend. Later, as you begin to feel more flexibility, you will want to test the bow's draw-weight to see how close you are getting to your desired poundage. Before you learn how to read that weight, let's first understand the meaning of "draw-weight."

## *Draw-Weight or Bow-Poundage*

Some bows are harder to pull back than others. These strengths are calibrated to accommodate the varying strengths of different archers. If a bow is said to be a fifty-pound bow, this does not mean the bow weighs fifty pounds. If the strung bow were suspended horizontally by wall pegs at its handle, a fifty-pound weight hooked to the string's midpoint would sag exactly twenty-eight inches, which happens to be the average American draw-length. (People have varied arm lengths and chest spans.) A factory-made bow of that strength is said to be "fifty pounds at twenty-eight inches" and marked on the bow this way: 50# @ 28".

A 40# bow set on the pegs would do the same with a forty-pound weight. To know what weight is right for you, you simply need to try out finished bows at an archery store. If you can pull the string back and touch the strong-side corner of your mouth with your index fingertip and hold this bow at full-draw for a few seconds without trembling (don't let go—or you may have to buy the bow . . . damaged!), try a higher poundage until you discover which bow strength is too much for you.

Now comes a dilemma: If the decision seems borderline, it is tempting to suggest that you go with the higher poundage, because as you grow into archery, your drawing strength will increase. Any archer should shoot as strong a bow as she can comfortably manage, because that bow will cast an arrow on a flatter trajectory compared to a weaker bow. A stronger bow makes aiming and accuracy easier.

But . . . using a bow that is too strong will most definitely prevent a beginner archer from learning the proper form. Going overboard on poundage is common, especially among males. Bad habits are sure to work their way into such an archer's technique, and once those habits are in place they are frustratingly difficult to purge. My best suggestion is this: Before you make or purchase a bow, start with a very comfortable bow provided by a teacher. Later, move up in poundage only after the perfect form has been earned. My adult male students rarely begin their lessons with a bow stronger than thirty pounds. Adult females average twenty pounds. After a month of practicing, each gender is likely more suited for a bow ten pounds stronger; however, it is doubtful they could have arrived at this accomplished form with a heavier bow from the beginning.

### Cutting the String Notches

To test the strength of your bow, carve string notches into the limbs a half-inch from the tips. These notches can be cut with a knife, but they should be smoothed to prevent sharp edges from abrading a string. Use any string that will not noticeably stretch. When you outfit the bow with a string at this point, don't try to bend the bow to the arc you see for its finished future. Bend it only enough to get the string positioned away from the handle area.

### Reading the Draw-Weight

Like you did earlier in this chapter (*Determining Your Bow's Length*), make a calibrated "arrow," this time out of a stiff dowel or strip of wood that will not flex. Cut a V-notch into one end to serve as a nock. From the valley of that nock, stretch a measuring tape and make marks on the wood starting at twenty inches, then twenty-and-a-half inches, then twenty-one inches,

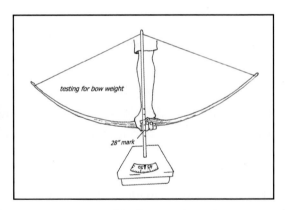

testing for bow weight

28" mark

twenty-one-and-a-half inches, etc., up to thirty-four inches. Cut away any excess dowel beyond thirty-four inches.

Load this calibrated shaft onto the string just as if you were planning to shoot it. Push the tip end straight down onto a bathroom scale. You can read the poundage at every draw-length. In this way you can patiently work toward the draw-weight you desire to achieve at a twenty-eight-inch draw or at your particular draw-length.

## *Tillering*

Getting the bow's limbs to bend equally is important. A tillering board is simply a bow support and a calibrated background of lines that allow you to fine-tune the limbs until their bends are mirror images of one another. The board can be drawn on a wall or on a sheet of plywood that you mount on a post or wall. The face of my tillering board is merely a grid of small squares that can be used to visually check the symmetry of a bow's bend by comparing one limb to the other while drawing the bow from a distance.

The grid helps you identify asymmetry, especially if you checkerboard the grid squares for easier visual study. I use identical symbols on corresponding mirror-image squares for even better recognition.

When you are nearing the end of the wood removal on your bow, use the tillering board frequently, but before you mount the bow each time, bend it a dozen times over your knee to loosen it up. Then after viewing the bend on the board, mark tight spots on the belly of the bow with a pencil and then rasp there. Repeat this process until the bow bends evenly.

## Making a Tillering Board

Unless you have a wall that can be used, all you need is a three-foot-by-six-foot sheet of plywood and a strong post (a two-inch by six-inch by six-foot board works well). Using a yardstick, make a grid of two-inch squares on the face of the plywood. For a group project each student could provide his own pair of symbols on the checkerboard squares. Each pair should show analogous mirror-image positions on the grid, measured from the vertical line of symmetry at the center of the board.

Attach two shelf brackets just below the top of the grid and centered three inches apart. Pad the brackets to protect the handle of the bow. When the tillering board is later propped up vertically, the bow must rest in these brackets in a perfectly horizontal position.

With the grid complete, drill and screw the plywood centered and squared to the post. Leave six inches of the post extending above the plywood. Cut notches in the sides of the post above the grid and near the post's bottom for lashing the tillering board to any substantial upright.

Using a tree or some other upright, lash the post vertically by tying the post at the upper and lower notches. Orient the board to face an open space where you can step back ten feet to view the grid. At the bottom notches on the post, tie a small pulley at the centerline of the post. Make sure that the unstrung bow lies perfectly horizontal on these supports.

An extra-long bow-string will be used exclusively for tillering. Make the loops for this string large enough to slip on and off the notches easily. Attach this string so it sags several inches beneath the unbent, horizontal bow in a shallow catenary.

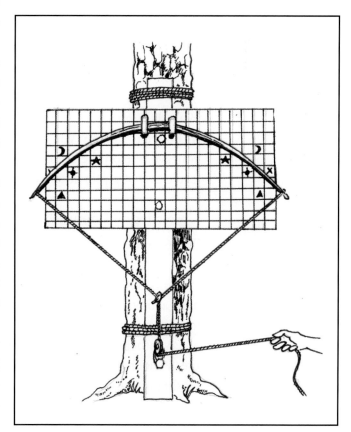

Now run a strong cord from your viewing spot, through the pulley, and up to the midpoint of the loose tillering bow-string where you will tie it with a reliable knot. By pulling on the other end of the cord (extending away from the tillering board) you can view the bending of the bow from a strategic distance. (This is also a safe place to be should the bow—heaven forbid—break!)

### Using the Tiller

Each time you wish to check the symmetry of the bow's bend, first bend it over your knee a dozen times to warm up the fibers. Then attach the loose tillering bow-string to the bow's notches and set the bow in the brackets. Before doing any bending, take time to adjust the relaxed bow until it lies in a perfectly horizontal position. This might mean shimming beneath the handle on one bow support with an extra wrap of padding.

Keeping a little tension on the pulley rope, walk back ten to fifteen feet for a good perspective and pull the long cord a few times to compare the bend of the two limbs of the bow. Use the correlating symbols as a visual guide for gauging whether or not there is a symmetrical, mirror-image bend of the limbs.

Wherever one limb appears too stiff to match the other limb's bend, mark that stiff spot with charcoal on the belly of the bow. Remove the bow from the tillering device and patiently scrape away a small layer of wood at the mark. Then return the bow to the tillering board to test it again.

Remember, don't overdraw the bow early in the project.

## Heat-Straightening and -Bending

Almost any odd bend in the wood can be satisfactorily straightened by steam or boiling water—except for two problematic cases: 1. a bow that arcs sideways as viewed from the belly; and 2. a bow with a propeller twist. In the case of the former, if the arc is shallow, you can let it work in your favor by shooting the bow with its concave side on the same side you plan to load an arrow. But, in my experience, the latter case of a propeller twist is a problem without a lasting solution.

### Correcting an Unwanted Bend in the Unstrung Bow

The primitive methods of shaping a bow by heat are problematic enough that I will offer the high-tech system that I eventually adopted for my classes. Too many of my students' bows became scorched by using the method of an open fire pit, hand-rubbed animal or vegetable oil, and radiant heat from hot coals. Scorching dooms a bow. It is a heart-breaking experience to ruin a bow after so much scraping and tillering.

Another primitive method calls for a tightly mud-packed trench filled with creek water that must be sustained at a boiling temperature for an hour or more by adding red-hot stones. Such a project would necessitate a tribe of helpers who must remain dedicated to the water supply, the fire, and the boiling. This is why I offer a less primitive technique that celebrates the wonderful efficiency of forged metal.

Acquire a long, heavy-duty, metal pipe with a six-inch diameter and weld a circular plate of metal on one end to seal it so it will hold water. The pipe's walls should be at least five-sixteenths of an inch thick. Prop this pipe inside an open-topped, metal, fifty-five-gallon drum in which you will build a fire. Cut a four-inch-by-four-inch air intake portal near the bottom on the rounded side of the barrel. Fill the pipe with water and the barrel with firewood and light the pyre through the air portal. When the water in the pipe comes to a boil, lower the bow into the water by using a wire handle wrapped around the top notches. Heat from forty minutes to an hour. (You'll have to experiment with boiling time for your particular bow.) Then lift the bow out and, using hot pads, gently bend the troublesome spot by using leverage gained from the crotch of a tree. Hold until it cools. It may take two or three boilings to get it just right.

If a limb has recurve—that is, if one tip curls upward while at rest on the tillering board—consider this an asset. Match the other limb to it by heating and bending. If the problem is a kink that can't be removed by boiling, match the other limb to it as best you can. A bow with symmetry is better than one with asymmetry.

## Finishing Touches

When the bow bends evenly on the tillering board . . . and the proper bow weight has been achieved . . . and when all heat-straightening is complete . . . erase any tool marks by gently scraping the bow with a perpendicular knife blade. (Any groove, divot, or gouge left on the bow is a potential breaking point.) Sand to a smooth finish using progressively finer "scraping rocks" (or sandpaper), and then burnish all the wood surfaces by rubbing every outer wood fiber with the rounded side of a small glass bottle or rounded bone.

Next, oil the bow by hand near a heat source—a good reason to make this craft a winter project. You can buy wood oils or render oil from the skin of a road-killed raccoon, beaver, or opossum. After removing the skin, lay the flesh side down in a frying pan on very low heat. As the fatty tissue in the pelt heats up, oil will begin to fill the pan.

Rub warm oil into your bow every night for two weeks, pressing more lubricant deeper into the fibers with each application. Doing this work next to a wood stove is ideal. One of these subsequent oiling sessions takes only fifteen minutes. Each time you finish, leave the bow propped several feet away from the wood stove, where it can still soak up some of the radiant heat that helps to drive the oil deeper into the wood.

This oiling process is a time when a first-time bowyer really bonds with his bow. A lot of hard work has gone into the bow's creation. It is fitting that this final step be soothing and contemplative and loyally applied on time.

After this initial oiling treatment on a new bow, reapply oil one night every two months for the life of the bow. As you can see, a relationship has begun—one that lasts the lifetime of the bow . . . and, perhaps, the lifetime of the bowyer.

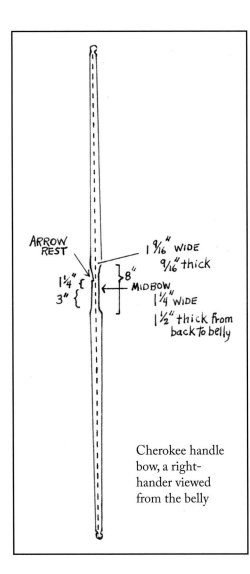

ARROW
REST

1¼" {

3" {

1 9/16" WIDE

9/16" thick

8"

MIDBOW

1¼" WIDE

1½" thick from back to belly

Cherokee handle
bow, a right-
hander viewed
from the belly

## The Handle Bow

A more evolved Cherokee bow design uses a bulked-up handle, much thicker (back to belly) and less wide than the limbs. To make this bow, after drawing the centerline on the stave, mark four inches from the midpoint in both directions for the handle. In addition, make a mark for the arrow-rest (or shelf) one-and-a-quarter inches above the midpoint. (Modern right-handed archers load on the left side of a bow; lefties on the right.) This shelf should be cut only a quarter-inch deep, so as not to endanger the bow. (In shooting the finished bow, cant the upper limb of the bow to your strong side to keep the arrow perched in its place on the shelf.) Make one more mark three inches below the midpoint. It is from these last two marks that the handle area will begin to widen to the two four-inch marks to begin the widest part of the limbs.

The thickness of the handle will eventually measure about one-and-a-half to one-and-three-quarters inches, depending on the size of your hand. The width of the handle will measure about one-and-a-quarter inches.

Each of the limbs of the handle bow can measure about one and nine-sixteenths inches wide at its widest point and then taper arbitrarily toward the limb tips. The thickness of the limbs at this widest point can be about nine-sixteenths of an inch and also arbitrarily taper. The limb thickness will have to be worked out in the tillering process, in which you will achieve the bow-strength (draw-weight) you desire.

# The String

The Cherokee preferred woodchuck (groundhog) skin made into rawhide for their bow-strings. (Refer to *Volume 3* for skinning, scraping, drying, and making a pelt into rawhide.)

### Making a Woodchuck Skin String

After cutting a woodchuck rawhide into an oval or circle, cut a three-sixteenths-of-an-inch-thin strip around the edge, continuing to spiral inward to achieve an impressive length of strip. For a six-foot bow you'll need two or three fourteen-foot strands, depending upon the strength of the bow. Use two strands for bows with less than 35# draw-weight.

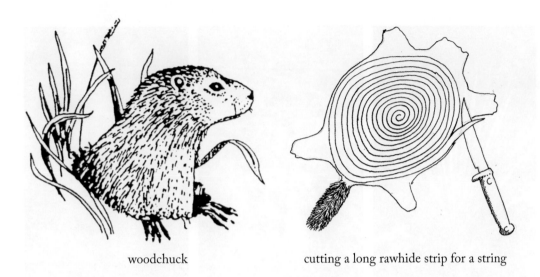

woodchuck                    cutting a long rawhide strip for a string

Wet the strands until pliable and double them by folding at the middle over the strong nub of a small broken branch. Start turning all the strands together (four or six, now that they are doubled) into a tight twist to make a four-inch-long section. Remove the small loop from the nub. Then take half of the loose strands and thread their free ends through the small loop. By pulling this tight, a new string loop forms and the old smaller loop becomes embedded in the twisted bow-string.

Now slip this new larger loop over a tall branch nub and tie the bottom ends of all the strands together in one common overhand knot. Secure this knotted end to a brick-sized rock so that the rock hovers slightly off the ground in order to maintain a constant stretching pressure on the string being made. Spin the rock so the wet strands twist and tighten. When the string is tightly wound, secure the rock to a tree trunk so it cannot unwind. When the string dries you have a bow-string that can be looped over the lower limb notches. Then tie the loose end to the upper limb notches while the bow is bent.

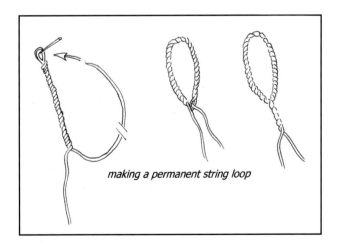

*making a permanent string loop*

yucca                    dogbane                  common milkweed

There are a few plant fibers that are strong enough to serve as bow-strings. All require multiple splicing to achieve the needed length for a bow. Among these are yucca, dogbane, and common milkweed. Refer to *Volume 1* for details.

## Determining Proper String Tension

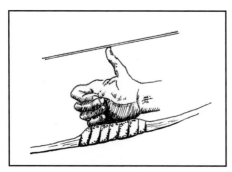

The distance from the belly of a strung bow to its string is called the "brace height," and its measurement varies with bow styles. The brace height of the longbows we have covered should be one "fist-mele." This old English term is a measure made by a fist and an extended thumb (about six inches). Such a "hitchhiker's fist" should fit between bow-handle and string. Adjust the bow's bend accordingly. (Recurve bows' brace heights average seven-and-a-half to nine-and-a-half inches.)

## Stringing and Unstringing Your Bow: The Bow-Stringer

There are several ways to bend the bow for stringing. The easiest by far is to use a bow-stringer. To use one of these handy devices, you need a pre-set loop on each end of your bow-string. The archer must, therefore, determine where to tie a second loop on the string to allow for a proper brace height. This is accomplished by trial and error. Make the second loop large enough to slide down the limb when not strung, so at rest the slack bow-string remains attached to the bow by both loops.

The bow-stringer is simply a strong cord (about five inches longer than your bow-string) with a leather pocket attached at each end—one pocket slightly larger than the other. The larger pocket fits over the fixed end of the bow-string (the lower limb notches) and the smaller pocket barely fits over the other limb's tip, leaving the *upper limb notches exposed.*

### Using the Bow-Stringer

With the bow-string relaxed on the bow (the small loop snug in the lower limb notches and the larger loop slid down the upper limb), attach the large pouch of the stringer over the lower limb tip. This pouch should cover the notches to help hold the lower loop in place. Cap the smaller pouch over the other tip, leaving the empty notches visible. Hold the bow by the handle with

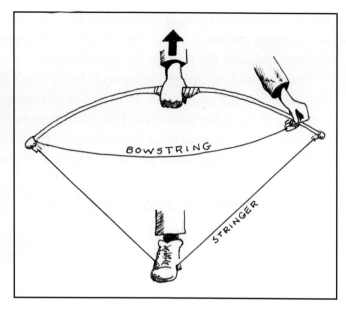

the back of the bow facing up. With the stringer sagging beneath bow and string, bend forward and step on the stringer. As you pull the handle upward, the stringer bends the bow, allowing you to slide the loose bow-string loop into its notches. Reverse the process to unstring the bow.

**Warning: Before shooting a bow always check to see that both bow-string loops are firmly embedded in their notches.**

## *Tightening a Finished Bow-String*

Once the bow-string has both ends tied with permanent loops, it can be left slack on the bow (when not in use), its small loop notched, its large loop slid down its limb. If ever the string stretches and the brace height is reduced, proper tension and brace height can be reclaimed by removing one loop from the bow entirely and then twisting the string to shorten it.

### Step-Through Stringing

This is a stringing technique to use when one end of your bow-string remains tied to the bow at all times and the other end is un-looped and must be tied each time it is strung. Instructions for right-handers: Stand with the bow held vertically in front of you with your right hand on the upper limb, belly of the bow facing left, the end of the bow with the fixed string loop touching the ground. In your left hand hold the free end of the string.

Keeping the belly to the left, place the bottom tip of the bow on the left side of your left boot. Holding the loose string well out to your left, step through the V made by bow and string with your right foot. Now your

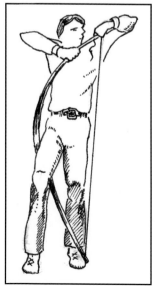

right leg becomes a fulcrum as you bend the top limb toward your left hand where you can wrap the loose end of the string into the upper notches and tie it off once you have eyeballed the fistmele for brace height.

The drawback to this stringing style is that each time you string the bow, only the top limb of the bow bends. To even out this monopoly on bending, change the fixed loop to the other end of the bow from time to time. In this way, the fibers of one limb will not be weakened faster than the other limb's fibers.

(If you are a lefty, reverse all these "lefts" and "rights.")

## *The Symmetrical-Bend Stringing Method*

This method of stringing is for bows having string loops at both ends, both loops remaining relaxed on the bow when unstrung. This technique bends both limbs of the bow simultaneously and symmetrically.

### Stringing Symmetrically

First, for safety, wear goggles to protect your eyes in case the bow's upper limb slips out of your hand—especially if yours is a recurve bow. Check the bottom loop of the string. It should be secure in its notches. If stringing a recurve bow, be sure the string touches only the belly of the bow all along the lower recurve.

Stand with your feet wider than your shoulders, and—if you are a righty—hold the bow in front of your torso with your right hand on the handle, belly of the bow facing away from you. Turn your torso and the bow's belly to the left and lower the bow almost to the ground. Touch the lower limb-tip to the instep of your right foot just above the sole of your boot. The belly of the bow should remain facing to your left. Now, as you lean from the waist, tilt the top of the bow over to the left so the back of the bow faces right and up. In this position the loose string sags beneath the bow's belly. Bend both legs for balance and stability.

With your right hand still on the handle, use your left to slide the slack string loop as high as it will go up the upper limb. Place the heel of your left hand on the back of the bow just beneath the slack loop, and then lower the top limb of the bow to the left until you can straighten your left arm. With the heel of that hand braced on the back of the bow, loosely support the sides of the upper string loop with the tips of thumb and index.

Bend the bow by pulling the handle up and to the right with your right hand while pushing down on the top limb with your left hand and stiffened arm. Make the bow bend enough until you can easily glide the string loop up the limb toward the upper notches.

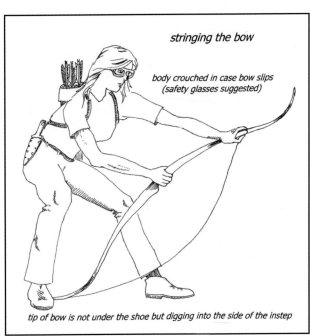

*stringing the bow*

*body crouched in case bow slips (safety glasses suggested)*

*tip of bow is not under the shoe but digging into the side of the instep*

If you find yourself forcefully pushing the loop upward with tension, you are not bending the bow enough. (You can't push a taut string upward; you can only bring the notches down to the loop by bending the bow. If you are not able to bend the bow enough to string it, it's time for the previously discussed bow-stringer.)

When the string loop snaps into place check both upper and lower notches to ensure that both loops are secure in their respective notches . . . and that the string is positioned only on the belly side of the bow.

**Warning: When using this method, never put your left-hand fingers between the string and the belly of the bow! And never allow the bent bow to slip from the hand or foot.**

## The Dry-Fire Disaster

Once the bow is strung, never pull back the unloaded (arrowless) string to full-draw and let go! This mistake is called a "dry-fire" and can break or fracture the bow . . . causing either an immediate catastrophe or a later one. Having a bow break in your hands while at full-draw is like being on the receiving end of a flying bola from an angry Argentinean gaucho!

# Shooting Your Primitive Bow

The first Cherokee self-bow described in this chapter has no arrow-rest or shelf except for your hand, the top of which roughly forms a right angle (an L) with the side of the bow. If the bow is held vertically, the arrow sits in that L, touching the vertical stem of the L and pressing its weight down onto the foot of the L. Since the handle portion of the bow is wide, the arrow will have to shoot around this width of the bow. This causes the arrow to wobble in the early part of its flight, though it will stabilize for the latter part of the flight. The bigger problem is that the bow's wood pushes the arrow to the left. (Modern bowyers eliminate this problem by cutting "sight-windows" into the wood, usually to the center of the bow, thus allowing the arrow to move straight ahead "through" the bow.)

Both parts of the L exert pressure on the arrow at release. The lift portion of this interference is not a problem, but the lateral movement is. (For a right-hander, this means the arrow is pushed to the left.) By canting the bow 45 degrees (top of the bow swinging to the strong side), the problem can be remedied. With this cant the shelf transforms from an L to a wide V arrow-rest. Both sides of the V exert pressure on the arrow when it is released. The sum of these two vectors is a vertical lift. Again, lift is not a problem.

The canted bow also opens up your field of vision. This is a decided advantage when shooting at a moving target, but I believe it makes for more pleasant shooting even at a stationary target simply because the width of the bow is not interfering with your view downrange.

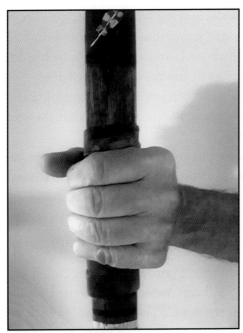

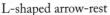
L-shaped arrow-rest                    V-shaped arrow-rest

The Cherokee handle bow does use a rest, but it is not cut to center. Cant it also to achieve the same good results. With a little experimentation, you will learn at what position your particular bow shoots best.

The self-bow is generally not capable of holding up to repeated sustained full-draws, which is why the Indian technique evolved toward a fluid shot without hesitation. With a self-bow, it is recommended to draw as you raise the bow and arrow to bear on the target . . . or as you push your left arm toward the shooting position with the arrow aiming at the target all along . . . or as you lower the bow after beginning with the arrow pointed skyward. In each case, the arrow should be released as soon as full-draw is reached. In other words, the drawing and the aiming are synchronized to be complete at the moment the arrow is fully drawn.

There will be much more to come in this book regarding shooting techniques. Even if you are using modern, factory-made bows with sight windows cut to the center, be sure to try the canted position for the bow. You may, as I do, prefer it.

*Do you see that crow . . . how straight he flies? When he drops a few feathers onto the forest floor for me to pick up and use as fletching, my arrow will fly straight, too.*

—Bobby Spotted Horse, *A Dance in the Devil's Rain*

# CHAPTER 5
# A Feathered Stick—Arrow-Making

## *Arrow-Shaft Materials*

An ideal arrow shaft follows the rule of the four Ls: It should be **linear**, **light**, **lithe**, and **ligneous**. 1. An arrow needs to be *straight* in order to follow a straight trajectory. A curved shaft will fly astray, just like a car with its front wheels slightly turned. 2. An arrow's *lightness* affords speed, which affects its gravitational drop for a given distance. An arrow too heavy moves off the bow sluggishly, its speed so diminished that it cannot reach an appreciable distance before gravity pulls it to the ground. 3. *Flexibility* allows the arrow to absorb the initial launch off the bow by bending back and forth before it gradually stabilizes in the air. Without this ability to flex back and forth (especially at the beginning of its flight), an arrow would take an unwanted lateral leap off the arrow-rest. In essence, because of this oscillation of the shaft, a fully drawn arrow will not pass through the exact position it held on the bow before it was drawn. (This is a brief introduction to a phenomenon called "the archer's paradox.") 4. The woody requirement of a shaft simply reflects durability. If an arrow is intended to be used time and again, it needs to hold up to the stress of impact. There are new materials in the world of archery that have replaced wood for arrow shafting, but the original arrows of history relied upon the wonders of wood for longevity.

There are a number of trees and shrubs in Southern Appalachia whose branches turn the heads of wandering archers for straightness alone: those dogwoods that love the stream banks, the shoots of blueberry, maples, wild rose, and certain viburnums (like "arrow-wood," *Viburnum dentatum*).

Sourwood presents a supreme oxymoron: In Southern Appalachia it is the most contorted of all the large trees, making impressive sculptures of trunk and limbs, yet when under stress it often produces perfectly straight shoots from the base of the tree and from reclined trunks. The downside of sourwood is its density and weight. Still, the Cherokee utilized it; because, in the thick forests of Southern Appalachia, a heavier arrow did not necessarily pose a problem. Hunters were forced by the landscape to move in close to prey in order to have a clean shot through so much foliage, vines, branches, and trunks. Long shots were rare. Stalking became more important than exemplary archery equipment. After stealthily moving within ten yards of a deer, a Cherokee hunter considered his sourwood arrow to be stout and dependable for such a close shot.

### Harvesting Arrow Shafts from Trees and Shrubs

From the trees and shrubs mentioned above, sourwood is easiest to locate in the mountains. Cut straight shoots in winter, and then scrape away the thin layer of bark by using a perpendicular knife blade. To prepare for thorough drying, alternate every other shaft's direction to make a more cylindrical bundle and then lash the bundle to a straight support and let dry for two months or longer. Later, if straightening is needed for any shafts, use the heating procedure explained below. To ensure a consistent thickness along the shaft, use a rock with a hole drilled through it as a caliper.

## *Rivercane*

A more abundant source of arrow-shaft material was available to the Cherokee, and this plant still thrives today along the streams of the Southeast and up into the Ohio Valley. Rivercane is a native grass that grows large enough for blowguns, but

rivercane

bamboo

it can seldom be found much larger. One variety of rivercane, often called "switch-cane," does not develop to arrow-shaft size. It might grow to be four feet tall, but its culm (the stem-like cane) is too thin and weak to serve as an arrow.

Rivercane is related to bamboo, a non-native grass (containing over a thousand species) introduced from Asia. Both plants are usable as arrow shafts, but rivercane is the superior material because it is tougher. To differentiate the two, look for river-cane's bushier, higher-angled branching and longer sections per given thickness of culm. Bamboo has more pronounced, bumpier joints at the nodes.

Like most bamboo, rivercane has hollow sections divided by solid septa at the joints. The resulting lightness—in addition to its flexibility and tough woody texture—makes this grass an exceptional

Dead rivercane showing its bushy branching

candidate for an arrow shaft. However, no matter how straight a specimen might appear from a distance, none is truly straight. This grass typically grows in a zigzag fashion—each section taking off in an alternating zig or zag . . . plus, each section is subtly arced. All this mixed misdirection can be overcome by heat-straightening—a craft performed around a campfire. Once you engage in it, the smell of heated cane will forever make you think of arrows.

Rivercane was an important craft material to the Cherokee people. They sometimes burned long stretches of floodplains to encourage its growth. Its underground rhizomes survived the fire, while other plants succumbed. This crude agricultural practice allowed rivercane to monopolize stream banks in botanical colonies that came to be known as "cane-brakes." Many such brakes still exist today along the creeks and rivers of Southern Appalachia.

What size cane will you need? This will require experimenting and will depend upon bow-strength, which leads us to a discussion about arrow stiffness, or spine-weight.

canebrake

## *Arrow Spine-Weight*

When an arrow is propelled forward by a bow-string, the arrow bends and flexes back and forth before eventually straightening out. To see this phenomenon on slow-motion film may be, at first viewing, a surprise. It seems improbable that such a whip-lashing projectile could be depended upon for accuracy. Yet the shaft does calm down, and the initial distortion is all a part of the plan.

If the arrow bends too much it will shoot wildly off to one side and high. If it bends not enough it will also jump to the side but fly sluggishly. I have seen Cherokee arrows almost as thick as my little finger and others the size of a pencil. The proof is in the shooting. When you have made an arrow that performs well off your bow—that is, it flies to the place you intend it to fly—use that arrow as your standard and measure its flex on a homemade spine tester.

### Making a Primitive Spine Tester

To a twenty-eight-inch-long board base attach a four-inch support on each end as seen in the illustration. Cut a one-inch-deep V-notch into the top of a five-inch support and attach it to the midpoint of the back of the base. Fashion a weight-platform with a triangular cross section to fit into this notch and to reach forward to the front of the base. Lash a brick or hefty stone permanently to the top of the platform near its front end.

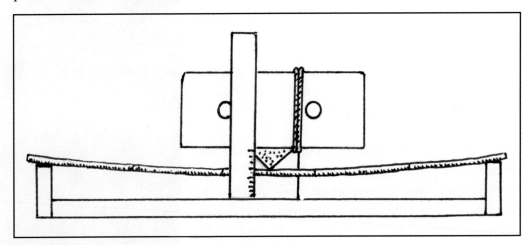

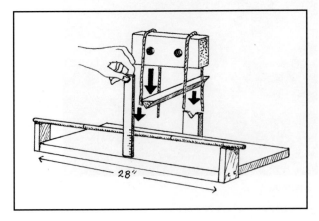

Lay a favored arrow shaft—one that has been proven to shoot true—on the two side supports. Fit the platform flush into its rear notch and lower its front end (with stone weight) to bear down on the middle of the shaft. Then look under the shaft at a vertical ruler to see how far the shaft bends. Now you have a standard by which to test other shafts before you go to the trouble of straightening. In time you'll not need to use this contraption as you simply test a shaft with your hands.

### Harvesting and Preparing a Cane Shaft

Cut your arrow-shaft cane in mid- to late summer when the woody tissue is hard. In the bow-making chapter you learned how to determine your draw-length. Add one to three inches to this measurement for your preferred arrow length. This extra length of the arrow—extending from the back of the bow at full-draw—serves the archer as she uses her peripheral vision to determine the left-right accuracy of her aim. Cut the appropriate shaft section from the harvested cane by notching a ring around it with a sharp knife until the cane breaks off cleanly.

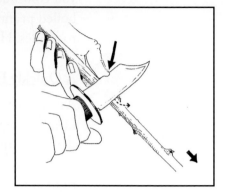

Carefully remove all branches and branch nubs by pushing the back of the knife blade with your thumb *toward the top end of the cane*. (See *Volume 2*, Chapter 5.)

With a perpendicular blade lightly scrape away the glazed, silica layer on the cane (this will augment the oiling process) and then carefully trim away the bulging rings at the nodes. Sand the shaft, paying extra attention to the nodes to achieve a uniform smoothness along the shaft.

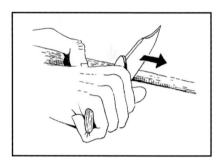

Now the cane is prepared to receive oil. (See *Finishing Touches* on page 43 for making oil from animal skin.) Around a campfire rub oil into the cane's surface, frequently exposing it to the radiant heat of the hot coals to persuade the oil to penetrate deeper into the cane walls.

*progression of cane straightening*

### Heat-Straightening the Shaft

Work on only one section of the cane at a time, starting with its "banana" curve. Hold the cane five to six inches over a bed of hardwood coals and rotate as you slowly thrust it forward and back, heating the section you wish to straighten at that time. It takes about a minute to reach the proper bending temperature. Test the heat content in the cane by guardedly (briefly) touching your fingers to the shaft. If it is too hot for a lingering touch, it's ready. Place the heated curved section in the fork of a tree and bend it just slightly beyond straight. Hold it in place until it cools. A second or third treatment may be necessary for the same section.

Next, do the same for a neighboring section. When each of these two sections are individually straight, it's time to heat the joint between them and align the two straight sections into a longer, straight double-section. And so this process goes as you continue to align the next section. The smell of heated cane is reminiscent of boiled peanuts, a popular and traditional snack of Southern Appalachia sold along roadsides. Have a snack handy. You might get hungry.

### A Quickly Finished Arrow

After achieving a straight shaft, carefully cut a slot into each end of the shaft—one ideally a half-inch in front of a septum to receive the arrowhead and the other three-eighths of an inch behind a septum to serve as the nock. To prevent splitting begin each slot by scratching out the cross-grain cut first. Initiate the other two cuts right at the cross-grain cut and apply pressure toward the end of the shaft. The nock will require lashing at its base with coils of thin cordage to prevent splitting into the main part of the shaft. Do this lashing as an extension of the feather lashing. Tie whole feathers a half-inch in front of the nock on opposite sides of the shaft, just as you did with the atlatl spear in Chapter 3. Continue this lashing slightly behind the nock's cross-grain cut so that the bow-string will contact that lashing when the arrow is loaded. Such padding by the lashing will prevent the bow-string from driving into and splitting the cane.

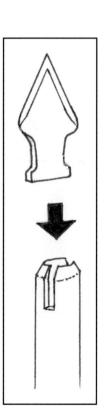

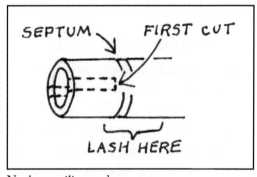
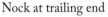

Nock at trailing end

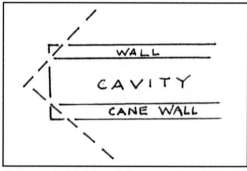

Penetrating angles at lead end

On the leading end of the shaft carve a beveled angle around the rim of the cane's opening. Without this angle the rim of the cane will balk at penetrating a target.

Stone-knapping—a science of its own—is beyond the scope of this book, but many materials can be scraped, carved, or filed into an arrowhead shape. Insert a stone, antler, turtle shell, metal, or hardwood point and lash it tightly from the neck to a quarter-inch beyond the slot.

You now have a basic and complete arrow. But we'll soon cover a smarter arrow with a wooden insert on each end.

### Making Multiple Shafts

Harvest a dozen appropriately sized canes and clean them of branching. Turn half upside down, mix them together, and bundle them all in a firm stack. Lash this stack to a straight post in a dry, ventilated place away from direct sunlight and season for two or more months until light and dry. Then finish as instructed above.

## Adding Fore-Shaft and Nock Inserts

So often when an arrow breaks on impact, that break occurs just an inch or two behind the point. Such an accident with the arrow described above would necessitate starting over with a new shaft of cane, because shortening the shaft by cutting away the broken part would increase the spine-weight and alter the up and down calculation for aiming. An improved arrow design involves making a replaceable fore-shaft. Likewise, making a nock insert provides a stronger tail end of the arrow.

Instead of cutting the ends of the shaft close to septa, allow for two inches of cane to extend beyond the point-end septum and one inch from the nock septum.

### Making a Fore-Shaft

Select a straight piece of dead hardwood—like dogwood, ash, locust, or oak—and carve it into a five-inch-long cylinder with a thickness that matches the outside diameter of the leading end of your cane. Reduce one end of this hardwood into a smaller cylinder as the insert, a two-inch plug that will slide inside the cane and just touch the first septum. This leaves three inches of exposed hardwood in front. Cut a slot into the leading end and then taper the sides for a beveled penetrating angle. Score grooves into the exposed surfaces a half-inch on either side of the ring where the cane and fore-shaft flange join. Apply a light layer of glue to the grooves and bind tightly with thread.

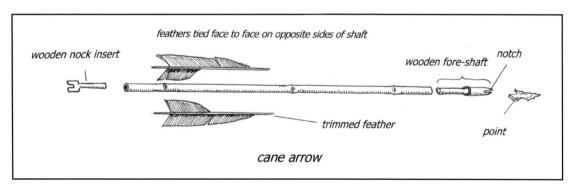

feathers tied face to face on opposite sides of shaft

wooden nock insert

wooden fore-shaft

notch

trimmed feather

point

cane arrow

### Making a Nock Insert

Repeat the above exercise, this time carving a one-inch plug and leaving a half-inch of exposed wood for the nock. There is no need to taper this piece at the slot. Score a half-inch of the cane and the leading end of the exposed wood of the nock to just behind the valley of the nock's groove. Glue and bind this scored area. By having the binding extend to and slightly trespass on the slot area, the bow-string will touch the binding when the arrow is loaded on the bow. Wait to perform this binding until you are ready to lash the rear of the fletching. One binding will serve both, securing the trailing quill of the feathers and the leading edge of the nock.

## *Improved Fletching*

The purpose of arrow fletching is twofold. First, the drag of feathers slows down the back end of the shaft, ensuring that the front end always leads. The fletching we have covered up to this point does accomplish this. But feathers can provide another asset if arranged in such a way that they cause the shaft to spin. Like a spiraling football, an arrow's flight can be stabilized by the gyroscopic effect.

The modern arrow uses like sections of split feathers glued at a helical angle to the shaft, prompting the arrow to spin as it flies. A primitive version of the gyroscopic effect can be accomplished by using whole feathers from the same wing (left or right, not a mix) with a simple removal of filaments from a portion of the quill.

### Preparing Feathers for a Gyroscopic Spin

Choose two feathers from the same wing of a turkey, vulture, goose, chicken, or any other large bird whose feather-use is not prohibited by federal law. (The great majority of birds are protected, including hawks, owls, condors, and songbirds. Most people do not realize that it is illegal to own a feather from a robin, woodpecker, sparrow, etc. A steep fine and imprisonment are possible.) Decide upon a four-inch to five-inch section of filaments to use from each feather, resulting in two similarly sized sections of feathers to be mounted. Leave a half-inch of quill extending from either end of the filaments. If the quill extensions are thick, trim the underside (concave side) so the remaining quill will lie flat against the shaft when mounted

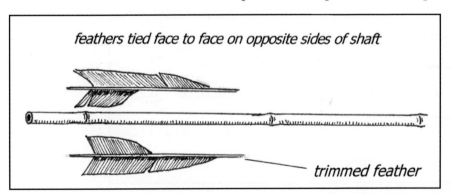

feathers tied face to face on opposite sides of shaft

trimmed feather

and lashed. Now remove the front half of the filaments from one side of each quill (same side for each feather before mounting). When the feathers are tied (concave side facing concave side) on opposite sides of the shaft, these gaps will appear on alternate sides of the fletching and create spin.

Another feather design that creates gyroscopic spin involves trimming all the filaments on the same side of each feather down to three-eighths of an inch. Again, when the two feathers are mounted to the shaft, these trimmed portions appear on alternate sides of the fletching. In other words, one section of trimmed filaments lies across from the other feather's full section of filaments.

## Attaching Feathers to the Shaft

Score the shaft (at the two bare quill areas) and bind the two feathers on opposite sides of the shaft, concave sides facing one another, the end of the quill three-quarters of an inch in front of the nock. Taper the leading edge of the quill with a knife and paint the scored area on the shaft with glue. Then bind the quill to the arrow shaft. This binding will protect your bow-hand when shooting. (A loose quill of feather can penetrate the hand when shooting.) Paint the scored area on the trailing end, bind the bare quill, and continue this binding to secure the nock.

For a three-feather, helical-spin arrangement, choose three feathers from same-side wings, section them as before, and then carefully slice the quill lengthwise to leave a flattish base for gluing to

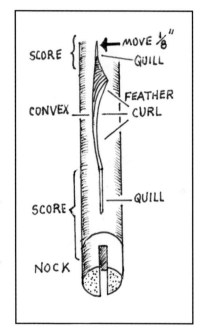

Turkey wing feathers trimmed asymmetrically for gyroscopic spin; turtle shell point on fore-shaft (both attached by sinew and topped with a dark band of pine pitch glue); tulip tree bark quiver sits nearby at upper right part of photo.

the shaft. Position each feather at a slight angle to the shaft, the leading end nudged one-eighth of an inch in the direction of the convex side of the feather's curl.

There is no moment quite like the one when a student loads a self-made arrow onto a self-made bow and launches the feathered arrow into the air. A piece of the archer's spirit flies with that arrow. Because the bow and arrow far exceeds the capacity of all other projectiles before it, perhaps this moment of firing the first arrow marks humankind's first dramatic venture into *flight*, paving the way for the Wrights at Kitty Hawk and every astronaut who would strap himself/herself into a rocket.

# *Arrowheads*

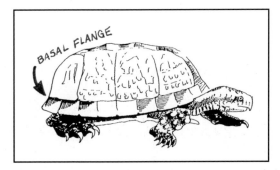

Points can be made of chipped or abraded stone, turtle shell, bone, hardwood, antler, filed metal, seashell, weighted stout thorns, spent bullet shells, pressure-flaked glass, or anything your imagination might conjure. For starters find a dead box turtle's shell and, using a stone, crack free an area around the thick, basal flange. Choose a likely shard and scrape it against flat facets and corners of a heavy stone to achieve a usable shape. Do the same with found bones.

### Attaching an Arrowhead

The notch cut into the fore-shaft must be wide enough and deep enough to receive the base of the arrowhead. This base needs at a minimum a half-inch-long constricted haft or neck that is exactly the width of the fore-shaft so the binding will hold the arrowhead fast to the shaft.

Point scraped from deer antler

Taper the leading edge of the fore-shaft so it does not present a blunt leading end that would be counterproductive to penetration. Score the exposed surfaces of the tapered fore-shaft around the slot for the point and then insert the arrowhead. Use sinew (see *Volume 3*) moistened by saliva to wrap the point in place. Or paint the scored area with glue and wrap the joined area with thin cordage. Continue wrapping back along the shaft for a half-inch.

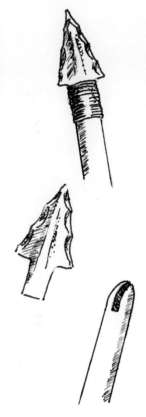

*"See the feathered stick fly,"* said the hawk proudly. *"The two-leggeds were wise to seek counsel from the wingeds."*

—the Goshawk's Tale

# CHAPTER 6

# Choosing Your Teaching Tools— Archery Equipment

## *Bows*

If you run classes in archery, you'll obviously need an arsenal of weaponry. Unless you are an accomplished, tireless, and prolific bowyer, I recommend that you purchase wood-laminate bows with fiberglass backing. Such bows shoot more smoothly and accurately than all-fiberglass bows. In short, they are more fun. Shop for bows with an aiming window cut to the center of the bow. Whether longbow or recurve, if treated with respect, these bows will last a teaching career and more.

For children you'll need bows ranging from 10# to 25# (measured at a twenty-eight-inch draw) in draw-weight. To accommodate those who cannot manage a 20# pull, you might need a few all-fiberglass bows of 15# or less. For adults the range of bows should run 18# to 35#. In order to absorb the proper shooting form, no novice should consider a bow heavier than these, even if he/she is a strong athlete.

Bows are made for right-handers (arrow shelf on the left), lefties (shelf on the right), and for either (some youth bows have shelves on both sides). Though length of bow is not a crucial calculation for lessons, for shooting stability consider bows forty-eight inches or longer for children and fifty-eight inches or longer for adults.

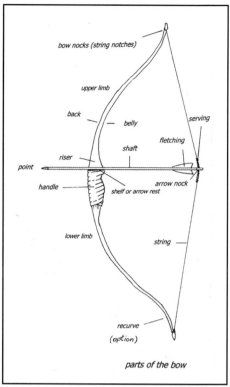

*parts of the bow*

Each archer must test bows of different strengths to determine which bow best suits her. If a bow is too weak, the archer will have to deal with more arc in the trajectory of arrow flight. This means that there is more room for error in long shots. If a bow is too strong, it will force the archer to struggle in the drawing of the string and in holding it at full-draw. Such struggling will cause excessive tensing of irrelevant muscles and make it impossible for the archer to attain perfect form.

### Choosing the Proper Bow Strength

Take the bow in your weak hand and determine which limb is the "upper" and which is the "lower." Do this by recognizing the shelf or arrow-rest that will support the arrow. Touch the string to the inside of your forearm and lower the arm to your side. Now the string should lie horizontally between forearm and hip. Spread your feet slightly wider than your shoulders. Spread your arms to either side like extended wings, your weak hand now holding the bow vertically, the string in front of the arm, not behind it.

Now pretend that you are standing in a creek, whose water level comes up to your chest. You do not want to get your arms "wet" during this exercise. Keep your arms level, as if lying upon an imaginary "tabletop" at shoulder-height. (Later, when we address shooting form, this tabletop will be a much-talked-about and much-used concept in the actual shooting of an arrow.)

Slightly bend your extended bow-arm in this wing position (still on the table-top). This subtle bend, as you will see, will serve as an important part of the proper shooting form. Now rotate your head to look at your bow. Twisting at the waist as little as possible, reach across your body with your free hand (keep that elbow "dry") to grasp the string in the distal creases of the middle three fingers. This particular finger attachment to the string is called the "English grip."

It is important to place your fingers on the string at the site where the arrow would be nocked. Visualize an arrow loaded on the bow and arrow-rest. Grasp the string accordingly. (In other words, not too high or too low on the string.) The thumb and pinky of the string-hand are never involved in the grip. Relax the thumb toward the palm. Be sure that both your bow-arm and string-arm are level on the tabletop. (To an observer, the string-arm is actually a little higher than the bow-arm. We could say that the string-arm lies on the tabletop while the bow-arm lies on the underside of the tabletop. But from the archer's perspective, it feels as if both arms lie on the tabletop.)

Bend the three finger joints over the string, relax your string-hand/wrist/forearm, and draw the string using your shoulder and back muscles—not your biceps. Do not make a fist . . . or any portion of a fist. As best you can at this point, allow the string-hand to be stretched flat, except for the outer joint of the three fingers that grip the string. (This feat is easier said than done, but strive for this relaxation now. Later, we will spend much more time perfecting this all-important paradox of utilizing the ends of the fingers while relaxing the rest of the hand, wrist, and forearm.)

As you draw the string, let the elbow lead the way. Throughout the draw, strive to keep the string-arm "dead" from your forearm to the first two-thirds of the gripping fingers. (Again, only the terminal finger joints are employed in holding the string.) Draw the string back until you can touch your index fingertip to the nearer corner of your mouth. Without changing the posture of your torso, tilt your head sideways toward the string-hand. You are now poised at full-draw. **Don't let go! Doing so would mean that you have performed the archer's taboo: a dry-fire!**

Throughout the draw, you'll want to feel *more* powerful than the bow. If the muscles do not tremble . . . and if you don't feel forced to crane your head forward . . . or arch your back . . . or grip the string with a fist . . . and if the pull feels substantially strong enough . . . this bow will work for you. Ease the string forward after testing.

## *Arrows*

If you are teaching young archers, you will probably want to buy premade youth arrows in bulk. There are some arrows on the market that bring nothing but frustration to a student. Do not buy any arrow with a plastic shaft or rubbery fletching. (Such a fletching is made as a solid pane without filaments.)

I suggest you buy arrows with Port Orford cedar shafts, real feather fletching, and crimped metallic points too dull even to scratch the skin. (3riversarchery.com and campexpress.com are two sources for cedar arrows.) When you order, ask for brightly colored shafts that will be easy to find when shots go astray in the grass or leaf litter.

Arrows are manufactured with specific spine-weights to match bows of varying draw-weights. But the "youth arrows" of cedar just mentioned have a spine-weight that can accommodate a mix of bows up to 35#.

## *Arrow Care*

To prevent breaking or losing arrows, there are suggested rules for all students to follow:

1. Never shoot at a target too dense or too hard to be easily penetrated.
2. Do not handle the arrow by its feathered section. Fletching must maintain its natural form. Touch a feather only when carefully preening it back into shape after being ruffled.
3. Never run to retrieve arrows, especially after a class makes shots into the ground at a distant target. Hasty retrievers might break arrows that fell short.
4. When pulling an arrow out of a target, grasp it near the penetration point and pull in a direction that is the perfect reverse of its entry direction. Pull with the elbow above the arrow, not below.
5. After releasing an arrow, keep your eyes on it throughout the entire flight and landing. If it misses the intended target, memorize a detail in the landscape that will help you locate it during retrieval: a clump of grass, a tree, a fallen branch, a shadow, etc.
6. Do not lay a spare arrow on the ground, where someone could step on it. To stand an arrow vertically in the ground, grip it three inches above the point and stab it gently into the earth. An excellent, inexpensive quiver-stand to use with students can be made of bamboo. See the illustrations in the margin.

# *Protective Gear*

1. **Safety glasse**s are recommended for stringing and unstringing. (The worst archery accident I have witnessed was a bow slipping from an instructor's hand while stringing. The recurve bow's upper limb-tip struck her in the eye.)

2. A leather **arm guard** protects the bow-arm from the slap of the string. This guard is generally necessary for a longbow shooter. A recurve shooter will experience "string sting" only if he fails to bend the bow-arm at full-draw, as the proper form recommends. For repeat offenders, offer an arm guard to prevent bruising and flinching. The student most vulnerable to "string sting" is the child or adult female who exhibits a degree of backward bend in the arm. In this case the string can slap behind the elbow. This is the student who must master the bent arm at full-draw. Meanwhile, supply her with an arm guard.

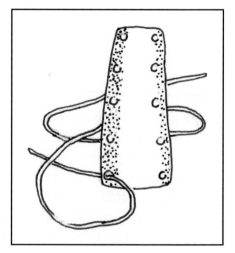

### Making an Arm Guard

To make an arm guard, cut a swatch of leather (say, eight inches long and tapering from four inches to three inches wide) to fit the inside of the forearm. Punch holes along the long borders and thread with cordage, leaving tails long enough to be tied.

3. Because a bow-string naturally scrapes across the fingertips at release, **finger protection** is needed. In addition, the pressure of the string in the finger creases at full-draw is considerable, especially for those new to archery. Both kinds of abrasion create an accumulative rawness and soreness. (As soon as that pain manifests, proper form in shooting is usually sabotaged by the archer's attempts to avoid the discomfort of release.)

Some youth bows offer **foam padding** sleeved over the string, but the thickness of the foam demands a finger-grip that engages tendons throughout the hand, which is contrary to performing a proper release. Inculcating this flawed form into a young archer is a great disservice, as attempts to overcome the habit will one day prove frustrating.

Another protective device is called a **"tab"**—a small patch of leather that loops loosely over the long finger to shield all three fingertips from the string. Because of its thickness and loose fit, it too can be problematic for beginners.

An archery glove is, arguably, a better solution. It fits tightly on the string-fingers and fastens at the wrist. Most veteran archers use one. Improved materials have made gloves much more user-friendly over time. Glove-fingers were once thick and stiff and counterproductive to an ideal release. Today, gloves can be supple, like the Damascus glove. Still, a glove is challenging for beginners, as it denies a sense of tactile contact with the string. A novice needs to have a more intimate connection with the equipment.

Athletic tape is my solution for new archers. Apply a three-inch by half-inch strip to each finger, wrapping twice around the distal crease so the crease falls at the strip's midline. After a few shots the tape will form its own crease.

## *Targets*

There are many commercial targets available to purchase. Perhaps the easiest and cheapest target material is a hay bale purchased for a few dollars. After buying a bale you will need to cinch it tighter with rope stronger than baling twine. Such a bale will remain compact enough to stop an arrow as long as you keep it dry. A cardboard face can be pinned or tied in front. Prop your bale on two logs and cover with a tarp when not in use.

You may invent your own targets. Just keep in mind that your arrows need to be stopped before the fletching can penetrate. Constant compression of feathers (or ripping off the shaft) will keep you busy in their repair rather than in the shooting.

There are expensive foam "animal" targets that are undeniably fun to shoot, even if an archer is not a hunter. Hunting has been necessary for survival throughout much of the human story; therefore, shooting at animal targets provides a sense of history. But there is another value to shooting at an animal target.

If a modern archer intends to be a hunter, his performance with such a target can dictate whether or not he is ready to engage in the hunt for a real animal. These targets are marked by a subtle groove (not visible from a reasonable shooting distance) that defines the animal's "kill zone." A "cruel wound" on a foam deer should be a revelation to an aspiring hunter and should be taken as seriously as a tragic wound in real flesh. Shots that do not strike the "kill zone" telegraph an ethical message to an archer: *You are not yet skilled enough to launch an arrow at a living creature.*

Hunting should not be an experimental event. Every hunter should afford his prey an instant kill to guarantee as little suffering as possible on the animal's part. To lose a wounded creature in the woods through inaccurate shooting and inept tracking is a shame indeed.

*You may think that shooting a bow is a forceful act, but that is simply the bow returning to its undrawn shape. The archer moves in a state of grace.*

—Robert Asherwood, from *A Tale Twice Told*

## CHAPTER 7

# Preparing to Be an Archer—
# Slipping into the Mantle of Grace

## *The Way*

There is no single "correct way" to shoot a bow. This I know only because I have seen many of the great American archers use methods that differ from one another. However, with my students I am a proponent of a very specific technique—one that I believe in whole-heartedly. This method uses a relaxed *string-release* that demands

an isolation of muscles in the hand, wrist, and forearm . . . and it produces a fluid and graceful *follow-through*. To distinguish it from all other shooting styles . . . and because it is the only technique I am willing to present in these pages . . . I will consider this method to be "the way."

Why do I teach this method? Because it has made me and my students more accurate and more consistent archers, and because I have seen it improve every archer who embraces it. Many veteran archers who attend my classes struggle with unlearning their old habits. Their muscle memory is deeply ingrained. It does take an effort to restructure a shooting style, especially after years of practicing another method. As is so often the case in one of my classes, these veterans may adopt the new lessons for that day and even improve their accuracy. Months later, however, when I encounter them at an archery shoot, I often find that they have reverted to their old, familiar ways. Along with this recidivism, I always see the return of their inconsistencies in accuracy. Old habits have a dogged tenacity. It takes a lot of dedication to convert.

This is why I like to receive students very early in their shooting career, if not before they have actually shot a bow. One student of mine, a young man most willing to absorb every facet of the technique, had never picked up a bow before the day of his first lesson. After taking the Art of Archery lesson once, he was smitten by the bow and arrow. He practiced with what seemed an innate devotion to the sport. He took the lesson a second time and then practiced for over a year, at which time he entered a regional competition and became the Southeastern Longbow Champion.

Enough said.

## Concepts to Digest Before Picking Up a Bow

When an accomplished archer releases an arrow, there is a certain balletic quality to the movement of the arms and hands. The bow and string, of course, snap forward quickly, perhaps even violently, releasing all the energy that was stored in the extra bend of the bow's limbs. But, in contrast to this sudden jolt of the weapon, the archer performs a gentle flowing movement that appears to be more a feminine motion than a masculine one. It is a decidedly artistic approach, which is why I call my class (and Chapter 9 of this volume) "The Art of Archery."

Watching a great archer as he shoots an arrow reminds me of a downy feather puffed off a table by the closing of a door. The feather makes a quick initial move and then floats gracefully to the floor. Even a big ox of a man—if he embraces the method in these pages—exhibits this dainty movement. Ask any veteran archer how he learned such a technique, and he is likely to reply: "I learned it from another archer."

Those of us who pick up a bow and teach ourselves how to shoot (myself included) do not discover this method of relaxed release and fluid follow-through on our own. It does not seem to be natural. It has to be taught. (I learned it that very way, from Tom Jeffrey in the back of his bow-making factory in Columbia, South Carolina.)

Left to our own devices, we self-taught archers teach ourselves bad habits that become lifelong demons that we must continue to exorcise from our shooting form. Even after we overcome them, these same demons can return, and we must purge them again. Muscle memory has a tenacious nature, it would seem. But there is good news: Eventually a dedicated flood of practice can drown out old muscle memory to establish a new memory for that same muscle.

For this reason, when someone new to archery contacts me about a lesson, I implore them to abstain from shooting until we meet. (This is no small request, because so often the new student has just purchased a new bow and is eager to shoot.) Otherwise, we will spend the first hour or two of the class trying to dismantle the bad habits that he has already learned.

The main challenge deals with how the archer releases the bow-string at full-draw. First, you should know that there are many historical techniques for gripping the string, some of which employ the thumb as the primary catch on the string. We will use the previously mentioned English grip, trapping the string in the outermost crease of the index, long, and ring fingers of the strong hand, securing the nocked arrow between the first two of those fingers just listed.

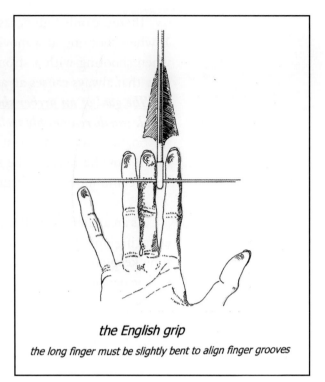

*the English grip*
*the long finger must be slightly bent to align finger grooves*

Likewise, to let go of the string, there are many techniques that have been used around the world; but, in my opinion, only one makes for consistent shooting. We'll get to it soon. First, here are the other most commonly self-invented releases, which invite error in every shot.

1. Opening the fingers as quickly as possible.
2. Plucking the string like a harpist.
3. Slowly opening stiff fingers until the string slips.

First of all, no one can move his fingers fast enough to get out of the string's forward path without obstructing that path. The string moves like lightning. Human fingers don't. At the instant that those so-called "fast" fingers have opened halfway, the string is already slipping laterally off the fingertips. If the string moves laterally one way, then the bow must pivot the other way. When that happens, a perfect aim is spoiled. This explains why #1 and #3 just mentioned are not recommended releases.

As for #2, this is an even cruder method of forcing the string around the fingertips. It would seem to be difficult, if not impossible, to perform it in the same way each time. And its margin of error is multiplied by a complete lack of finesse in jerking on the string when stability in aiming is all-important.

An archer who consistently shoots left of the target is, of course, tempted to aim in the other direction, as if to negate the lateral flaw. The same is true for one who shoots consistently to the right. This planned "off-side-aiming" is called "*lateral compensation.*" Such a method can be entirely subconscious. Lateral compensation is, in my opinion, a terrible practice to embrace, because every different distance will require a different degree of lateral compensation. This is too much to ask of any archer, especially when "the way" described here in these pages negates the need for any lateral compensation, no matter the distance.

There are only four occasions in which lateral compensation should be employed: 1. when shooting at a moving target; 2. when shooting from a moving vehicle; 3. when shooting with a strong wind from one side; and 4. when shooting a flawed bow that always causes an arrow to veer to one side.

*__The goal of an archer should be this:__ After achieving a perfect aim (which most people can do reasonably well), get out of the bow's way and let the bow do all the work.*

So, how does a successful archer get out of the way of the bow? One aspect of this is how he releases the string. The four-word description of a proper release is often confounding to a beginner. Easy to say; hard to perform. Here it is:

*"Stop holding the string."*

As an archer you will learn to isolate muscles in your string-forearm/wrist/hand, engaging only the last joints of three fingers to grip the string, while at the same time keeping the rest of the hand, wrist, and forearm relaxed. Releasing the string will be performed by instantly relaxing those fingertips. All this will be covered later, but plant that seed in your mind now.

## Seven More Archery Seeds to Plant Inside Your Head

1. **Never draw back the string of an unloaded bow and let go of the string.** The previously explained "dry-fire" can break or crack a bow. A bow cannot tolerate recovering too fast from its bend and stopping suddenly. The straightening of the bow at release must be cushioned by the mass of the arrow being launched. When you test the strength of a bow by drawing the string, always return the string to its original position by easing it forward to its straight-line position.

2. **How you let go of the string and what your body does during and after the letting-go are, after aiming, the most critical points in archery.** These two movements are called "release" and "follow-through." Almost everyone is an accomplished pointer, which means that—if an archer's head is in the proper position relative to the arrow—she is probably aiming well (at least on the left-right aspect) while at full-draw. Her job at the moment of release is to get out of the way of the bow to let it do its work. Instead, it is more common to see a beginner disturb that "perfect aim" by introducing an interruptive movement.

3. **Use the strongest bow you are capable of using . . . without straining.** Strength in archery contains a technical advantage. The stronger a bow, the flatter the shot. In other words, no great arc of trajectory is needed because the arrow is traveling so fast. An archer should draw his bow with strength to spare; that is, he should use more strength in the draw than is actually necessary, pouring the excess strength into smoothness and control.

4. **The left-right consideration is the easiest part of aiming an arrow; the up-down aspect is more complicated.** Unless wind is a factor, the left-right dimension (windage) of aiming at a stationary target never changes, no matter how close or far your target. But the up-and-down (elevation) part of aiming changes with every different distance and with every different bow.

5. **Once the aiming has been accomplished, get out of the bow's way and let it do all the work of launching the arrow.** The best archers do not display dramatic movement when they shoot. The heroes of movies, on the other hand, are compelled to look heroic. On the big screen, an archer tries to appear dynamic and action-packed—as though he/she is transferring personal fortitude and will into the act of shooting by telegraphing it through the bow. Nothing could be further from good form. In reality, a great archer's movements are minimal and graceful rather than forceful, so he does not compromise the perfect aim he has already achieved.

6. **In the early days of learning to shoot, practice the proper form in front of a large backstop without a bull's-eye.** A bull's-eye has the power to turn on a desperate competitive edge and erase the lessons of form.

7. **Practice and perfect your form to the point of knowing that you will hit your target.** Confidence comes only from practice. All archers lose it from time to time when they cannot practice regularly. But once an archer regains it, she *owns* her expertise. There is a tendency for a novice archer to *hope* that her shot might be good. This wish is tantamount to admitting that archery proficiency is lacking. *This attitude is diametrically opposed to confidence.*

## Grace and a Tabletop

The archer's first quest on the path to excellence is to achieve a grace that is isolated in certain parts of the arms and hands. The purpose of this grace is to get the archer *out of the way of the bow and string* to allow the bow to do the work that the archer has invested into the drawing and aiming. More than steadiness is necessary. *Fluidity* allows the violent motion of a bow at string-release to be independent of the archer.

   Grace—just like strength and visual alignment—is the archer's tool. Aiming is relatively easy. Everyone is good at pointing toward something. Strength allows the archer to achieve steadiness at full-draw. This strength is not abandoned at release, but instantaneously channeled with grace into what is called the archer's "*follow-through.*" The follow-through is not a manipulation but a continuation of the push and pull that was already in progress during the draw and while holding at full-draw.

## Follow-Through

When an archer applies push to the bow and pull to the string and reaches the point of equilibrium known as "full-draw" (the point at which the bow is fully bent and the archer and bow are both stationary), <u>the archer is still pushing and pulling, though not moving</u>. (If an archer were not still pushing and pulling at full-draw, his arms would fold up from the force of the drawn bow.)

Most who try to pick up the skill without benefit of instruction assume that the bow-arm should lock straight as a wooden post, making the draw simply a pull against a fixed support. In fact, an archer should not lock the bow-arm straight. If she shoots with a stiffened arm, the recoil of the bow will cause a jostling of that arm at release. The direction of this jolt could manifest to the left, to the right, up, or down . . . or any direction in between. However, a slightly bent bow-arm at full-draw allows room for that arm to thrust *forward* one to two inches at the moment of release. (This bend also puts the forearm out of harm's way from the slap of the string.) The forward follow-through of the bow-arm at release is not something manufactured and added to the shot. It should be the natural result of that *static pushing* on the bow and the sudden disappearance of the resistance by the string.

Even though it seems a given that an archer's arm should automatically follow-through **straight ahead**—as it should—beginners frequently (and unconsciously) push in some other direction while at full-draw. (This wayward push does not manifest itself until the release.) In such a case, the bow-arm might jump to the left or right a few inches. By far the most common flaw is a downward motion. To remedy this the archer must imagine her arms working on a tabletop throughout the act of shooting. Still, even using this image, an archer at full-draw must *consciously* push her bow-hand directly toward the spot she plans to hit.

Positioning the arms on the tabletop

The other half of the follow-through involves the pull of the strong arm. When the archer suddenly relaxes her string-hand (aka stops holding the string), another instantaneous, natural movement should occur, this one diametrically opposed to the bow-arm but in the same line and on the tabletop. Because it was supplying considerable force to hold the string in static place, the string-arm should leap backward, a movement from four to eight inches depending upon bow poundage.

Note: In reality, the string-arm is above the tabletop and the bow-arm just below it. To the archer, it feels as if both arms are on top of it.

An archer who strives to be a statue at full-draw cannot achieve the follow-through. He is locked in a muscular tension all over his body, especially his biceps, which should never be used in shooting. There seems to be an instinct telling him to flex every muscle and to move as little as possible, except, of course, opening the fingers to release, which compounds the problem even more. When, finally, such a "statue archer" does experience the follow-through's natural leap of arms in opposing directions, he reaches an important milestone as an archer.

The follow-through is merely a completion of what the arms were already doing at full-draw—pushing and pulling. In other words, full-draw is a temporary "holding-pattern" in the whole process of pushing and pulling. The grand finale—full extension of the bow-arm and the complete backward journey of the string-arm—occurs immediately *after* the release.

The follow-through is tri-partite. Besides the bow-arm straightening *forward* and the string-arm jumping *backward*, there is one more movement: The relaxed string-hand drops *downward* at the wrist, flopping "through the tabletop" by gravity alone. There it simply dangles. Achieving that freefall of the string-hand is another milestone in a beginning archer's career.

The follow-through is not forced. It merely happens. And it happens with grace because string-release is not a surprise. The archer plans it. The follow-through is something one expects and embraces . . . with grace.

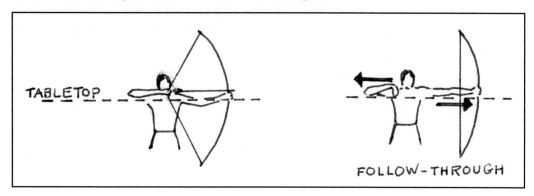

To learn how to perform the follow-through, it helps to identify the two factors that make it difficult to learn. Both are challenges that deal with isolating muscles. That should not be too scary. We do it all the time. We can run fast and at the same time gently catch a ball. We can evenly lift a suitcase with one hand and a pencil with the other at the same time. The muscle isolation needed in archery is simply one a beginner archer has probably not encountered.

Obviously, muscle is used to keep the arms horizontal on the tabletop. The muscles supplying this support are primarily in the shoulders. The bow-arm is also using its triceps to push the bow. But neither arm should use the biceps to lock itself in place. Flexing the biceps of either arm would be a braking action that prevents follow-through.

Of course, the last joint of the string-arm's fingers must be engaged to hold the bow-string, but the rest of the hand, wrist, and forearm should be treated as if it is a thick piece of rope. Rope cannot flex, but it can be pulled taut. This is the tricky part, because it is an unfamiliar isolation of muscle/tendon. Do not give up on learning this. It is a vital part of the form. You *can* master it. The next exercise will show you how to begin.

## A Follow-Through Exercise (when a flop is a success!)

Stand with your feet spread a little more than shoulder-width. Raise your strong arm so the elbow is jutting out to your strong side, palm facing toward your chin about five inches in front of your face. This arm should appear to be resting on the imaginary tabletop.

Raise your weak arm straight up above your head, then bend it at the elbow to lower the hand, palm toward you, toward the other hand. With your weak hand, take a firm grip on the three string-fingers of your strong hand. The weak hand's palm should touch the backs of the strong hand's fingers. Maintaining that grip, lower the weak elbow to make a mirror image of the strong arm. Now both arms are on the tabletop.

**Part A:** Holding this grip on the string-fingers, begin pulling as if you are trying to "pull the fingers off the strong hand." Before reading further, apply this tension now and ask a friend to watch the wrist of your strong arm for any elongation of the joint. If no friend is present, stand before a mirror to study this joint.

In this first experience with this exercise, it is natural that your instincts have instructed you to tighten the wrist of your strong arm to protect that wrist joint. Everyone does this. The person observing you will see no extension in the wrist joint.

**Part B:** This time your goal will be to relax the wrist so the joint makes a visible elongation when pulled. Begin the exercise again, slowly, this time not allowing the strong wrist to flex. Pull gradually with enough force that you can feel the wrist joint expand ever so slightly. An observer will see a definite elongation of the wrist joint. You yourself can see it if you crane your head forward, but it is most obvious when viewing the motion in a mirror.

When you can achieve this relaxation of the wrist while firmly pulling, suddenly release the grip on your fingers, maintaining your position on top of the table. Watch your hand flop downward (through the tabletop). If the hand dangles once or twice before coming to rest, you have performed the proper release. If not, you have tensed the muscles. To perform this drill correctly, it is essential to relax your strong wrist _before_ you begin to pull.

When you suddenly let go of the grip, three things should happen:

1. Both arms should suddenly fly outward, the *elbows leading the way*. (Don't unhinge the forearms to swing the hands outward. Allow the elbows to lead.) Both arms should slide along the tabletop until you feel the "bounce" in your shoulders that defines the limits of your range of motion.

2. Your strong hand should flop down from the wrist, fall through the tabletop, and dangle. This dangling should be natural, driven by gravity, not contrived. (As proof that the movement is natural, look for two tiny pendulum swings as the hand comes to rest.)
3. The rest of your arms should remain on the tabletop.

   Practice this exercise until this movement becomes ingrained in muscle memory.

---

### The "Bag of Chips" Metaphor

If you are having trouble understanding the follow-through exercise, a sealed bag of potato chips might help. To get at the snack we have learned to grasp the top of the bag on either side of the seam and very slowly pull in opposite directions but prepare for the sudden tear that could shower potato chips everywhere. We prepare by flexing our biceps, readying for the moment when the seam tears, so we can reverse directions as quickly as possible to keep the bag from ripping further. **This is the opposite of the archer's follow-through! Do not use your biceps. Let the chips fly!**

---

## The Archer's Shooting Demeanor

Archery's inherent act of violent motion—the limbs of the bow unleashing their stored energy and whipping the string forward to launch the arrow—causes some folks to enter into the firing of an arrow with some degree of apprehension . . . even fear. Such an approach is likely to develop a *flinch*, which, if allowed to become a habit, will undermine any hope of achieving pre-shot confidence. These two concepts—flinching and confidence—are important aspects of archery. The former must be conquered. The latter must be earned.

While some students enter the lesson with timidity, others, invariably males, meet this violent action by matching it with their own—pouring an unnecessary dynamic action into the shooting, flexing muscles that should not be tensed, gritting teeth, flashing a new facial expression, throwing body weight into the firing of the arrow as if that method might boost the arrow to a higher speed or will of purpose. All of these approaches to shooting are misguided.

A lot of energy can be stored in the drawn bow, but it should be handled by graceful, deliberate, and economical body movement. When the string is released, the fast action that follows should be **enveloped** by that same grace. The archer's movements are flowing and calm, the face composed, showing no surprise. The head does not move. The eyes do not widen. Knowing you will hit what you are aiming at is a big part of success.

## This Method of Grace

Back in history there were archers who sat down on the ground, braced the bow on the soles of their feet, and pulled back the string with both hands. Some Native American tribes loaded their arrows on the "wrong" side of the bow and canted the bow the "wrong" way. Some drew the string with a bent thumb, others with a pinch-grip between thumb and index. Archers have used two-, three-, and four-fingered grips on the string, sometimes straddling the nock, other times bunching all fingers below the string.

Even today, within any group of veteran archers, a variety of methods might be employed. But I have rarely seen an archer excel *with consistency* without the release and follow-through covered in these pages.

The most common flaw in form is a stiff string-hand at release. Such a hand, rather than dropping by gravity in a relaxed fashion, jumps stiffly out to the side looking like talons tensed for a kill. The second most common flaw is the stiff bow-arm that tries to hold the bow rigidly out in front like a wooden post.

For veteran, self-taught archers the eradication of old habits is a formidable task. It takes a lot of willpower to convert. A student who is new to archery learns the method of grace much faster than a seasoned archer. Novices get results faster. Well into a class I often see the green archer outshoot the experienced one.

## The Evils of Lateral Compensation

As stated earlier, an archer who consistently shoots just left of her intended target may be tempted to aim just to the right. It is a profound mistake to employ such lateral compensation. When that archer moves back five yards, she will need to increase the compensation. Five more yards will necessitate even more. This imposes an impossible burden on the archer. A much more effective remedy would be to analyze the shooting form to discover the root of the flaw . . . and then correct it. Other than moving targets, moving shooting platforms, and cross-winds, the only exception to this rule applies to a bow that is so wide at the middle that it interferes with the arrow flight every shot. Unfortunately, such a bow would force lateral compensation upon the archer. Rather than surrender to this frustrating task, one would be wise to replace the bow with a better-designed weapon.

In this modern age of center-cut windows in bow risers (the handle area), lateral compensation should never be needed for the left-right aspect of shooting. However, the elevation aspect of shooting does require compensation from all varied distances. This *vertical compensation* is a demand placed on the archer by gravity. The longer the shot, the more time the arrow is in the air, and the more time gravity has to pull the arrow toward Earth.

*Look up at the thin curve of the moon holding steady in the night sky . . . and you see the patience of the Great Spirit as He aims His bow.*

—Crow Little John, *Requiem to the Silent Stars*

# CHAPTER 8

# Shooting the Bow—The First Shots

Establishing the safety rules

Let us first address the archery teacher's top priority for a group lesson: safety.

---

**Safety Rules For Your Archery Class**

1. Never load an arrow to a bow unless you are standing at the shooters' line.
2. Never point your loaded arrow in any direction except downrange toward the target.
3. Never draw the string of a loaded bow before this signal: "All clear to shoot!"
4. Never step over the shooters' line until you have heard: "All clear to retrieve arrows!"
5. Students should always be their own judge about what is safe. They should inform the instructor if they believe some potential danger has been overlooked.

---

6. Never perform a dry-fire.
7. Handle your bow as if it is made of glass. (Actually, it is. The outer lamination of factory bows consists of fiberglass.) Do not auger your bow into the earth by twirling it from the top. (This seems to be the universal tendency.) When you want to prop your bow on something while waiting for your turn to shoot, prop it on your foot. When not in use, hang it from a strong nub of a broken tree branch. (Archery ranges are typically equipped with bow racks with pegs for hanging up a bow on a wall.)
8. Never hold or move your arrow(s) in such a way that someone could move into your vicinity and be accidentally stabbed.
9. Never hold your arrow by the fletching. Feathers are fragile.
10. Never run to retrieve arrows, whether they are impaled in the ground, hiding under the grass, or protruding from a standing target.
11. Unless you are under instructions to perform an action shot with your bow, never run with an arrow in hand.

### Loading the Arrow (written for right-handers; lefties reverse "left-right" directions)

Hold the bow in the left hand in front of your belly, bow horizontal, big fist-knuckles up, string under the forearm and not touching your body. The bow's upper limb should be to the right, lower limb to the left, the arrow shelf visible on the upper side. With the right thumb and index hold an arrow by its nock in front of you, the point aiming skyward with the odd-colored feather (nock feather on a three-fletched arrow) jutting toward you.

By holding the nock between your fingers you can learn to load without looking at your bow-string—a skill that might be invaluable if ever you need to keep your eyes on something else . . . or should you ever need to load in the dark. The feathers should never be handled unless they have been ruffled and need careful preening.

Swing the arrow point down until the shaft taps down onto the bow next to the shelf or arrow-rest. The nock feather should now point up. (In this position, when the arrow is shot, the other two feathers gently brush past the bow with little disturbance. Loading the arrow upside down would put the nock feather in a position to bump the bow as it leaves to take a disturbed flight.)

Bend your wrist to fit the nock's groove firmly onto the string to make a perpendicular angle between arrow shaft and string. Push the nock firmly against the string, enough to feel some tension from the slightly "bent" string. Holding this tension, raise your left index finger from the bow-handle and place its fingertip on the uppermost surface of the shaft and push straight down toward the earth. Do not wrap your finger around the shaft—one of the most common tendencies for beginner archers (see the photo above)—as this may cause the nock to slide on the string. You now have the arrow locked in place by the combined tensions of finger and string.

Test this lock by holding bow and arrow with your left hand only, pointing the arrow down by your side. Give it the "shake-test" to prove you have a firm grip. Bow and arrow should feel as one unit. No looseness, no rattling.

## The Locksley

Adjusting the arrow perpendicularly is merely a starting point for loading. If an arrow is fully drawn and launched from this 90-degree angle, its flight will be undulating, not smooth. Archers call this flight distortion "porpoising." (There is only one type of shot that uses a perpendicular load—the lob—which we'll cover soon.) To prepare the arrow for a smooth trajectory, its angle on the string must be altered by a measure called the "Locksley."

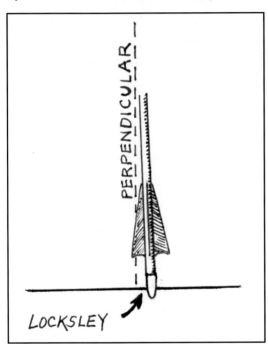

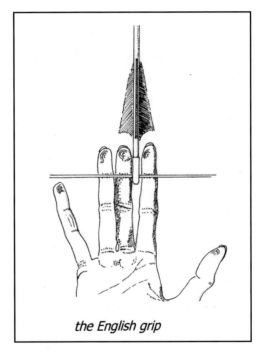

*the English grip*

### Setting the Locksley

The thickness of an arrow shaft defines the calibration of the Locksley. Estimate the arrow width (simply eyeball it) and slide the nock that same amount on the string to your strong side as you hold the bow in the horizontal loading position. Now when the bow is raised to the vertical shooting position, the arrow point should angle slightly downward toward the ground.

### Gripping the String

With the bow/arrow in the "locked" horizontal loaded position, bring your string-hand—palm up—under the string and split the index from the long finger so the arrow nock will lie between them. The ring finger takes its place on the string next to the long finger. Take the string with these three fingers in the "archer's creases" (the outermost bending lines). Granted these creases do not make a connected straight line across the extended fingers, but the adjustment to align them is easy and natural on the string. You will *never* use your thumb or little finger in the grip.

Insert the string into the creases and squeeze the nock with a little pressure from the insides of the two fingers touching the nock. Now bend the distal joints of all three fingers, enough to hook onto the string. Now you have a new lock on the arrow. *Immediately release the left-hand index-lock and let that finger wrap around the bow handle with the others.* If you don't, the slightest tug back on the string can pull the string out of the nock and the pressure of the left-hand index-lock will push the arrow down off the bow and you will, though subtly, "shoot yourself in the foot." It happens to everyone in the beginning days.

---

**Warning: Failure to promptly release the left-hand index-lock could result in a dry-fire! With the arrow locked in place, if an archer pulls back the string far enough to remove it from the nock but barely maintains a grip on the nock with his fingers, he may be tricked into thinking the arrow is still nocked to the string. Shooting the arrow in this "false-load" position results in a dry-fire!**

---

With this new right-hand lock securing the arrow to the string, point the arrow downward again and try the shake-test. This time your combined gear may not feel quite so snug. The arrow can rattle against the shelf, but it should not fall off the bow.

## First Shots

The first shots I ask my students to perform are tiny ones. The arrows travel only a few yards away from their weak side before falling to earth. We spend twenty to thirty minutes with this partial-draw warmup as a way of easing into the concept of a relaxed string-hand. By doing this, we first address the most difficult part of archery—the release. (We address this first in order to preclude any bad release habits that are, otherwise, sure to form.)

The exercise that follows requires an awkward shooting position. It is designed to help a student learn the proper release while 1. drawing against slight resistance and 2. seeing the release. (Learning the release at a full-draw is much more difficult.)

Before beginning the exercise below, lay down your bow and practice *A Follow-Through Exercise* found in the previous chapter. Repeat until your string-hand is regularly flopping and dangling by gravity alone.

### First Release Shots

Stand with your feet spread wider than your shoulders. With the bow loaded and your string-fingers in place on the string, turn the bow vertically in front of you, the arrow pointed to your weak side. To achieve this position, rotate the bow inside your

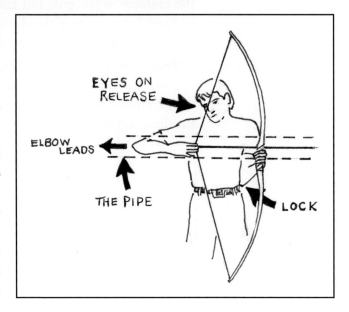

grip on the handle as needed. Slide the bow-arm elbow back along your side and brace it against the side of your ribs. Now hinge the horizontal forearm 10 degrees to your weak side while keeping the elbow against the ribs. Again, if needed, rotate the bow inside your grip on the handle until the arrow points directly to your weak side.

Now align your strong forearm <u>in line with the arrow</u>. Flatten the hand as much as possible (except, of course, the last joints of the string-gripping fingers). This arm from elbow to fingers should be poised in the air like a rear extension of the arrow.

Your bent bow-arm will serve only as a fixed support in this exercise. Concentrate fully on the drawing arm and hand. Dig the string deeply into the archer's creases.

***Before*** you begin to make a two- to three-inch draw with the string/arrow, completely relax your right forearm, wrist, and all but the gripping segments (the distal joints) of the fingers. Concentrate mostly on relaxing the wrist and the rest will follow. Isolating the flex of the fingertips is the trick. Imagine your drawing arm as amputated at the elbow and attached to it is a thick rope (your forearm) with three hooks (the string-fingers) at the end. As you draw, lead with the elbow. Use no biceps in the drawing, only shoulder muscle. During this draw, guide the arm back

in a perfect line with the arrow, as if your arm and the arrow are encased inside the same hollow pipe.

Because the string is drawn back only a few inches, you'll have a good view of your string-hand. During this draw you should see your hand flatten out from the tautness of the pull, but there should be no flexing of muscles in the hand or forearm (except where the distal finger joints grip the string). When you decide to release, stop holding the string. (Remember, this does not mean opening the fingers. It means that you let your string-holding effort suddenly die.)

You should see two things happen: 1. The string-hand flops downward and dangles from the wrist. 2. The leading elbow of the string-arm makes a little leap in the direction it had been drawing. This movement should occur inside the "pipe."

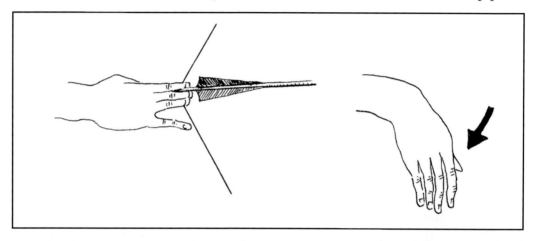

If these two movements cannot be witnessed, you have tensed muscles that should not be used. This usually includes the biceps.

**The most common mistakes made in this exercise are:**

1. Not drawing in line with the arrow. Solution: Imagine that the arrow and your forearm are inside the same four-inch-wide PVC pipe. As you draw, <u>keep the arm inside the pipe.</u>

2. Cupping the hand, causing the arrow to swivel off the rest. Solution: Do not use the "fisting" muscles in the palm. <u>Relax everything in the hand except the last joints of the three gripping fingers.</u> Let this hand be pulled taut by the tension between the string and the drawing elbow.

3. Forgetting to watch the hand at release. *Solution:* Shoot in a safe direction so you do not have to watch the arrow. <u>Watch your hand!</u>

4. Flexing the biceps to draw. *Solution:* Draw by <u>leading with the elbow,</u> using the shoulder muscles only.

5. Hinging downward from the elbow at release, letting the lower half of the arm drop. *Solution:* Use the pipe imagery again. <u>Only the hand can fall through the pipe.</u>

6. Failing to flop the hand. *Solution:* Relax the wrist <u>before</u> you begin the draw.

Repeat this exercise until you achieve the proper relaxation, hand flop and dangle, and slight follow-through by the string-arm.

## *The Lob Shot*

lob

For a beginner the lob is the simplest type of shot to launch from a bow, but it is seldom used by today's archers for two reasons: 1. It delivers a relatively weak impact (not useful in hunting), and 2. it is a moderately difficult shot to deliver with great accuracy unless one practices it. Most modern archers have no need for this shot and so do not practice it.

It is my belief that a working knowledge of the full spectrum of the bow makes one a better archer. This includes esoteric shots like the lob and clout. Starting with the lob is prudent for two reasons: 1. It is easy (physically) to perform, and 2. during the entire process, the string-hand is visible so the archer can watch and critique his own release.

Historically, the lob shot had its practical place among hunters, forest outlaws of medieval times, and soldiers. A lob was a means of creating a diversionary sound, sending a signal or message, or safely passing along needed ammunition to a comrade who might be pinned down at a distance. The lob shot basically follows the path of a long, arcing football pass and should land at an angle with the feathers easily spotted from a distance. It does not require a full-draw. In fact, the length of draw is discretionary and part of the mystery of this shot. Getting a feel for how much to pull back the string is all part of getting to know your bow.

Demonstrating the lob shot, forearm in line with the arrow

The lob is the only archery shot in which we launch the arrow loaded perpendicular to the string. In other words, a Locksley angle is not used. And it is the only shot in which the archer's torso faces the target.

In my three-acre meadow I have my students fan out in a flank and lob their first real shots (following the practice session of three-inch-draw and release) toward a totem pole thirty-five yards away. Our goal is to have the arrows pin the earth close to the base of the pole. The totem lies in the middle of the meadow so there is ample room for the predictable first-time over-kill shots that sail too far. There will be a number of grossly under-shot arrows too, but eventually each student gets a feel for the proper length of draw for that distance.

There are two mechanical principles that have to be gauged by the archer to attain lob accuracy: 1. how far to pull back the string and 2. at what angle to elevate the arrow while aiming. The angle poses an interesting problem. Let's say your lob-draw is consistently ten inches. If you shoot at the totem and the arrow falls short, on your next attempt you might raise the angle to get more distance. (The other option would be to draw the string back farther.) But there is a threshold at which raising the angle higher will eventually cause the arrow to lose linear distance as measured across the meadow. Physics teaches us that the maximum achievable distance of a projectile with a constant send-off force is 45 degrees.

When this archer elevates her bow to see her target below the handle, her forearm will easily align with the arrow.

Launch angle and draw-length are intimately interwoven in aiming a lob. Each affects the other. For example, at a given distance an archer has more than one option on how to improve a lob. Consider shooting with the arrow raised at a certain angle, X, which is above 45 degrees, and pulling back a certain distance, Y. If the lob shot is perfect with these calibrations, perfection can also be achieved if X is increased . . . but only if Y is increased also.

If X is initially less than 45 degrees, to increase it (up to but no more than 45 degrees) and maintain the same accurate shot would require decreasing Y. If this sounds complicated, don't let the math scare you away from the lob. It is best understood by simply playing around with lob shots to let the physics sink in experientially.

To gain practical proficiency with the lob, an archer must practice shooting at a constant distance with a variety of launch angles and a variety of draw-lengths. If one day the need arises to send a lob shot through the forest, the archer's "flight-window" through the tree canopy (a passageway in the foliage through which the arrow can travel without obstruction) may dictate the aiming angle without any other choices. In other words, the angle is set by limitations of the tree canopy. The only way to change this angle would be for the archer to move closer to or farther from the intended target.

In a fixed-angle scenario, the archer has only one factor to help him solve the riddle of accuracy—draw-length. Therefore, it would behoove an archer to practice in the woods. The varied "flight-windows" available will teach a great many lessons about the lob shot.

### Shooting a Lob

Load an arrow without the Locksley, face your target, and spread your feet for balance. Hold your bow horizontally in front at arm's length and raise it up until you can see the target beneath your bow. With the lob, a straight bow-arm will suffice, as the recoil of shooting this kind of shot is minimal. No follow-through with the bow-arm is necessary. For the lob shot only, think of your bow-arm as a fixed post.

Bring your three string-fingers under the string—palm up—and grip the string/ nock normally. If now, standing perfectly upright, you were to align your string-forearm with the arrow (as you did in *First Release Shots*) you would have limited space for drawing due to your elbow running into your belly. A change in posture is the remedy.

Shift your hips to the weak side, and your shoulders and head will shift to the strong side, putting your string-arm elbow in a position to slide past your ribs in the draw. Be sure that your bow slides to the strong side also, to maintain the necessary straight line of aiming that connects eyes to arrow to target.

Align your flattened drawing hand and forearm with the arrow. To draw, begin by relaxing the wrist. Then lead with the elbow as if both arrow and forearm share space inside the same hollow pipe. *Do not draw by using the biceps in a barbell-curling motion toward the chest.* Strength for the draw should come from the shoulder and back muscles. Maintain relaxation in the wrist. As you draw keep your eyes on your target while using peripheral vision to keep your arrow aimed in the proper left-right alignment toward the target. Position your head so eyes, arrow point, and target all lie on the same straight line.

the hip-shift and posture for the lob

To release: *Stop holding the string.* Allow the hand to relax instantaneously, flop, turn palm-down, and dangle naturally from the wrist by the pull of gravity. *This string-arm should naturally perform the backward follow-through along the path of the imaginary pipe.* To improve accuracy on the next shot, use the same arrow angle with a new draw-length. After ten shots, experiment with different aiming angles while keeping the draw consistent. Ask a friend to monitor your hand flop at the moment of release.

A lower bow position is used on close shots.

### First Lob Competition

In a meadow, set up two hay bales forty yards apart (or less, depending upon bow-strengths) and name one bale as the shooters' line for archers to stand behind. Have archers stand in a flank and lob toward the far bale at your signal. All arrows should sail in a fairly high arc—say, over an imaginary twenty-foot-high wall. When all have shot, carry the bows downfield to retrieve arrows. Now the bales reverse roles. Lob back toward the first bale using the close bale as a marker for the shooters' line. Keep going back and forth until everyone has achieved, first, a relaxed hand flop at release and, second, a reasonable proximity of arrow to target.

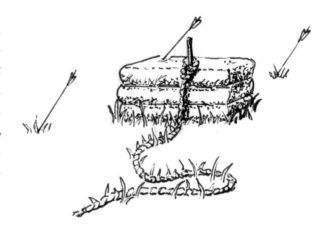

With students so fixated on how close their arrows come to the bale, many will forget about form. Pull them back into an attentiveness to form. Remind them of specifics: body lean, string-arm alignment with arrow, string-grip, and natural hand flop at release.

### Lob Accuracy

Form two teams, each of varied skill levels in an attempt to balance the average proficiency of the two teams. Using the same two hay bales, stab into the top of each a sharpened stick with the end of a fifteen-foot-long rope tied to each. These ropes will be used as a radius to determine scores: three points for arrows that land within the circle defined by the rope; five points for arrows within a bow-length of the bale; ten for hitting the bale. For arrows that fall outside the rope radius, archers try to score one point by throwing into the bale from the point of impalement. (During each throw, clear everyone else out of harm's way.) In this way, those shooting poorly are having fun with their throws. Keep a running score for a given number of rounds.

Whether the teacher makes the lesson competitive or noncompetitive, archery is fun!

*"Don't just pull on the string, boyo. You must push the bow, as well. You, lad, are standing outside these two forces. Stand at the center of them. Control them. Don't let these forces control you."*

—the old Welsh fletcher to young Robin

# CHAPTER 9

# The Art of Archery— Perfecting Shooting the Bow

Up to now, by beginning with the three-inch-draw release-practice shots and the lob shots, we have purposely avoided the increased tension of the fully drawn bow. It is much more difficult to learn the proper release while contending with the full strength of a bow. (Beginners tend to flex many more muscles than necessary when fully drawing a bow, making the follow-through impossible.)

## *The Direct Shot*

Now that you have experienced the dedicated relaxation needed for a perfect release, it is time to apply this accomplishment to archery's most famous arrow flight—the *direct shot*. Such a flat and fast trajectory is the familiar shot of the hunter, the warrior, the Olympic archer . . . sending the arrow on the most direct line possible to the target.

Though a direct shot may appear virtually "flat," gravity steadily pulls it down, just as it pulls on a bullet shot from a rifle. To allow for this drop, the archer learns to raise his arrow angle ever upward as the shooting distance increases, which causes the arrow to follow a long, shallow arc. The

*direct shot*

greater the distance, the higher the archer must aim. The greatest challenge in aiming is learning how to change the arrow angle to accommodate all these different distances.

The greater the distance the arrow has to travel, the greater will be the arrow's initial angle from the horizon—up to 45 degrees, that is, at which point the bow can deliver no more distance without overdrawing or breaking form to thrust the bow recklessly forward. Neither adaptation is advised.

## Initial Pointers for the Direct Shot

The direct shot is performed with the archer turned sideways, left shoulder to the target for right-handers. This and all the other types of shooting that use a full-draw require the Locksley loading angle. With modern, factory-made bows, the bow can be held either in a canted shooting position (top limb tilted to your strong side) or in a vertical position. It's your choice. If you are shooting a primitive bow, which features an arrow shelf that is not cut into the center of the bow, the canted position is necessary for left-right accuracy.

With a class of archers about to perform their first direct shots, I stand students in a flank just a few yards from a large backstop. (A wall of stacked hay bales works well.) After the signal "All clear to shoot!" I let them shoot at their leisure from the same shooters' line. I encourage them to go slowly, to invest time and thought into each shot. I never stipulate any specific target or bull's-eye. Archers ought not to be burdened by thoughts of accuracy at this point in the lesson . . . only form. (However, because most beginners shoot too high, it is prudent to ask everyone to send their arrows into the lower half of the backstop.)

A bull's-eye would only stir up a competitive spirit and distract the archer from a more important focus—a thing she cannot see at full-draw: her release hand. She must blind herself to the hay bale and "see" her hand with her inner eye. That hand, wrist, and forearm must be stretched taut at full-draw (like a rope) by the tension between the backward-leading elbow and the resistance of the string. Only then can the proper release be accomplished.

The secret of achieving full-draw with a relaxed hand/wrist/arm is to ***initiate the relaxation in the wrist <u>before</u> the draw begins.*** It is extremely difficult, if not impossible, to draw the string with tense muscles and then to try to relax them in preparation for the release.

## *Anchor Point*

Before performing a full-draw, you must know exactly how far back to pull the string. There are a number of spots that can be used as an *anchor point*, but never the ear nor eye. A good starting place is the (strong-side) corner of the mouth. Touch the tip of the index finger to that corner. With the slightest *tilt* of the head to the strong side, this places the strong-side eye directly *above* the arrow at full-draw—exactly where it should be. Be loyal to this anchor point. Archery can be a confounding game of variables, and an archer's objective is to eradicate all variables to achieve a chain of constants in form. Changing how far you pull back the string is one such variable. Be consistent with this dedicated anchor point.

As you evolve as an archer, you may prefer a different spot for an anchor point. Whatever position you settle on, it must situate the arrow directly under the strong-side eye—which, hopefully, is your dominant eye. If it isn't, you'll need to close the dominant (weak-side) eye while aiming so the non-dominant eye alone is forced into use. An archer who can't close that eye must resort to an eye patch. Beyond that would come the formidable task of learning to shoot with the bow in the other hand.

### Finding Your Dominant Eye

Choose some distinct object in the distance—a squirrel's nest, a crest of a treetop, a small cloud. Make a triangular window by crossing your hands as shown in the illustration below. This window should be the size of a large hen's egg. Raise this window with outstretched arms, and with both eyes open focus on the distant object until you see it clearly. Now close your left eye. If the object remains inside the window, you are right-eye-dominant. If it disappears from the window, you are left-eye-dominant.

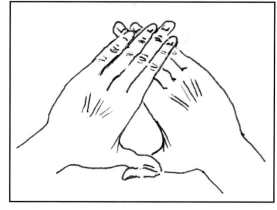

If this test proves inconclusive, rather than closing an eye to assess your eye dominance, very slowly bend your arms to let the window approach your face as you keep focused on the object. If you keep the target object in sight, your hands should gravitate toward your dominant eye.

Some archery teachers claim that closing an eye removes depth perception, but I disagree. An archer studies his target with both eyes open and then may close an eye for aiming. For the brief time spent at full-draw, the brain retains the depth perception just previously registered by both eyes.

When handed a bow and arrow without benefit of instruction, most beginners will pull the arrow to the side of the head, level with the eyes, and toward the strong-side ear, thereby aiming along the *side of the arrow*. Such a position prevents the most fundamental aspect of aiming—the horizontal (left-right) discernment. This is surprising, because almost everyone has an instinct to point at an object with a finger held *beneath* the eyes. The below exercise is proof of that.

### Instinctive Pointing

Without revealing a purpose to this exercise, stand before a flank of students and tell them that you are going to test their reflexes. At the word "draw" they should go into action like Old West gunfighters, draw their "six-gun" (index fingers), point at your chest, and then immediately freeze. Tell them you are planning to beat them all to the draw so they will be thinking about nothing but speed.

Say "draw!" and as soon as all fingers are pointed at you, as a reminder, call out "Freeze!" Look around at all the fingers accurately pointed at your chest. Point out to your students that they have instinctively positioned their pointing fingers *on a vertical line with and beneath their eyes* as they hold their arms extended. Rarely does a student position that pointing finger off to one side of that vertical line.

### The Horizontal Dimension of Aiming of the Arrow

Pair up students and ask partners to face one another while standing ten yards apart. Taking turns, each partner will support an arrow at mid-shaft (from underneath with strong-side fingertips) and rest the arrow nock on the strong-side ear while keeping her head directly facing the partner. (This arrow should be now situated *beside* the pointer's eyes.) Without pivoting her head, the arrow-holder attempts to point the arrow at the partner's nose. The partner then makes a circle of his thumb and index to show where the arrow is actually pointed. The error will surprise the pointer. (I've never met anyone who could accurately aim this way.)

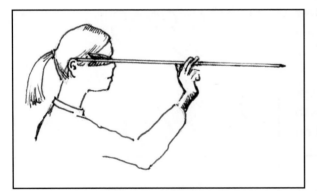

Reverse the roles. Let the one who just aimed now assess her partner's beside-the-eyes aim. His aim will prove just as flawed.

Repeat the exercise with the nock *carefully* positioned two inches *below the strong-side eye* on the front of the cheek. Try again to aim at the partner's nose. Bull's-eye!

### Solo Proof of the Eye Above the Arrow

You can prove this principle by yourself. Impale two sharpened, forked sticks firmly into the earth, the forks in line twenty inches apart, twelve inches off the ground, and twenty yards from a large backstop. Lay an arrow in the forks so it points in the direction of the backstop. Lie down behind and beside the arrow so the nock almost touches the right ear while both eyes are squarely facing the backstop and positioned on the left side of the arrow. Take note of some speck on the backstop where you judge the arrow to be pointing. Walk to the backstop and pin a small scrap of paper to that spot. Go back to the arrow and position yourself exactly as before and double-check that you have pinned the marker in the correct place.

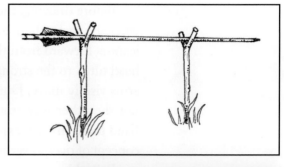

Being careful not to jostle the arrow, reposition yourself behind the shaft with your strong-side eye two inches <u>above</u> the nock. You will discover that your first aim was well off to the side.

These last two exercises prove that you must tilt your head sideways over the arrow when at full-draw. Your aiming eye must be in a vertical line with the arrow shaft.

## At the <u>Center</u> of the Forces of the Bow

A common misconception about shooting an arrow from a bow is that the archer holds a bow with a stiff arm at full-draw. Such a shooter becomes a statue, moving as little as humanly possible when he lets go of the string. Only his fingers move when they open for the release. This mistaken concept of "statue-shooting" prevents the shooter from learning the proper release and follow-through.

The act of drawing and releasing is full of motion. The process is quite fluid, but all movement is confined to the arms and string-hand. The rest of the body serves as a relaxed foundation for that movement. The head, neck, spine, hips, and legs should remain absolutely still. The most common infraction of this rule of form is raising the head at release, as if to better see the flight of the arrow. The second most common flaw is trying to thrust the entire body forward, as if trying to boost the power of the bow.

Tilting the head to get the eye above the arrow is a necessity for a true aim.

While drawing the bow—*pushing* the bow and *pulling* the string—the archer should not feel that these two forces are causing him to assume a defensive struggle. He should feel stronger than the bow, drawing it *around* his body, pouring his excess strength into the smooth movement of reaching full-draw. If he can't do this, it would be prudent to select a lighter-poundage bow.

Archers who feel overpowered by the bow might show one of these symptoms at full-draw: 1. the shoulder of the bow-arm collapses awkwardly toward his chin, 2. the bow-hand strangles the handle, 3. the string-hand tightens like a fist, 4. the spine arches backward (hyper-extending), 5. the head/neck arch backward, 6. the head/neck crane forward toward the target, and 7. the biceps are engaged, flexed, and hard to the touch.

An archer should not let a bow bully him into one of these just mentioned deviations from good form. The offending bow is simply too strong for him. Choose a bow that the archer can overpower.

Before drawing, the archer should first spread his feet and set his torso and head where he wants them to be at full-draw. Generally speaking, this stance is very slightly leaning forward from the waist, body sideways, weak shoulder toward the target, and head tilted to the strong side. This pose should not change during the draw. Only the arms visibly move. During the draw, the archer makes the bow *work around him . . .* not the other way around. **The archer's strength should gracefully swell from his fixed torso into an expanded position of the arms that dominates the bow.** If this concept of overpowering the bow is not possible, that bow is too strong for the archer.

Poised between these two opposing forces of push and pull, the archer should not feel the threat of implosion. Instead, he should feel a confident and contained domination over the bow by his torso and arms. If he does not feel that he is standing at the center of these two forces of push and pull, then he may not be turned fully sideways to his target. Adjust the shooting stance to get the feet and shoulders more in line with the target.

## Pushing the Bow, Pulling the String

Once the string-hand, wrist, and forearm are relaxed, pull the string back by leading with the elbow in a diametric direction from the push on the bow toward the target. The muscles of the back and shoulder perform this pulling work. The string-arm—from the elbow outward to (but not including) the terminal finger joints—should feel like a thick rope pulled taut by the opposing forces of bow and string. That part

feeling the push and pull

of the arm should *not* be taut from flexing the muscles of that arm. This feat requires an isolation of muscle that will at first seem unnatural and challenging. Stay with it. You can achieve it. Many archers have, all for the betterment of their shooting.

The push of the bow is equally important. This push should accompany the pull and it should be done by the heel of the hand while gripping the handle *loosely*. With a gentle grip, push the heel of your bow-hand directly at the tiniest mark you can distinguish at the center of the target you wish to hit, but stop the forward progress of the bow before fully extending the arm, leaving room for the follow-through.

If you are having a hard time feeling the proper swell of muscle in drawing, try this: Point the arrow at the target at the beginning of the draw and then draw slowly, keeping the arrow on target throughout the draw—as if the arrow might fire unexpectedly at any moment and you want to be sure that it hits the target.

At full-draw, the bow-arm should not be locked out but slightly bent at the elbow. A stiff arm will invite a jolt at release—either to one side, up, or down. There *should* be movement with this arm at release, but this movement should be directed *straight toward the target* as the bent arm naturally pushes into the follow-through. Therefore, it is crucial that while you are at full-draw, *all of the force applied by your bow-arm should be exclusively directed toward the target* using the same vector as the arrow. Such instruction might seem obvious, but it is common to discover that an archer, while pushing the bow forward, also unconsciously engages muscles that will cause the bow to jump sideways once the tension is released. An observer can assess this flaw by standing behind a shooter and watching the bow-hand at release. Does it move straight forward? Practice until it does. ***It is not a given that, by pushing the bow at full-draw, an archer is pushing with precision toward the target.***

## Arrow Pivot

One of the most common beginner frustrations involves coming to full-draw only to have the arrow pivot off the rest away from the bow. (Releasing at this moment could be dangerous.) This flaw occurs when the string-hand is tense and probably cupped. It is difficult to coax the arrow back to its proper place while straining with the bow at full-draw. The safest solution calls for easing the string forward to start a draw again *with a relaxed, flattened hand*. Maintain that relaxation as you draw again, and the arrow will remain on the shelf.

### A Critique on Push Direction

While at full-draw, with a relaxed grip on the bow, push directly toward the target with the heel of your bow-hand. Because the bow and bow-arm are not actually moving at full-draw, it might be tempting to believe that you are automatically pushing toward the target. But perhaps you are not.

Have a witness stand at your back. When you reach full-draw, this observer should line up some distant object with a knuckle of your bow-hand so he can judge how far your bow-hand moves laterally at release. Most often this unwanted jerk of the hand moves toward the archer's weak side or down. But it can happen toward the strong side, too. Correct this problem by consciously staying *on the tabletop* and directing your push *toward the target*. It is simply a matter of will.

Once you have mastered the push of the bow, your observer will report that the only motion of your hand is forward, directly toward the target.

## How Long to Aim

Some archers come to full-draw and then bob the bow and arrow up and down, settling into their aim, like a golfer making little approach strokes with his club head toward the ball

Often the student can benefit from the push and pull supplied by the teacher.

before the shot. In archery this is wasted energy while holding at full-draw. It may rob the archer of the necessary strength needed for steadiness once the desired aim is achieved. And it will steal from that archer's endurance on a given day.

Other archers, who like to call their style "instinctive," simply draw the bow while raising it into position and release as soon as the arrow angle seems correct. This is a perfectly good technique that some of America's best archers have employed.

I suggest that we start somewhere in between these two methods. By holding at full-draw for two to three seconds, a beginner will have time to review the points of form on which he is working. During this sighting, be sure your head tilts sideways over the arrow to ensure that your aiming eye is directly above the shaft.

# The Four Zones of the Direct Shot

Because virtually all people are capable aimers (once they have learned to place their eye above the arrow), the release and follow-through become the most important aspects of shooting an arrow. It is too much to ask a beginner archer to perform every aspect of the direct shot from the start. There are simply too many points of the proper form to digest and deliver so early in the game. For this reason we'll enter into the direct shot by stages.

### Zone 1: The Release

To understand the release, it helps to know what a release is not:
1. It is not a pluck—as if you were twanging a harp string.
2. It is not a quick, tendon-powered straightening of the fingers to open the hand.
3. It is not an easing of the string forward until it slips loose.
4. It is not jerking the hand out to the side to get out of the way.
5. It is not a surprise.

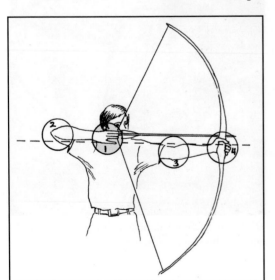

**Releasing the string should be a split-second decision to stop holding the string by relaxing the part of the fingers hooked over the string.** It is not adding something new to your drawn-string position; it is the cessation of something you were already doing. This information, as elementary as it may read, is profoundly important for consistency with successful shots.

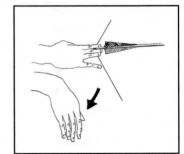

### The Success of a Flop

One of the best ways to guarantee that an archer will pour his concentration into his release is to ask the class to witness it and assess it. Ask the group to rate each demonstrator for two movements:

1. "Arrow creep" or "retreat" is the flaw that allows the arrow to move forward slowly on the arrow-rest at full-draw before the release. This is a sign that the string-hand is not relaxed. In fact, it is flexed and slowly beginning to straighten out fingers in preparation of letting the string slip. (Often when new students begin to develop sore fingers—probably because of improper string-releases—they will be tempted to retreat at the moment of release, as an attempt to lessen the abrasion. This is why tender fingers are counterproductive to learning archery form. It would be best to let those fingers heal before continuing.)

"Arrow creep" is also called "retreat" because the drawing arm should never move toward the target during a given shot. That arm should draw back, then pause at full-draw, and finally complete its backward movement in the follow-through.

2. The dangle of the relaxed string-hand (immediately after release) is the most prized accomplishment that a neophyte archer can demonstrate. That movement should show the slightest pendulum swing (back and forth) powered by gravity alone. This subtle swinging motion varies in intensity from one archer to another, depending upon the size of the wrist and, in some cases, the occupation of the archer. Generally speaking, the thicker the wrist, the less the range of motion and the less the dangle.

In one sense, this will be an easier flop to accomplish than the lob shot's release because the hand does not need to turn over from a palm-up position. On the other hand, all the new tension from a full-draw makes it more difficult for a beginner to maintain a relaxed hand and wrist while drawing.

One error during the release is very difficult to detect because it happens so fast. An archer might quickly open her fingers for the release (rather than *stopping the holding of the string*) and <u>then</u> let her hand flop at the wrist. This student is performing a token, after-the-fact dangle that serves no purpose. Her incorrect finger release has already doomed the shot. (A teacher can spot this by watching for arrow-retreat in the instant before the release. If watching for retreat proves inconclusive, focus on the student's elbow [of the string-arm] to detect this mistake.)

## Zone 2: String-Arm Follow-Through

Since the elbow leads the vector of force that draws the string (and is still in the act of leading that force at full-draw even though it is no longer moving), when that split-second relaxing of the fingertips occurs, the elbow should fly backward due to losing its resistance with the string. Simply watch the elbow of the string-arm to assess this. The motion should be immediate and natural, jumping backward from four to eight inches, depending upon bow-strength. (A stronger bow produces a longer follow-through.)

### Critiquing the String-Arm

Ask each archer to perform direct shots before the scrutinizing eyes of the others again. All eyes should be on the string-arm. The forearm should not drop on its

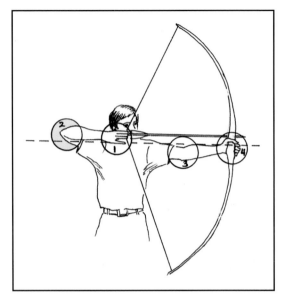

hinge at the elbow. Instead, like the bow-arm, the string-arm should remain on the tabletop. (Only the string-hand should fall through the tabletop.) At full-draw it is permissible to have the string-arm elbow slightly higher than the hand, even though the archer might not be aware of this elevated position. As long as the elbow jumps backward (not up) in the follow-through, this position at full-draw works well. This variation of forearm angle seems to be, for some, a matter of anatomical inclination.

There may be some rotation of the string-arm elbow toward the archer's back, but it should be minimal. There should be no rotation of the torso around the spine.

A proper follow-through allows the release-hand to dangle in the vicinity of the shoulder. Some very limber archers actually touch the shoulder during the hand flop.

### Proving the String-Arm Follow-Through

While a given student is at full-draw, quietly step up behind her and position your palm two inches behind her elbow to receive the impact of her follow-through. Her elbow should smack into your palm naturally.

## *Zone 3: Bow-Arm Follow-Through*

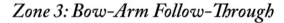

A bird's-eye view of an accomplished archer releasing an arrow shows the forward and backward movements of the follow-through occurring in the same line only in diametric directions. The forward motion of the bow-arm is much more subtle than the string-arm's but no less important. More than 90 percent of all archers I have observed—both beginners and veterans—drop their bow-arms at release, sometimes as much as 10 inches. Instead, keep that arm on the tabletop and, above all, be sure that you are actually pushing directly at your intended target rather than vaguely exerting pressure somewhere downrange.

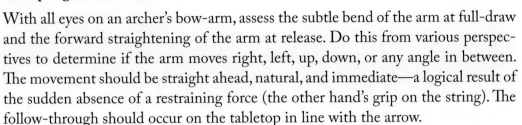

## Critiquing the Bow-Arm

With all eyes on an archer's bow-arm, assess the subtle bend of the arm at full-draw and the forward straightening of the arm at release. Do this from various perspectives to determine if the arm moves right, left, up, down, or any angle in between. The movement should be straight ahead, natural, and immediate—a logical result of the sudden absence of a restraining force (the other hand's grip on the string). The follow-through should occur on the tabletop in line with the arrow.

## Seeing the Entire Follow-Through

During the follow-through the spine should not lurch forward as though to push the arrow. The head should not move. Only the arms move . . . in contrast to the fixed anchor of torso, head, and legs.

To witness the flow of *both* arms and assess the stability of the rest of the body, stare at the chest of an archer at full-draw. Relax your vision to observe the entire archer with peripheral vision. At release the only motion visible should come from the arms and the bow.

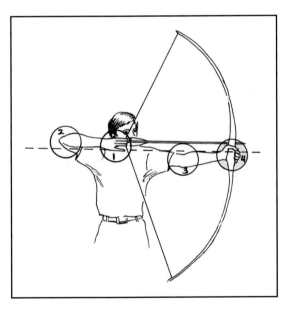

## *Zone 4: The Bow-Hand*

At full-draw the bow's handle exerts pressure on the heel of the hand, but the hand, in turn, should employ a very loose grip as it pushes toward the target, the fingers only caressing the handle. (Squeezing the handle telegraphs tension into the bow and can affect shooting accuracy at the instant of release.)

## Critiquing the Bow-Hand

At release the bow should be given free rein to bobble, dance, twist, rock, or slip in the hand. (Olympic archers often wear wrist-straps attached to their bows to prevent dropping their expensive equipment at release.) During such movement, the hand remains on the tabletop. Direct all eyes to the bow-hand of an archer and assess this loose grip by watching the lively response of the bow.

## Solo Work

The release and follow-through cannot be practiced too much. Veteran archers work on it regularly, because the grace of it can be lost after an absence from the archery range. Practice shooting five yards from a backstop without a bull's-eye, thinking only of the form of the four zones.

### Blind Shooting

Organize your students in a safe formation and have individual archers perform the release blindfolded, while only a few yards from the target. Stand behind the archer as a safeguard to make sure that the arrow remains pointed downrange. Because most people are challenged with balance when blindfolded, make sure the archer's feet are well spread for stability. Placing your hands on the waist of each archer provides good ballast. Have the audience students critique the release.

*Loose thy bolt first in thy mind, and thy shaft shall follow as an afterthought.*

—Robin o' the Hood

### CHAPTER 10

# The Fine Points of Shooting—And the Second Dimension of Aiming

So far in these lessons we have amassed quite a number of principles to think about while at full-draw. On the next page is a checklist of the important pieces of the whole.

1. Grip the string *deeply* in the archer's grooves. With the terminal joints of the string-fingers hooked on the string, *relax the rest of the hand, wrist, and forearm before attempting to draw.*
2. Draw the string by *leading with the elbow*. Push the bow with the heel of the hand. Both arms should work *on the imaginary tabletop.*
3. Draw with more strength than needed, *channeling the excess strength into maintaining smoothness, control, and form.*
4. At full-draw push the static bow directly *toward the target*. Even though the bow is no longer moving, the direction of push is crucial.
5. Keep the bow-arm *slightly bent* at the elbow.
6. Anchor the index fingertip *at the corner of the mouth.*
7. Tilt the head over the arrow to ensure that the aiming eye is *vertically above the arrow.*
8. The string-hand elbow should exert its vector of force *exactly backward from and in line with the arrow.*
9. Keep both arms on the imaginary *tabletop* throughout the shot. Only the string-hand falls through this plane.
10. Keep the torso, legs, and head absolutely stable. Only the arms move in shooting the bow by performing the follow-through.

## The Flow *of the Release*

At the moment of releasing the string, there should be no sensation of surprise. An archer's release is deliberate. The torso and head should not move. Even the facial expression should not change. Around the unmoving anchor of legs, torso, and head, the arm movement that results should be fluid. Both arms lurch away from one another in opposing directions on the tabletop. The initial movement makes me think of a thread popping, followed by a graceful extension of the arms and the movement as the string-hand and bow dangle gently.

Raising the head just after release is tantamount to the archer removing himself as a participant in the shot in order to become a spectator. Stay with the arrow as a shooter until it hits its destination.

Watching an accomplished archer release an arrow, one sees artistic liberation in the act. Even though the bow reacts violently, even though the string tears from the hand, even though the arrow rockets away . . . the archer maintains grace. Think of the release as the sudden tear of wet, stretched newspaper.

When you embrace the flow of the follow-through, you allow the bow to execute the shot without your getting in the way of the perfect aim invested at full-draw. If the string-hand truly relaxes at release, the string will bull its way through the space that your fingertips had just occupied. The string simply throws the limp fingers aside. Relaxed fingers will not disturb the path of a released string, especially as bow weight increases. If the fingers are not relaxed, they will alter the string's forward path and contribute to inaccuracy in the shot.

The *flow* of the follow-through instills a satisfying feeling, for the archer has harnessed the powerful explosion of the bow's stored energy inside a dedication to grace. The archer feels none of the violence of thrust or recoil. He feels . . . *release*.

Pushing and pulling. These are the two forces that create *the flow*. When the release abruptly breaks that tension, let your arms gently, gracefully follow their predetermined courses of their own will. The resulting follow-through will carry your bow-arm toward the target from one to two inches, and the string-elbow will leap backward four to eight inches, depending upon bow-poundage. Both movements occur in the same line that the arrow travels, only in opposite directions. Add no flair or extraneous movement to the follow-through. Stay on the tabletop.

---

### The Most Common Release Mistakes

1. Tensing the string-hand with the fierceness of talons.
2. Causing the string-hand to jump out to the side away from the face.
3. Locking the string-hand into the side of the face and "gluing" it there.
4. Letting the string-arm elbow hinge so the forearm drops through the tabletop rather than just the hand dropping.
5. A stiffened bow-arm lurching up, down, or sideways.
6. Raising the head quickly as if to spectate.
7. Squeezing the bow-handle in a death grip.
8. Lurching forward with the spine.
9. Showing surprise as if the release was unexpected.

---

## Bad Releases

The most common cause of an archer's inaccuracy is, no doubt, a bad release. Even the great archers perform one from time to time. Most of archery practice is about training the string-hand to release properly. What follows is a list of more details that make for bad releases.

---

### More Release Errors

1. Tensing the body into the rigidity of a statue and trying for minimal movement in the release by merely opening the fingertips. Some students are so rigid that I can step behind them, hold my open palm a half-inch behind their elbows at full-draw and never feel their elbows punch into my hand at the release.
2. Adding flair to the release, such as raising the release-hand in the air in a *voila* gesture.

3. Sending the release hand forcefully downward like a karate chop.

4. Flinging open the fingers and then belatedly flopping the hand. In this case, the archer flops the hand *because* he has released. The reverse should be true: The release should happen *because* the hand flops. This flawed release is the most difficult for a teacher to spot. It is performed in two steps so quickly that the eye has a hard time separating the two.

5. Children will often tire of pulling back for a full-draw and allow the arrow to creep forward before release. In other words, they do not stay true to the anchor point . . . or perhaps they are slowly opening up a tensed hand.

6. Children are also prone to inject magnum force into the shot by wildly thrusting the bow forward . . . or by allowing torque of the torso . . . or by suddenly pulling the string back an extra inch or two just before release (a giant pluck). They need to learn to trust their bows. The bow should do all the work at release. The archer's work is to get the bow cocked and aimed and then get out of its way. "Trust your bow" becomes a repeatable teaching motto.

7. Raising the head at release is a very common problem. This motion usually causes the bow-arm to drop. The head-bob interrupts *the flow*. Mentally stay with your arrow in flight and do not move your head or torso until the arrow has come to rest.

# Aiming

When shooting at a target, your eyes should remain fixed on the target, not on your equipment. All that you need to see of the arrow is the long pointing shaft in the lower section of your peripheral vision.

Always choose the smallest speck you can make out at the center of your target, and shoot at *that*. If a bull's-eye on a traditional target is six inches across, aim not at that but at an existing puncture hole or particle of the fabric at the center of the bull's-eye.

A good deer hunter does not loose an arrow *at a deer*. He shoots at a tiny clump of hair or shadow in the fur within the kill zone. A popular adage says it best: "Aim small, miss small. Aim big, miss big."

## The Vertical Line

The most fundamental aspect of aiming is the left-right accuracy (horizontal aiming or *windage*). If your eye is positioned over the arrow and your release and flow are performed well, your arrows will always fall somewhere on a *vertical line* that runs through the center of the bull's-eye. Think of a very long "rope" that begins at the archer's feet and runs along the ground directly to the target, up its face through the center of the bull's-eye, and then beyond the target along the ground. An archer with a good release and follow-through should always hit somewhere near this rope, even if her shot falls short or sails high. This left-right accuracy is the first aspect of archery to master. An archer's most difficult computation in aiming is *elevation*.

At this point, while your beginner students are shooting from rather close, all they need to know about up and down aiming (elevation) is that there is a tendency to aim too high at a close target. Instruct them to aim lower than instinct suggests.

The reason for this illusion is that, during aiming, the eye is above the arrow. Beginners tend to believe that the arrow will go to that spot where they see the tip of the fully drawn arrow *appear to touch* the target. In fact, such an arrow is angled well above that spot.

In the beginning days of shooting, don't let a student feel dismayed about shooting too high or low. Compliment her on her left/right aim—even if she shoots over or under the backstop intended to stop the arrow.

## The Wand

In medieval England impromptu contests of bow and arrow could crop up almost anywhere at any time. At a tavern meal two men might squabble over the right to the last drumstick of goose. Or three forest outlaws could argue over their first choice for sentry duty. When such an argument broke out, someone might say, "Let's do a wand!"

For this contest a willow branch was cut and peeled of its bark to expose the bright, light-colored wood beneath. This linear target was impaled vertically into the earth at the bottom of a berm of earth. The archers agreed upon a shooting distance, and each man shot once from that mark. Whoever hit closest to the wand won the argument.

It was not unusual to split the wand, for a vertical target is the easiest to hit. As it still is today, left/right aiming was the easier calibration of a shot. With the wand being a meter or so long, the up and down margin for error was not so problematic. It did not matter where the arrow neared the wand— low, in the middle, or high. What mattered was the distance from arrow to wand after the shot was made.

In my beginner classes it is common for students to split a one-and-a-half-inch-thick wand of dried bamboo from seven yards. They do it rather frequently. Hitting a six-inch-diameter bull's-eye is a different story, however, because of the demand for accurate elevation.

Splitting the wand probably spawned the legends of splitting arrows at will, which is not an easy proposition . . . largely luck, in fact, even for an expert bowman to precisely cleave the arrow's nock. The wand is still an excellent exercise for archers. And it's a lot of fun, especially if stakes are included . . . like a leg of goose.

### Shooting the Wand

Pin a four-foot-long, one-and-a-half-inch-thick cane of <u>dried</u> bamboo vertically to a backstop. From the bottom of the cane tie a sunburst of four separate ropes that spread to the shooters' line where four archers will stand. In this way, a shot that falls short can be judged, too. The rope is merely an extension of the cane from that archer's perspective. It should not matter how high or low the arrow goes. The objective is to hit the line that includes cane and rope.

# Elevation Aiming

I don't know that anyone can teach another how to aim high enough or low enough for a given target on the first try. Bows come in different strengths. Archers' arms come in different lengths. Arrows come in different lengths and weights. All of these factors affect arrow flight and the up-down aiming. A teacher cannot center a shot in a bull's-eye at a given distance and then, based upon that shot, describe to a student exactly how to angle her arrow. This knowledge must come with the experience of a given person with a given bow and arrow at a given distance. Over time an archer gets a feel for the elevation factor with a particular bow at a particular distance. The prescription for any young archer is to shoot a lot of arrows . . . from the same distance . . . and then from a variety of distances.

Some archers use complicated methods for achieving perfect elevation. They learn to estimate distance yardage quite accurately and translate that into usable information in sighting. Though rare with traditional archers, there are those who attach sighting pins to their bows, each pin used like a rifle sight for a calibrated distance.

Others think not at all about distance. They simply allow their instincts to guide them. Yet, that instinct is fed by their experiences shooting from many different distances. The brain remembers shooting at distance X. It also remembers the correct relationship between the point of the arrow and the target at that distance (as seen by the archer's eye at full-draw) in order to produce a successful shot. After all, an archer can't really see the angle of his own arrow at full-draw. He would have to be standing beside himself to accomplish that.

What this archer is actually remembering is the <u>space</u> seen separating arrow point from bull's-eye at full-draw. This space is called "***the gap***." The assessment of the gap is somewhat abstract because it could be measured either at the tip of the arrow or at the target. There are no numbers or specific calibrations used—just a sight picture that asks for aiming-memory to well up from experience.

## Shooting with the Gap

Take the example of an archer who has become proficient at keeping her shots on the vertical line. Picture her shooting repeatedly at a plastic milk jug exactly fifteen yards away. This jug sits on the top rail of a four-rail fence. Her first several shots sail over or through or strike the rails. Eventually, whether or not she can explain the process, she learns to hit the jug consistently. (With enough practice any archer could achieve this.)

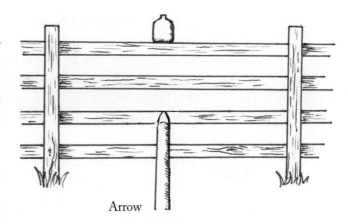

Let's join her after she has begun to consistently hit the target. If we ask her how she is positioning her arrow for these successful shots, she may not be able to answer. She is not aware of the details.

So let's imagine that a tiny camera has now been implanted in her dominant eye. Each time she aims—just before release at full-draw—the shutter snaps and takes a picture. Once developed, the print shows the arrow as a short, thick, slightly tapering vertical line centered at the bottom of the frame, its point hovering on the fence at the top of rail number two directly below the milk jug. The space between the arrow point and the milk jug is *the gap*.

Measuring this distance with a ruler on the photographic print might show a seven-eighths-inch reading. But if the archer takes a tape measure to the fence and stretches it from the jug to the top of rail number two, the distance might measure twenty-three inches. Herein lies the conundrum of describing the gap.

But in shooting with the gap we will never use inches or any other mathematical calibration. Nor will we use fence rails, because other targets will not be sitting on a fence. We will simply use the *gestalt* memory of a successful gap at a given distance.

*The gap* is the only variable with which an archer contends (at least concerning a stationary target on a windless day). Horizontal aiming is easy. It never changes with distance. The gap changes with every different distance.

The fence rails, in this example, give the archer a way to figure out *the gap* in concrete terms. In essence, the rails serve as sighting devices. If the jug sits in the grass, there is nothing but grass in the photo between the arrow tip and the jug; therefore, establishing the proper gap is all about the *perceived space* between point and target.

Every time you shoot repeatedly from a certain distance, your brain begins its rote education about the proper gap for that distance. It is best not to use objects (like a fence rail or a straw on a target face) as a reference upon which to settle the arrow point, but instead to use a remembered space—a gap. Why? Because when shooting at another target in another setting from an identical distance, there will be no such reference.

In other words, it is *not* judicious to look at a target and choose a predisposed marker (like a certain blade of grass) upon which to rest your arrow point at full-draw. Such a marker will not serve you at another target. The process is better approached by ascertaining the gap at full-draw—not in inches but in a general recognition of space.

Whether you hit a bull's-eye or not, if you are aiming and releasing and following-through well, all your shots should fall in a good vertical line with the target. Eventually, at a given shooting distance, you will become familiar with the gap between point and target that delivers an accurate shot. At that point in time your trial-and-error episode has written its first chapter in your book of experience. Another day, in another place, shooting at a different target but at that same distance, your memory will well up with the spatial information that you need. This is why the truest test of an archer is a series of single shots from varying distances without practice.

### Learning the Many Gaps

Pace off seven walking strides from a foil pie plate pinned to a large backstop (an earthen bank, a wall of cubic hay bales, or the round, flat end of a cylindrical hay bale). Shoot as many times as needed to achieve consistent hits on the plate, being sure to pay attention to the gap.

Move back four paces and repeat until you can consistently hit the bull's-eye.

Return to the original seven-pace mark and give yourself three tries to remember the proper gap that delivers an accurate shot. If successful, move back to the eleven-pace mark again and do the same. If you fail, start this activity from its beginning.

When finally you achieve success, stand at the fifteen-pace mark and shoot until you can hit the plate three out of five tries. Then return to the seven-pace marker and take three tries to hit the plate. If successful, take three tries at the eleven-pace mark. If successful again, move to the fifteen-pace mark.

## Long Distance Shooting

When an archer steps back to a formidable distance, there is a temptation to put more *oomph* into the push of the bow or the pull of the string. Never before has it been so important to adhere to perfect form and let the bow do all the work. A tiny jolt at such a distance translates into a major error at the target. Don't let distance intimidate you. Compared to a shot from eight paces, there is nothing different about a shot from sixty paces except that you must aim higher. Release by instantly giving up your hold on the string. Let your fingers fall away like downy feathers. Embrace the flow of the follow-through.

As you move back farther from your target, the gap necessarily gets smaller because you must elevate your aim to give the arrow more time in the air. At some point you reach "the golden distance," at which you must "touch" your arrow point to the bull's-eye. In other words, at this distance the gap is zero. This can be a fun distance from which to shoot.

To move back farther means that you will need to sight with your arrow point above the target. Now you will have to deal with a "negative gap." Seeing that gap is not possible at full-draw because your bow-hand is in the way. Now you must resort to using landmarks in the background scenery above the target. Such landmarks might include a fork in a tree, a shadow in the canopy, or a small bright patch of sky between leafy boughs.

To be sure that your landmarks are on a true vertical line with the target, stand in your shooter's stance with the loaded bow lowered by your side, keeping your head exactly in the position where it will be during the shooting. Then raise your locked and loaded arrow vertically at arm's length with the bottom of the shaft bisecting the target. Potential landmarks lie along the upper portion of the shaft. Now learn by trial and error. Again, only experience will finally teach you about using these negative gaps for other distant targets with different background sceneries. The difference now is that you must study your gap after each successful shot in order to get a feel for its spatial recognition.

## Shooting Indian-Style

There is no one technique of shooting that can be called *the* Native American way. Methods varied from tribe to tribe. But generally speaking, the draw-length of native archers was shorter than today's average full-draw. The arrow was drawn back lower on the body, probably without a loyal anchor point. There may not have been a detailed aiming process while holding at full-draw—one reason being that full-draw is considered a potentially dangerous bend that could break a self-bow.

The common Indian draw was smooth and quick with the arrow pointed at the target from the beginning of the draw, as if the need to release might occur even before reaching the intended draw-length.

Some historians believe that the Indian draw was executed while raising the bow—the arrow released as soon as the desired angle of trajectory was reached. I don't doubt that such a technique was employed, but it does add one more variable to the act of shooting. I believe that most native archers would have naturally gravitated away from such a method and leveled the arrow at the target *while drawing*. (That said, America's most celebrated archer, Howard Hill, used the draw-on-the-rise method with impressive effect.)

### How to Shoot Indian-Style

There were many string-grips among the various tribes of North America. We will stay loyal to the English grip while learning this variation on bow/arrow position and draw. Load the bow (with Locksley) and stand with the weak-side leg forward, that foot pointed at the target, both legs bent for stability, the body slightly hunched forward to allow space for the draw into the body. Bring the bow up and out in front with both arms bent until the arrow is chest-high and pointing dead-on at the target. Your chest should angle toward your strong side, slightly away from the target.

Now consider the arrow's alignment at the target a constant. It never changes. As you draw, your body must make every adjustment to ensure that the arrow does not move from this alignment. *The loaded arrow floats out front on the one true line of accuracy.* Push the bow forward and draw the string back toward the chest, keeping the string-hand and forearm in line with the arrow. The eyes remain positioned vertically above the arrow and fixed upon the intended target. The string-hand and wrist should be relaxed and ropelike. In drawing the string, the torso rotates around the axis of the spine somewhat. Make the push and pull remain servants of the *true line.* All movements of the body are fluid and graceful. When your drawing hand has come back almost as far as the sternum, *while you are still pushing and pulling,* release. The follow-through is exactly as you have learned earlier in these pages, only performed on a lower tabletop.

### Making a Belt-Quiver

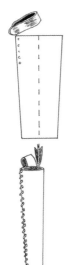

Making your own quiver is a good way to get more personally connected to archery. Adorn it with designs that are meaningful to you. Inspirational symbols from Nature are appropriate for this art: a lightning bolt, a stooping hawk, the catapulting stamens of a mountain laurel flower, the archer fish, as examples.

A quiver is simply a long pouch of any lightweight material. It can be cylindrical or flattened, rectangular or tapered. I have seen homemade quivers of cardboard, pant legs of old jeans, purchased leather, printed curtain fabric, vinyl, tulip tree bark, cane-splints, and brain-tanned deer hide.

Measure one of your arrows from its point to the leading edge of its fletching and cut a piece of material that length. Decide how wide you would like this quiver to be, multiply that measurement by two, and cut accordingly, letting the bottom of each side taper enough to result in a quiver with a wider mouth than a bottom of the pouch. When this material is folded lengthwise, it will resemble a giant knife sheath. Clamp the edges together temporarily by using clothespins.

Decide where you would like to wear the quiver: on your back or on your belt? If on the belt, which side of your body? Most right-handers who use a belt quiver wear it on the right hip with the fletching tilted slightly forward.

If a belt quiver is preferred, cut a wide, sturdy, leather belt loop and mark how it will be angled on the material to create the tilt. Unclamp the material, open it up, and sew the belt loop to the quiver. Now refold the material to match the sides and sew the seam.

### Making a Back-Quiver

If a back quiver is chosen, I recommend a double-strap—just like a daypack but lopsided. Single-strap back-quivers are frustrating, as they tend to relocate lower on the back unless you secure them to a trouser belt or around the torso. When such a single-strap quiver rotates around the body, the arrows become unreachable at the back.

Have a friend hold the temporarily clamped quiver angled against your back (righties have the fletching rise over the right shoulder) and practice pulling arrows out until you have ascertained a good position on your back for easy drawing.

Use sturdy, durable, comfortable material for straps. Leather is ideal. Fit these straps over your shoulders so your friend can see how they lie against the side of the quiver resting against your back. This orientation of strap to quiver is important in maintaining the proper tilt angle of the quiver as it hangs on your back. Your helper can hold each strap in place and outline it on the quiver. Each strap should be temporarily sewn in two separate places on the side of the quiver that touches the back. Rather than have the straps overlap on the quiver itself, have one sewn higher than the other at each end. For a righty, sew the left strap-ends lower than the right strap-ends. This will help maintain the proper tilt of the quiver.

Test the fit. Slip your arms into the strap loops and determine if the quiver holds your arrows at the proper tilt. If so, permanently sew on the straps and the quiver seam.

Some quivers are heavier—designed as protective containers. Others are light—serving only to carry the arrows conveniently. In the latter case, it is the bulk of arrows that provides strength and protection for the individual arrow. ("United we stand.")

The quiver shown in the photo is much longer than its arrows. A rag has been stuffed into the bottom to prop the arrows high enough to keep the feathers free. In the event of rain, the rag is pulled out to let the arrows sink out of sight, and the flaps at the top of the quiver are folded over and tied to protect the arrows. If desired, you can alter your quiver template accordingly to include extra length and rain-cover flaps.

*"Hit the leaf and you discard an acorn. If you miss by no more than this . . ."*
*Now she spread her hand, extending thumb and little finger in a measuring*
*gesture, "you stand pat. Hit outside that distance, you pick up a new acorn.*
*We'll take turns roving for a target. First archer to empty a pocket of acorns*
*is champion of the day."*

—M. Warren, *A Tale Twice Told*

## CHAPTER 11

# At Play in the Fields of the Archer—
# Games with Bow and Arrow

### A Wand of Accountability

As a teacher of young archers, keep your ears open for any point of disagreement among your students. It might be an argument about who is right or wrong about some half-remembered fact; or perhaps it's about who gets to be first in line for this or that; or it might be over the right to the last piece of fruit. Surprise them with a dramatic announcement. Point at the two in discord and declare: "Let's do a wand!"

Set up a vertical cane of dead bamboo against a good backstop and decide upon a shooting distance. Each archer gets only one shot with one arrow. The better shot rules.

### King Arthur's Bandoleer (Rovers)

In *The Once and Future King*, T. H. White has young Arthur and Kay playing "rovers" in the forest. They roam with their bows until someone chooses a reasonable target. ("Reasonable" includes targets that are safe to all living things and to the arrows themselves: a bright leaf on the ground, a rotten stump, a shadow. "Unreasonable" would include a rock, a living tree, a dead, semi-petrified Virginia pine.) Whoever hits the target or comes closest to the center names the next target.

A variation on this game can be played with a homemade bandoleer (webbing) adorned with regal "jewelry" and painted symbols of royalty. Design the belt to slip diagonally over the torso of any of your students.

Roam the forest and search for a target. Perhaps you, the teacher, spot a hand-sized patch of moss on the dirt bank of an old road-cut. One at a time, all archers shoot from a distance that you choose. Whoever makes the best shot ceremoniously receives the bandoleer on bended knee. She then wears it and leads the group to name the next challenge. If ever anyone holds onto the prized belt for three consecutive shots, the game is over. The rest of the party must kneel and raise their bows to this archer's accomplishment.

### Seven Stones

Every archer collects seven pebbles (or acorns or pieces of broken stick, etc.) and stores them in a pocket. The winner is the first to empty that pocket. As the group roams through woods and field, archers take turns naming a reasonable target. If anyone objects to the safety of a shot—that is, the welfare of human, live plant, animal, or arrow—another target must be chosen by the same archer.

When an archer names a bull's-eye (say, a woodpecker's excavation in a rotten log), she must name one more parameter outside the bull's-eye (perhaps a hand's span from the hole). This is the neutral zone. One at a time the archers shoot from

the same place, under the same conditions. Sometimes the caller makes a stipulation to the challenge: a time limit that involves a count-down; or a lob; or holding your breath up to the release; or kneeling while shooting, etc.

If an archer hits the hole (bull's-eye), she throws away a stone. If another archer hits in the neutral zone, he holds fast to what he has in his pocket. If someone hits outside that zone, he picks up a new rock and adds it to his collection.

## The Four Corners Tribes

Set up a two-and-a-half-foot by two-and-a-half-foot square of condensed foam as a target, and then, using a black marker bisect the target face horizontally and verti-cally to make four quadrants. At the center draw a saucer-sized circle. In any one of the quadrants draw another circle the size of the mouth of a coffee cup. Inside this circle draw a symbol that represents George Custer and the 7th Cavalry. A sword, or a seven will do . . . or if you're up for it, a portrait of Custer himself. (If using hay bales, affix two bamboo canes as the dividing lines for quadrants, an aluminum pie plate pegged behind the crossing of the canes as the center bull's-eye, and a paper cup pinned to any quadrant to serve as the Custer target.)

Divide your students into two teams and name them after Native American tribes who were present at the Little Big Horn (Cheyenne, Lakota, or Arapaho). Place the shooters' line at a reasonable but challenging distance from the target. Each tribe lines up side by side so the archer at the head of each line will shoot first from the shooters' line. When the signal "All clear to shoot" is given, there is no hurry. Each archer shoots at the lower right (southeast) quadrant. A successful shot cannot touch a line or the center circle. (Therefore each quadrant is not a true square. It is a square with a bite taken out of one corner.)

When the next two archers step up to shoot, if a previous tribal member successfully hit the southeastern quadrant, then the present archer shoots for the southwest (moving clockwise). But if not, this archer must shoot at the southeast (again, for his tribe). Each tribe must hit the assigned quad-rant before advancing to the next.

The order is southeast, southwest, northwest, northeast, then the south-east again, and finally the center circle for the win. There is no hurry to shoot unless both tribes have shot all around the four corners and are now trying for the center circle. At that point, the archers cannot load until you have announced "All clear to load and shoot." The arrow that hits the circle first wins the contest for that tribe.

What makes the game more interesting is the ability to delay the opposing tribe's progress. An archer stepping up for her turn to shoot may call out "Crazy Horse!" This is the signal that she wishes to erase the opposing tribe's last effective shot. This challenger (the "Crazy Horse" caller) shoots first. If she hits the Custer circle (any part of it including the rim), the other tribe—before continuing around the four corners—must re-shoot the last quadrant that they had successfully hit. If the Crazy Horse challenger misses the Custer circle, her shot cannot count for hitting any quadrant or bull's-eye. This is merely a shot lost by that tribe. Then the archer of the other tribe takes his normal shot.

### The Bubonic Rat

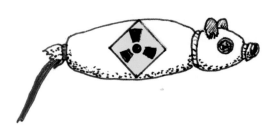

Stuff an old gray sock with rags and sew on white button eyes, black button nose, flap ears, and a bright red ribbon for a tail. Once made, keep this noxious rodent hidden in a bag.

Use a rake to define a thirty-yard trail in the forest. (Keep that rake nearby. You're going to need it again later.) Walk your students down the path so they become familiar with the route. Gather everyone together at the beginning of the trail and send your assistant (with a stopwatch and the bagged Bubonic Rat) to the other end of the trail. On her way down the trail (and out of the students' sight) the assistant plants the rat in a safe place, somewhere on the ground five to eight yards off the trail. The rat's lair should not be blatantly obvious, nor should it be too well hidden. The rat and its red tail, however, must be at least visible from the path.

Now it's time to tell the students about the rogue rat that has been spotted in this forest . . . and about their mission to eliminate it: "We have been appointed by a joint commission of CDC and the National Security Council to exterminate the Bubonic Rat. Death by arrow, it has been shown, is the surest way to dispatch a rat that has survived since the Dark Ages. But we must be careful of the rat's pathogens in the Bubonic Zone."

"The what?" someone asks.

"The Bubonic Zone," you repeat. "That's the trail you just walked with me. The rat is somewhere near that trail, and each of you is going in alone to kill it. No matter what happens, don't get off the trail! Your risk of infection is greater off the trail."

### The Rules of the Hunt

1. Each archer carries one arrow and can spend only twenty seconds on the trail. This limited time will protect the archer from exposure to pathogens. The assistant will call out the start and time the archer, counting aloud only the last five numbers to help the hunter leave the toxic area on time.
2. An archer cannot load his arrow until he spots the rat.
3. The archer cannot leave the trail.
4. If the archer shoots the rat, he must deliver the hero's cry of victory. Game number one is over.
   Time to re-hide the rat and try again, starting with the archers who have not yet had a turn.

5. If the archer misses his shot, he must hurry to the end of the trail before time runs out.
6. If a hunter does not arrive at trail's end within twenty seconds, he is infected and loses the ability to speak for one hour. This is a little-known symptom of early-stage bubonic plague called RATS! (Rodent-Activated Tongue-Swelling!)

Choose one archer to be the first hunter to venture alone into the Bubonic Zone. Then call out to your assistant to tell her that a student is ready to travel down the trail. When she checks her watch and gives the signal, the first hunter moves down the trail with bow in one hand and an arrow in the other.

One at a time each archer will take a turn at finding and shooting the rat from the trail in the allotted time. When a hunter arrives at trail's end, the assistant will signal for a new hunter.

After each game, retrieve all arrows from the woods. This will be a group effort. (Time to bring out that rake again.)

## Watermelon Hunt

This variation on the Bubonic Rat hunt substitutes a watermelon for the rat. It's a perfect game for a hot summer afternoon. This time, when the target has been shot, the successful hunter earns the honor of slicing the melon and serving to all.

## Quick Shot

Set up a one-and-a-half-foot hoop of grapevine on a backstop. Eight yards back from this target define a shooters' line. Form two or three students in a flank at the line. They will have nine seconds to grab an arrow from a quiver (or an arrow pinned beside the ankle inside a shoe), load, and shoot into the hoop. Until the start signal is given, no archer should be touching an arrow with a hand. Repeat this a few times and then reduce the time to eight seconds. Continue to reduce the number of seconds until it is not possible to get off a shot.

Sometimes working quickly can encourage bad form. And often the pressure of limited time makes archers fumble the loading. Encourage the students to work smoothly, economically, without wasting time. This exercise can cement the importance of the lessons you have been teaching. It can also eliminate some habits that are simply a waste of time—like spending unnecessary time aiming at full-draw.

Follow up this exercise with a round of shooting that is not under the clock. Encourage the students to use the economical lessons just learned—now without the constraints of the countdown.

## The Rainbow Race

If you have a traditional target of concentric, multicolored rings, drape a rope vertically down its center (or use masking tape) to divide the target into left and right territorial halves. Have two archers (or two teams) stand at the shooters' line

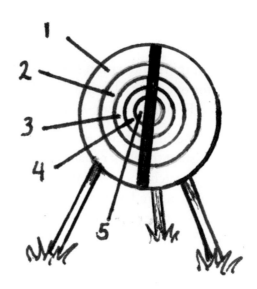

and—alternating shot-for-shot—move from the outer ring to the next neighboring color and so on to the half bull's-eye.

## Swinging Target

Throw a rope over a twenty-foot-high tree limb and tie it off. On the free end tie a plastic milk jug stuffed with rags, so it is suspended one foot off the ground. Pour enough water into the jug to wet the rags. (This will supply the weight needed to keep the jug swinging.) With the jug at rest, hammer two markers into the ground on opposite sides of the jug, each two feet from the jug. These markers delineate a four-foot-wide no-shooting zone.

Carry the jug to one side along its arc to the height of your chest. Ten to fifteen yards away an archer stands with an unloaded bow. At your signal to commence shooting, release the jug and move away into a safe zone. Meanwhile, the archer loads and attempts to hit the swinging jug. She can shoot as many arrows as possible until the jug's swing has dwindled down inside the no-shooting zone. Repeat with a new archer. This is a good spectator sport for waiting archers.

## Run and Shoot

On a backstop set up three targets, all differently sized. The largest is worth one point. The middle is worth three. The smallest is worth five. An archer with no equipment stands forty yards from a target. Twenty yards from the target lies his bow. At ten yards an arrow is lightly impaled into the ground.

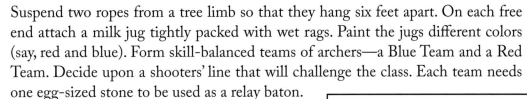

When the teacher begins counting down from fifteen, the archer runs to his bow, picks it up, and carries it to his arrow. There he loads and then shoots. The arrow must be released before the countdown reaches zero. After each round, subtract one second for the next round.

## Dueling Pendulums

Suspend two ropes from a tree limb so that they hang six feet apart. On each free end attach a milk jug tightly packed with wet rags. Paint the jugs different colors (say, red and blue). Form skill-balanced teams of archers—a Blue Team and a Red Team. Decide upon a shooters' line that will challenge the class. Each team needs one egg-sized stone to be used as a relay baton.

Two archers (one from each team) stand ready to compete, each with a stone in a pocket and a bow in hand. Standing next in line behind each archer, a team member holds a bundle of twenty arrows. (The arrow-holder will be the second team shooter.)

Just before the contest begins, pull the jugs in the same lateral direction—each jug moved three feet from its resting place—and release them to swing in side-by-side arcs.

When all people are in a safe location, give the signal to begin. Each arrow-holder gives one arrow to his team-shooter. The archers load and shoot—the Reds aiming at the blue jug, the Blues aiming at the red jug. Only one shot is allowed. The object of the game is to keep the opponent's jug swinging by the smack of an arrow. If a jug comes to rest, the team of the same color wins.

As the first archer is in the process of shooting, her arrow-holder passes the bundle of arrows to the teammate behind him. Once the present shooter has fired one shot, she turns and holds out her stone to her arrow-holder, who pockets the rock, and steps to the shooters' line with his bow. The first archer walks to the back end of her team's line to await another try. When the second archer takes his stance at the shooters' line, the archer in line behind him (his arrow-holder) supplies him with an arrow. He can then load and shoot as fast or as slowly as he likes.

For the sake of safety, maintain a strict order for team rotations, exchange of rocks and arrows, and attention of archers to the shooters' line.

### Tic-Tac-Bow

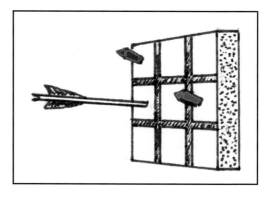

Divide your class into balanced teams, Red and Blue. On a cardboard target face draw in heavy black lines a large version of the traditional tic-tac-toe game. Wrap the head of six tent stakes in red surveyor's tape and six more in blue. Choose your distance based upon the proficiency of the archers. Two teams alternate shots (one shot per archer, then it's back to the end of the team line) as they try for a win. There is no time limit in this game. Each archer shoots in a leisurely fashion when it is her turn. Each time after an arrow is shot into the grid, suspend the game long enough to remove the arrow. If this arrow hit cleanly inside a square (without cutting a line), replace it with the appropriately colored stake. Play until one team completes a same-color tic-tac-toe straight line across three squares.

## The Clout Shot

Perhaps the most esoteric shot of all—and, arguably, the most fascinating for spectators and shooters alike—requires a lot of open space and enhanced dedication to safety. The clout shot is a fully drawn shot that is raised well above the 45-degree maximum-distance angle so the arrow sails skyward, stalls, turns, and drops by gravity to an intended target.

Accuracy with the clout shot demands more practice than any other shot. Obviously, the clout is archery's shot with the greatest potential for error. This—and the lack of available open space—may be the reason that most modern archers do not ordinarily use it.

In the crowning days of the English longbow, the clout shot had a militaristic role during castle siege. Hundreds of arrows rained down inside the castle walls of the enemy, wreaking havoc and intimidating the sequestered army.

It has also been suggested through oral history that a great oak in Sherwood Forest once served as a "signal tree," where medieval outlaws sent arrows marked with a message. (This could perhaps be the "Major Oak," which still stands in Sherwood Forest outside of Edwinstowe in Nottinghamshire.) The only way to send such a

missive from a distant point was the clout, as the arrow had to make its journey above the obstructions of the tree canopy. These "signal-arrows" would have been fitted with blunt points to prevent sticking high up in the branches. (Today an empty cartridge shell glued or taped over the point works nicely in the forest.) Such an arrow was launched cleanly through a canopy "window." When it reentered the forest it fell clattering through the tree limbs delivering an audible, primitive version of a ringing telephone.

When the first clout shots are made by students, the teacher must verbally approve to "okay" the release. This signal verifies that an arrow is angled neither straight-up nor too low. (Thankfully, a first-time clout shooter rarely shoots straight-up. He will be under the illusion that his arrow is aimed extremely high when it is actually angled lower.)

There are varied posture preferences for performing the clout. The specialized stance that I propose is designed to help the archer gain a high angle with the arrow *without bending at the waist*. For most people, the spine does not easily bend sideways. As an archer attempts it, the spine tends to rotate to one side or the other so the bend becomes more frontward or backward rather than sideways. Such a shift takes the arrow off aim. By using the posture described below, the spine never has to bend at all.

## Learning the Clout Shot Stance

Load as usual with the Locksley. Stand sideways to the distant target as with a direct shot but spread your feet apart twice as wide.

The leading leg should bend only a negligible amount for balance control as the back leg bends dramatically with the foot turned to allow the knee to bend away from the target. Lowering yourself on this bent back leg allows the spine to recline away from the target. With the legs positioned this way, recline your spine *until it is aligned with the front leg*.

Grip the string without drawing and stretch the bow-arm toward the target. Using the tip of your undrawn arrow as a "paintbrush," take practice sweeps vertically from the target up into the sky and back down again as if you are sketching a vertical line on the landscape before you. (To do this correctly, the arm should pivot from the shoulder, so the spine and shoulders do not move.) These

*clout shot*

"practice strokes" with the arrow go up and down a few times to determine a true vertical line. These strokes work best if done in a smooth flowing motion rather than slowly creeping the arrow up and down.

The determination of arrow-angle (elevation) is somewhat abstract and can only come with practice. Initial clout shots by beginners are generally far too long, as measured across the land. Ironically, the closer the target, the more difficult (and dangerous) the clout shot. As a target gets farther away, your clout shot (the most challenging shot in archery) begins to approach an angle more like a long direct shot (the most accurate shot in archery). When the target is close, establishing the vertical line with the practice strokes becomes much more difficult. Furthermore, angling the arrow so high becomes less defined with nothing to look at but sky.

Also, the stronger the bow, the more difficult the clout. (The farther the arrow travels up, the more room for error.)

You'll want to limit young or beginner adult students to relatively distant clout shots so as not to endanger anyone with a shot performed too near the vertical.

### Shooting Your First Clouts

You and a friend should situate yourselves in a field where you have good visibility in every direction. Start off with a distant flag target. This definition of distance will vary with different bow weights. Consider a yardage that is two-and-a-half times the poundage of your bow. (If using a 30# bow, set your flag at seventy-five yards.)

Take the proper stance and sweep your loaded (but not drawn) arrow through practice strokes several times to ascertain a good vertical alignment with the target. On one of these sweeps bring the arrow very high . . . perhaps 70 to 80 degrees. **Ask your friend to verify that your arrow is not pointed straight up!**

As you draw keep your eyes on the arrow's angle against the sky and be sure that it does not change left or right, up or down. (A sky with near-stationary clouds is most helpful.) To achieve this steadiness, rotate your shoulders *around the fixed axis of your spine*. The release and follow-through for the clout shot are the same as for the direct shot.

In this exercise you have started with a very high elevation, hopefully to shoot your first clout shot short of the target. Now you can work subsequent shots toward the target by sequentially lowering the launch angle (elevation).

### *Clout Windage*

Because the clout shot suspends an arrow in the air longer than any other type of shot . . . and because the arrow slows at the apex of the flight, a clout shot can be most vulnerable to the wind at the top of its trajectory and during the first moments of its freefall. Watch your clout arrow just after it points back to earth and observe to see if the wind pushes the feathered end of the shaft to one side. Clout-shot arrows in wind can drift off line quite a distance, so this must be factored into the aiming equation. An archer has no choice but to compensate by aiming upwind.

Wind direction at ground level can be measured by dropping a hair or fistful of crumbled leaves and dust from an extended arm and hand. However, be prepared for surprises with wind direction. If the field in which you are shooting is surrounded by a wall of forest, the wind direction above the trees might be opposite from the wind direction below the canopy. Trees form a barrier to the wind. As the wind rushes over the treetops, when it encounters a vacuum below (the treeless meadow), wind rushes down and backward at ground level, forming an eddy just like water flowing backward behind a rock in a stream. If your clout shot takes the arrow above treetop level, it is the wind current above the trees that will most affect your arrow. Factor that loftier current into your aiming.

### Castle Siege

Stake four poles in a fifty-foot-by-fifty-foot square, each pole topped by a streamer of surveyor's tape. This square defines an imaginary castle in the meadow. At a distance suitable for the bows being used, make an identical castle. Assign five arrows per archer. Stand inside castle #1 and attempt to launch clout shots into castle #2. When all the arrows have been shot, walk down and survey the battlefield. All arrows that successfully entered the domain of the fortress may be shot again (by their owners) from this castle into the first. Continue this elimination game until a clout champion emerges.

### Tournament of the Medicine Bow

A contest that involves quickness and accuracy (and the challenge of shooting at a swinging target) is covered in *Volume 2* in the storytelling section. See *The Legend of the Medicine Bow.*

## *Arrow-Throwing Techniques*

Throwing an arrow is undeniably fun . . . and challenging. Hurling the arrow without use of the bow is all part of getting to know your archery equipment. I have seen a number of throwing styles: javelin, point over nock flip, underhand with the index hooked behind the nock, atlatl-style over the shoulder (again using the index hooked behind the nock), etc. But nothing beats the discus technique for distance. Using this technique most people can throw three or four times their javelin-style distance. The drawback of the discus style is its difficulty in controlling the aim.

### Throwing the Arrow for Distance

To perform the sidearm discus throw, first move all spectators out of harm's way *in every direction*. Take the shaft of the arrow in your flattened stronger hand, the thumb pressing into the shaft just in front of the fletching. While letting the shaft rest on the middle finger, barely nestle the sides of the shaft with the index and ring fingers. This hand will serve as a launching platform. Some of the fletching may lie against the forearm.

With your body turned sideways (weak side toward target), elevate the weak arm as a counterbalance and cock back the extended arrow-arm with the arrow pointed at a spot on the ground about five yards away. Take a skipping start toward the target area and, by rotating the body a quarter-turn, whip the straight arrow-arm around, rising to a 45-degree angle, with all the power and grace you can muster. Release the arrow early . . . *before* the arm completes its half-circle around the body . . . *before* it points toward the target. The first time you try it, you will likely release too late and throw to your weak side. Keep trying with an earlier release.

A variation of this throw is an underhanded pendulum version. Distance suffers somewhat, but directional accuracy increases. For accuracy throws that don't require distance, the spear style is probably best. (See spear-throwing in Chapter 2.)

### Using All of the Shots of Archery—Archery Golf

Archers take turns naming a challenge that requires multiple shots or a single shot under unique conditions. A starting spot is named, and each archer, in his turn, must touch a foot to that spot. Here are a few examples:

First archer's challenge: Start with a clout shot from this rock. The ultimate bull's-eye for this challenge is the paper cup at the far end of the meadow in the shadow of the ash tree. Wherever your clout arrow lands you will pull it, place a foot over the hole it made in the ground, and throw it for your second advancement toward the bull's-eye. From there you will direct shoot until you hit the cup, keeping count of your shots.

The challenger begins with his clout and then the others follow. Then all walk to their clout arrows and decide the safest order to perform the throwing. Each throw counts as a stroke. (If someone hits the cup on the throw, her score is two.) Then come the direct shots. If an archer hits the paper cup on his first direct shot, his score is three. If it takes an archer three direct shots to hit the cup, her score is five. As in golf, low score wins. If ever an archer's score exceeds eight on a given hole, he's done. Give him a mercy-score of eight.

Second archer's challenge: The ultimate target—for a score—is the milk jug hanging from the persimmon tree. Before we shoot at it, first the shooting distance from the jug must be earned. From this tuft of grass shoot five arrows at the hay bale. Every arrow that hits the bale affords five paces to be walked from here toward the milk jug. No matter how many paces are earned and taken, hitting the jug with the first direct shot is a "hole-in-one" (one point). Hitting on the second try is worth two points. And so on.

Third archer's challenge: From this stump, lob three arrows into the triangle defined by the picnic table, the willow tree, and the corner of the fence. Each arrow that goes into the triangle can then be thrown from the triangle back toward the big tournament target. Arrows that missed the triangle can't be used at all. Where the thrown arrows land, make direct shots for the target face. The target's color rings are scored this way: outermost white, five; black, four; blue, three; red, two; yellow bull's-eye, one. With each thrown arrow, try for a bull's-eye. An archer who earned multiple shots at the bull's-eye can use her best arrow as the one that counts.

Fourth archer's challenge: From this circle of rope, make a clout shot for the totem pole. Before that arrow hits the ground, spin around, load, and shoot at the tournament target's bull's-eye: bull's-eye, one point; red ring, two; and so on. If the direct shot is not made before the clout lands, all the assigned target color points are multiplied by three. Once your color points have been assessed, pace off the distance from totem to clout arrow. Every ten paces (or portion of ten) adds a point to the score. A best possible score on this challenge is two.

# Moving Targets

After lob, direct, and clout shots, the moving-target completes our shooting methodology. Basically, it uses the principles of the direct shot with a few modifications forced upon us by a new dimension—a target in constant motion.

To give your eye a full view of the landscape through which the moving target is traveling, cant your bow, top limb tilted to your strong side. Plan ahead for the moment in which you will release, and plant your feet and stance for that orientation. In other words, don't set your stance based upon where the target is before it moves, and don't move your feet to accommodate the target as it flies by. Set your stance for a predetermined moment in the target's movement. But, rather than setting up to wait at full-draw for the target to enter this planned spot and appear in your sights, you will want to follow it with your arrow as you rotate your torso and draw while the target is moving. The best method for hitting a moving target is one similar to the Indian style covered in Chapter 9.

## Hitting a Moving Target

Before the target begins its movement, set your stance for the position at which you plan to shoot. Twist at the waist back toward the target so your undrawn arrow is pointed at the target. When you call for the target to be released, follow its path by smoothly rotating your torso; and, as you do, begin a comfortable draw. It is important to stay loose and relaxed as your torso pivots to follow the target. Keep both eyes open throughout the entire run of the target.

Set your body-pivot speed to the target speed. If the speed is slow-to-moderate and if you are only ten yards away from its path, you won't need to allow for leading the target with a relatively high-poundage bow. If the target is fast or if you are at some distance, leading is a necessity. Gauging that lead is challenging at distances of, say, fifteen yards for a speedy target. It takes practice.

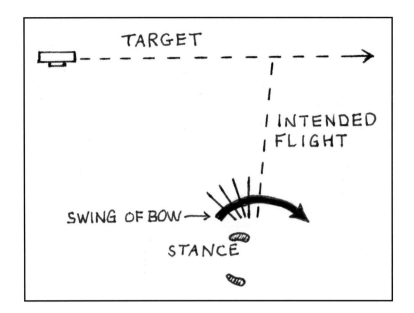

**Note: The pivot of the body and bow must continue <u>through</u> and <u>after</u> the release! The bow should continue to follow the target even though the arrow has been shot.**

There is a strong tendency among beginners to stop the swing of the bow at the moment of release. This is a signal of tension in the archer's form and will usually result in shooting behind the target. Keep the bow moving after release. This gives the arrow the lateral movement it needs in flight to keep up with the target.

### Making a Horizontally Moving Target

Slip a two-and-a-half-foot section of one-foot diameter PVC pipe over a thin, bare metal cable or wire (not plastic-coated) and stretch the cable between two posts or trees. (If using trees, protect the outer and inner barks with a section of garden hose as a protective sleeve over the wire.) Attach the target (a rectangle of Ethafoam will do) to the pipe. You can do this by pushing a short section of PVC through each top corner of the foam, running a short rope through each, and lashing to the pipe. Cover each lashing with duct tape to hold it fast to the PVC.

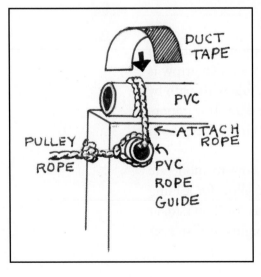

We'll consider a target that runs left to right from post one to post two. Attach a long piece of rubbery surgical tubing (or other stretchy, elastic band) to the front of the foam target and tie the free end of the tubing to post two. Adjust the length of tubing to complement the length of cable. Make practice runs from post one to see that the tubing pulls the target the full length of the cable.

Attach a long, eighth-inch-thick pull-rope to the back of the foam and run it through a small pulley tied to post one. From there the rope runs out to the archer's shooting position.

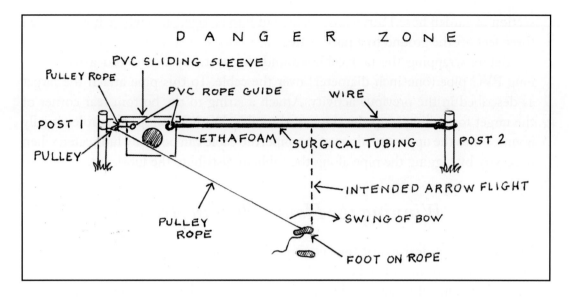

To shoot when alone, pull the target back on its track by the pulley-rope and stand on the end of the rope. When you are set to shoot, ease pressure off the rope.

The weak part of this system is the surgical tubing, which weakens by use (and by exposure to sunlight) and then, inevitably, breaks. Tubing should be removed and kept inside when not in use. The gravity-powered target below requires less maintenance.

### Making a Gravity-Powered Moving Target

This simply designed setup moves the target on a downward gradient. Tie one end of an eighty-foot-long, multi-stranded, eighth-inch-thick (uncoated) cable twenty-five feet up a tree trunk. (Protect the tree by running the cable through a short

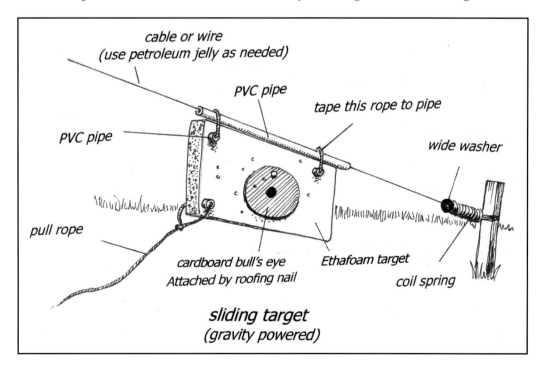

section of garden hose.) Stretch the cable out into an open area where it will be tied three feet off the ground to a post or tree.

Before wrapping the taut cable around the post, slip a two-and-a-half-foot-long PVC pipe (one-inch diameter) over the cable. To this pipe attach the target as described in the previous activity. Attach a string to the bottom rear corner of the target for pulling it up the slope of the cable. With a dollop of petroleum jelly jammed into the upper openings of the pipe, the cable can be easily lubricated when necessary by tugging the pipe along the cable to distribute the lubricant.

# Winning the Honor Shirt in Archery

In *Volume 2,* you learned of the ceremonial shirt that is offered at Medicine Bow as a challenge to students who have been self-motivated to excel in certain areas of woods lore. One of these is archery. What follows is a detailed description of these challenges for you to use or modify to suit your group, whether it be for a day of shooting adventure or for earning such a shirt and standing.

### A Measure of Excellence

There are eleven challenges in this trial of bow and arrow. All are performed in my three-acre meadow where targets are set up for testing the full spectrum of handling bow and arrow. If a challenger goes through all the tests and misses only one challenge, she may repeat that challenge at the end and make it up to win the shirt. Only one attempt at the shirt is allowed in one day. Refer to the drawing of the archery field to get a sense of distances and difficulty of the requirements.

**Challenge 1: _Long Clouts_**—From the tournament target, the archer shoots four clout shots the length of the meadow, landing as close as possible to a plastic, ten-inch-wide, Halloween pumpkin hanging by a string from the top of a three-foot-long, slanted post. The clout distance is about 150 yards. For challengers with very light bows (say, twenty-five pounds and under), reduce that distance by a third to make sure the target is within range of the bow's capability.

The archer then walks to these arrows and, one at a time, pulls an arrow from the ground, places a foot over its hole in the earth, and shoots a direct shot at the pumpkin. He must hit the pumpkin with three of the four arrows.

**Challenge 2: _Clout and Lob_**—A clout shot is made from a shooters' line to anywhere the archer desires, so long as the shot is safe. Before that arrow hits the earth, she must draw a second arrow, load, and shoot a lob (it must be released before the clout lands) to the place she judges the clout shot will land. Another pair of arrows is shot in a repeat performance. The archer then walks to the first pair of arrows, pulls one from the earth, stands on its perforation hole, and throws the arrow to stick as close as possible to its mate. She does this again with the other pair of arrows. After each throw, one pair of arrows must be as close together as two hand-spans (thumb-tips together, little fingers stretching outward) and one pair must be close enough for one hand-span. If the thrown arrow does not stick into the ground, the measurement is made from that arrow's first point of contact with the ground.

**Challenge 3: *Three Clouts*—**From the swamp-target at the southwest corner of the meadow, three clout shots are made in this order: to the walnut-target, to the tournament-bale, and to the creek-target. These targets lie at varying distances from the shooter. If at the end of these shots the archer is disappointed with one of those clouts, he can elect to redo it, but his make-up clout must be used in lieu of the one that was replaced. Each clout arrow must then be used on its assigned target as a direct shot at the ten-inch bull's-eye.

**Challenge 4: *Turn and Shoot*—**Thirteen yards from the tournament-bale the archer puts her back to this target and shoots a clout shot for the mound-target. Before this arrow lands she must turn, draw another arrow, load, and shoot the bull's-eye on the tournament-bale. To complete this challenge, she walks to her clout shot and shoots it at the mound-target. Both direct shots must strike bull's-eyes.

**Challenge 5: *Seven Arrows*—**In this challenge an archer uses a total of seven arrows. With the first six he can earn his way toward the target that will eventually count toward passing or failing the challenge. To begin: Thirteen yards from the tournament-bale, the archer shoots at its bull's-eye. If he is successful he moves back five yards. (If he misses the bull's-eye, he remains in place and shoots his second arrow from the same distance. Only when the bull's-eye is hit does he move back for a longer shot.) The seventh arrow must be shot in the opposite direction toward the mound-target. An archer with six misses at the tournament-bale bull's-eye could still pass the test with a long, accurate shot at the mound-target. But an archer who did well with his first six arrows could be shooting the all-important seventh arrow from thirty yards closer.

**Challenge 6: *The Moving Target*—**From twelve yards, the archer has three tries (three slides, one arrow per slide) to hit the sliding-target's two-and-a-half-foot by one-and-a-half-foot foam once and its ten-inch bull's-eye once.

**Challenge 7: *Throw and Shoot*—**From behind the mound, male archers throw an arrow toward the swamp-target as a setup for a direct shot. Females throw from in front of the mound. From where this arrow lands, the archer shoots the swamp-target bull's-eye.

**Challenge 8: *Countdown*—**At any place desired, the archer hammers a stake into the ground somewhere inside the polygon defined by the pumpkin, the target-in-the-pines, the bucket (a medium-sized plastic planter), and the mound-target. (This last target—because it lies forty yards away—uses its full two-foot-by-two-foot square as the bull's-eye.) A six-foot rope tether connects the stake to the archer's ankle, giving him twelve feet of leeway for positioning himself for shooting. Starting with an arrow nocked to string, he has thirty-two seconds to shoot all four targets using as many arrows as he is able to get off in that time.

**Challenge 9: *Long Flights*—**From the same stake, the archer has four attempts to shoot the tournament-bale (not the bull's-eye, but any part of the bale) for a single hit. Though long, this is a direct shot (not a clout) that forces the archer to

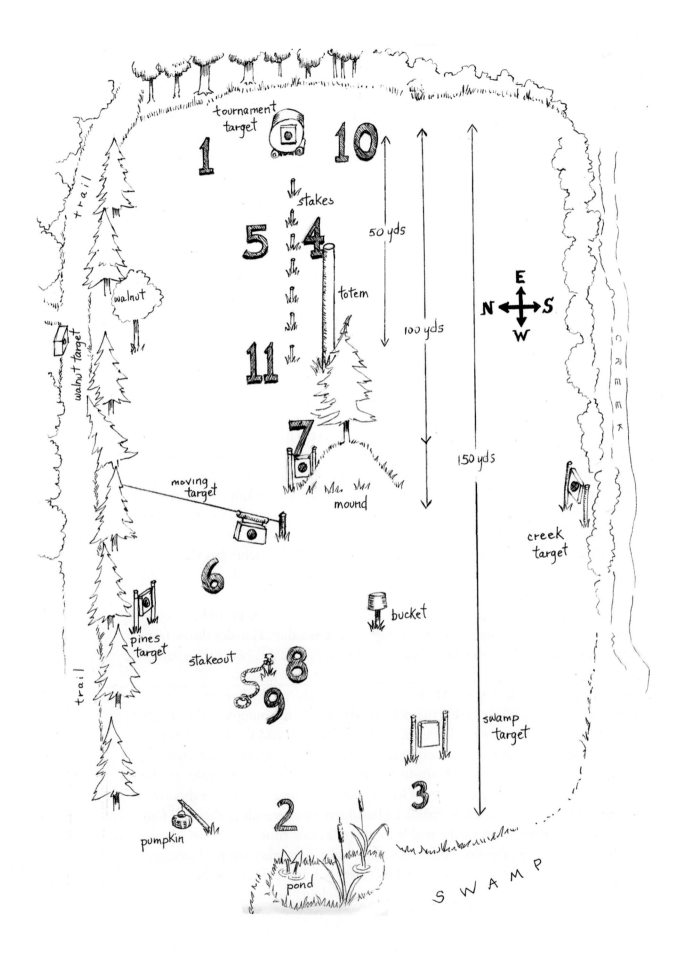

sight high above the target in the backdrop of trees. For bows twenty-five pounds or less, reduce the distance by one-third.

**Challenge 10:** *Micro-Shot*—A small circle (one-and-a-half-inch diameter) of string is laid upon the ground. Standing three feet from this string loop, the archer takes a full-draw and attempts to shoot inside the circle. He can lean in toward the target, but when at full-draw his arrow point must be two feet or more from the loop. Two out of three shots must penetrate the circle.

**Challenge 11:** *Adding Up Lobs*—From the tournament-bale an archer lobs five arrows to land as close as possible to the totem. Then he paces off each arrow's distance from the base of the totem. These five numbers are added together to arrive at the number of paces to be walked from the tournament-bale. (Any lob shot that hits the totem—no matter how high or low on the pole—counts as "zero paces.") With only one direct shot from that paced-off distance, he must strike the bull's-eye.

*The Makeup*—If the challenger has missed just one of these previous tests, he now attempts to rectify it to pass the Honor Shirt challenge. If he fails in the make-up shot, he must wait for another day to try for the shirt again.

Lenton Abbey 1279
~Robin shooteth his last shaft~

*To see a boy throw a rock at a tree stump is to witness his natural right at claiming atavistic ties to the ancient hunters of his family lineage. When he throws a knife and sticks it, now we see something else. There is magic in it. And joy. And there is no explaining it.*

—Robert Spotted Horse from *A Copperhead Summer*

# CHAPTER 12

# Slinging Steel—
# Knife and Tomahawk Throwing

Inspired by the legend of James Bowie, I started throwing knives when I was nine years old. I took to it with a passion—not an uncommon phenomenon for many males I have known. Not owning a large metal knife (though I carved scores of wooden bowie knifes with my pocketknife, none were feasible for throwing), I threw anything metallic that faintly resembled a projectile: screwdrivers, scissors, paint scrapers, mill files, and so on. Much to my mother's consternation, our kitchen was a treasure trove of flying weaponry: butter knives, dinner knives, paring knives, steak knives, butcher knives. All those instruments took their turns cartwheeling from my hand into the loblolly pines of my backyard.

This chapter should be dedicated to those dozen big loblolly pine trees that served as my targets for all the years of my youth. All of them, it should be noted, survived the abuse, which says a lot about the wound-healing capacity of pines. However, when I grew to understand the plight of all trees in fending off fungal infection, I never again threw at a living tree.

When I finally owned a respectable throwing knife at the age of eleven, I had already plotted several knife-throwing "courses" laid out in my yard from tree to tree to tree. Some of the intervals between trees required triple flips. On those days when I achieved a perfect round on one of those courses, life was grand. Six decades later, I continue to feel that same sense of satisfaction when I sink a knife into my intended target. And still, there's no explaining it.

# The Knife

Only a small percentage of store-bought knives are suitable for throwing. Generally most handles are too heavy and the blades too short. Most blades are not tough enough for the abuse of mis-throws. Cheap knives are usually just that . . . cheap. If thrown, their blades are going to bend or break because the quality of the metal cannot stand up to the stress.

Some so-called throwing knives are not well suited for the task either, because they are too light. A good throwing knife needs to be hefty for control, for driving force to stick, and for a slower spinning speed.

A good woodsman's knife to be used for camp jobs is as poor for throwing as a good throwing knife is poor for camp jobs. Basically, a bowie knife that feels good in the hand for jobs requiring hacking (like a hatchet) will be well balanced for throwing, simply because a bowie has a lot of blade, which means more weight forward in the blade. This is the blade-heavy balance we want for throwing a knife by its handle.

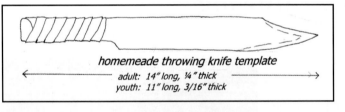

*homemeade throwing knife template*
adult: 14" long, ¼" thick
youth: 11" long, 3/16" thick

The original handle grips might break, but this is of little consequence as you can wrap thick strips of leather to replace the handle. If the metal bends, you'll have to bend or gently hammer it back into shape.

But today there are well-constructed throwing knives (hefty, balanced for throwing, made of high-grade steel, and equipped with virtually unbreakable handles) available for purchase over the Internet. Go online and search for "Cold Steel throwing knife." That's a good place to start.

In my teen years, long before the Internet and all its opportunities, I approached a metal worker about helping me to construct a throwing knife. I handed him a quarter-inch-thick leaf spring from an abandoned truck and a template I had drawn on paper. That slab of steel cost five dollars at a junkyard. The rough cut-out of knife cost ten dollars, making my first indestructible throwing knife a fifteen-dollar investment. The edges and point were not at all finely honed, so I went to work with a file.

## Acquiring a Throwing Knife

Today finding a knife made for throwing is easy. There are lots to choose from, but I will suggest one that I consider to be one of the best because it is well suited for new knife throwers ages thirteen and up. The "Cold Steel Perfect Balance Thrower" measures just under fourteen inches and weighs just under one pound. It sells for around twenty dollars. Its carbon steel composition supplies durability and its design well suits its function. Any knife lighter than or shorter than this one might prove to be unsatisfying to a serious thrower. This is only my opinion, of course, and perhaps I am swayed by the fact that I began my knife-sticking career wanting to learn the "battle throw."

## The Battle Throw—The Bowie Throwing Style

Of the many skills that I have entered in the "first man" mode (figuring out the technique on my own, i.e., "winging it"), knife-throwing might be the first one that I successfully fashioned out of whole cloth. I grip and throw today exactly as I did when I was nine years old—only with a stronger hurl. No other thrower has convinced me that I should change my methodology.

I was well into adulthood before I saw professional throwers perform. There are now competitions that include a World Championship tournament. When I first witnessed these masters of flying knives, the differences in their form and mine became quickly evident. It had to do with force. They were throwing at a target. Because I was raised on the legend of Mr. Bowie—and because I was a typical American boy looking for adventure—I was throwing at an imagined enemy.

The style that I developed for such a battle throw is one that allows for maximum impact and penetration. The grip is far from natural, but by using it, the knife flies true without any spinning around its long axis. And it hits hard. The proof of its driving force is manifested by the depth of blade in the target. Prying the battle-thrown knife out of wood requires considerable effort.

## Target

If you prefer a broad target that is sure to stop even the most wayward of throws, build a wall of rough-sawn boards that run vertically so the grain is oriented in the same direction as the penetration marks your knife will be making.

### <u>Making a Wall Target</u>

Buy rough-sawn pine from a saw mill to construct an eight-foot-tall, forty-inch-wide frame of two-inch by six-inch boards. Inside this rectangle add two two-inch by six-inch braces to trisect the space vertically. Onto the front of the frame nail a sheet of plywood. From the back of this plywood you will be able to nail the face-boards that will receive thrown knives. Use nails that penetrate only halfway through the face-boards to minimize the possibility for contact of knife points with nail points. Use four two-inch by ten-inch face-boards (rough sawn) and do nail the borders of the receiving face through the boards, through the plywood, and into the frame. These borders at the edge of the target lie where knives are least likely to hit.

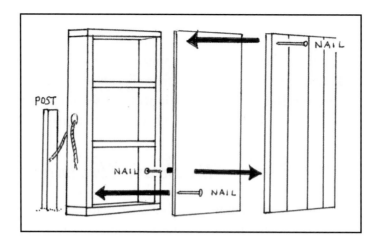

To keep the structure upright and ensure that it cannot fall forward, lash it to two fixed posts or prop the frame vertically against a tree and tie it off. To protect it from the weather, prop it off the ground using a few logs and cover the wall with a tarp when not in use.

### Portable Targets

For a lighter, less bulky target, chainsaw an eight-inch-thick disk from a dead pine or soft hardwood tree with a two-foot by two-and-a-half-foot trunk diameter. Drill holes on the rounded sides of the disk at the two o'clock and ten o'clock positions to insert large wood screws with round eyelets. Attach ropes to the eyelets and suspend the disk four feet off the ground from two neighboring trees in a safe area. Use scrap lengths of garden hose to cushion the rope's grip on the trees.

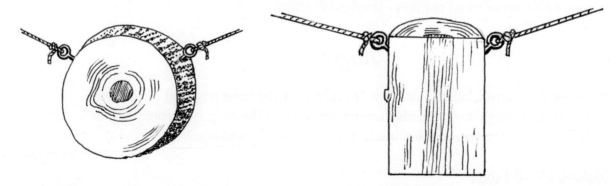

A variation of this target can be made from a cylindrical section of a dead pine log with a two-foot by two-and-a-half-foot diameter. After sawing a two-and-a-half-foot-long section, split the cylinder lengthwise by using wedges and sledgehammer, producing two targets, each with a long flat surface on one side to be used as the front of the target. Screw two eyelets at the top of the curved sides and hang between trees to receive knife throws.

---

**Before Throwing a Metal Weapon**

The first hour of a knife-throwing class is best served by throwing projectiles that spin slower than knives. This helps the student to become more adept at following the rotation of the weapon with the eye. It also cuts down on unintentional abuse to the collection of knives, which, in a beginner class, would be smacking into wood targets in every possible position. Instead of steel, use throwing sticks. Instead of a wooden target, use an earthen bank.

---

## Wood Before Metal

Cut straight sections of dead (but firm) hardwood branches, each stick two feet long and varying in diameter from three-quarter-inch to one-and-a-quarter-inch to accommodate a variety of strengths and hand sizes. On the heavier end of each stick cut an angle to make a one-sided shovel-point and on the other end cut a blunt squared end. Basically, these are rabbit sticks (see *Volume 1*). In a knife and tomahawk class, I pull out all the rabbit sticks that I normally store for my survival classes and hand out these same sticks to introduce the lessons for throwing steel.

Take your class to a road-cut or other place where the students can throw from flat ground to a near-vertical bank. At this site, give them the throwing lessons detailed below (*Throwing Form*) and have them practice throwing their sticks into the bank. Their goal is to throw a full revolution by the handle end and witness the pointed end penetrating the earth with the stick in a horizontal position.

After they have had fifteen minutes of independent practice, visit each student and point out how his form can be improved. (All the points of form will be covered soon.) Then have each thrower set up a frame of four sticks to use as a one-foot-by-one-foot square target.

After thirty more minutes set up a group target in a new place and call the students together for a show-and-tell time for throwing. Every audience member can be assigned one aspect of form to be assessing. In this way a full spectrum of critiques can be offered to each thrower.

After hurling wood the students have earned their way toward throwing steel. Not only have they learned something about throwing form but also about capturing an instantaneous mental "photograph" of the weapon at impact so they will better know how to adjust their individual throwing distances.

# *Throwing Form*

There is a basic similarity to spear-throwing. We still want the hand and elbow (slightly bent) to pass directly over the shoulder. Imagine a large pane of glass situated just outside the throwing arm . . . and another pane running through the body just inside the shoulder. Neither arm nor weapon should touch either glass.

### Prelude to a Knife

As an experimental place to start with wooden starter "knives," stand about eighteen to twenty-one feet from an earthen bank and scratch a line into the dirt at your toes. If you are right-handed, put your right toes on the line and the left foot behind you with your body weight mostly on the front leg. Both legs should be bent for balance and stability. Hold the stick down beside the forward leg, letting it swing in an easy pendulum arc, forward and back, within the six-inch space between the "panes of glass." The thrower should not touch the glass . . . not with an arm, a hand, or the stick *in both the windup and the throw.* (In this way the backward windup prepares the throwing arm for the proper route of the same arm during the forward throw.)

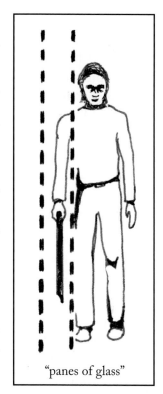

"panes of glass"

Bring the stick up high between the glass sheets until the elbow rises directly over the shoulder and the stick is high above and slightly behind the elbow. Allow the elbow to bend slightly. (To attempt to throw with a stiffened arm is an impotent experience.) Just an inch or two to the rear of this position is the range-limit of the arm. Use this limitation as a place to "bounce" the arm to begin its forward movement for the throw.

The back foot should begin its step forward for the throw at the same time that the windup begins. The "bounce" and forward thrust of the arm should occur in the instant *before* the foot touches down. The timing and coordination of this might require practice.

At full-cock (the backward limit of the windup) don't let the wrist "break" to allow the stick to hang down behind the back. At full-cock the stick should be angled at the sky behind you. And don't let the elbow dramatically bend toward the target. (An elbow pointed at the target while at full-cock is one of the most common tendencies for a beginner.) Keep the elbow above the shoulder and the stick high. By doing so you will be using your arm as a longer radius in the arc of the throw (with your shoulder as the center). If you bend your arm too much at full-cock, the radius of the throw becomes the forearm with the elbow at the center, resulting in a much weaker throw.

The step forward with the rear foot should be graceful—a smooth, controlled, floating motion cushioned by using both legs as shock absorbers. Don't bend at the waist when you hurl the stick. Keep the spine upright as you throw. This taken-step is similar to the thrusting lunge of a fencer.

Let the stick slip from your grip naturally. Don't try to flip it by snapping the wrist forward. We want a slow rotation. The stick will flip on its own.

## The Timing of the Release

It surprises beginners that the hand should allow the stick to slip away fairly high in the hand's throwing arc; that is, the stick should be released well before the extended arm points toward the target. Just like elevation aiming in archery, this fine point of release has to be learned and earned through experience until the muscles absorb it. And again like archery, this point changes with distance. (If later with a knife you progress to double and triple revolutions, the increased distance will require that the knife's trajectory be a more curved arc. The single-revolution throw follows a trajectory that is close to a straight line.) The longer the throw, the higher the arc of the projectile and the earlier it will disengage from your hand—just like throwing a ball except that it's done over the shoulder instead of above an elbow positioned out to the side of the shoulder.

Once you have achieved a successful single-flip throw with the stick, it's time to trade wood for steel.

## Throwing the Knife

All the above instruction for hurling a stick overhand can be applied directly to a throwing knife. Only the grip differs. My method of holding the knife handle is designed to eliminate two throwing flaws: 1. flipping the wrist to make the weapon spin faster (end over end in the air); and 2. creating any torque around the knife's long axis. (In other words, the knife should flip in a vertical, end-over-end, flat plane a quarter-inch wide, never twisting like an Olympic diver adding twists to his heels-over-head flips.)

The knife needs to come off the hand without any pressure from palm or fingers that might make it twist. Twisting can result in the knife not sticking. Or worse, the tip of the blade can break when it sticks horizontally, because the revolution-momentum continues, putting undue pressure on the most fragile portion of the blade—the tip. The trick is to think of your hand as the open mouth of a smooth PVC pipe. Throwing the knife is a little like slinging the weapon from this imaginary pipe.

### Gripping the Handle for a Throw

All throws covered in this book are made by gripping the handle, not the blade. The latter is too risky, too awkward to firmly grasp, and, therefore, too weakly delivered as a throw.

To orient the knife for gripping, hold the knife by the handle in front of you at the level of your waist. The knife point should point forward and angled slightly to your weak side, sharp edge down. With your weak hand cocked back at the wrist, take a grip on the blade from above, fingertips on the strong side, thumb on the weak side, thick edge of the palm toward the knife point. Now let go of the handle with the strong hand in order to begin taking the proper grip.

The narrow part of the handle facing upward is called the *spine*. Bring your strong hand down on the handle so the spine touches the callus on the palm directly beneath the index knuckle and diagonally bisects the palm to the heel of the hand, where the outside curve of the hand meets the wrist on the little finger side.

In this position take only a loose grip, then bend the wrist toward your strong side to align the knife with the forearm, as seen from both above and from the side. Now, maintaining this loose grip, let the knife hang down by your side as you assume the throwing stance.

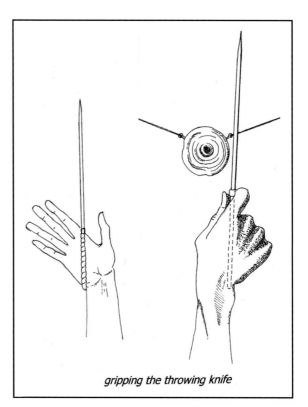

*gripping the throwing knife*

### First Throw with the Knife

As an experimental starting distance try standing thirteen to eighteen feet from the target and mark a line in the dirt. Begin the forward step of the weak leg as you begin the windup. Raise the knife between the panes of glass as previously described, bringing the elbow above the shoulder and the knife above the elbow, the arm slightly bent. An instant before the stepping foot touches down, the arm should reach its range limit and bounce off that limit for the forward thrust. Keep the arm in its slightly bent position in this bounce-back. Do not allow a dramatic arm bend.

Just after the stepping foot touches down, thrust the throwing arm forward. Think of your arm as a pipe into which the knife has been loosely loaded. Let it fly out of the mouth of the pipe (your loosely open hand) without any tightening of muscle or tendon. That point of release on the arc of the hand movement will be higher than expected. Don't push the knife forward. Don't try to flip it. *Sling it out*

*of the pipe!* Let it fly out of your hand without any bias from you except for keeping the pipe true to the path between the glass panes.

Keep your chest facing the target, as if you have mounted on your sternum a camera with which to take a video of the knife in its flight to the target. In other words, don't torque the torso.

After the knife leaves your hand, continue a follow-through with a continuous motion of your hand. Do not allow your hand to recoil and reverse direction, as so many beginners are wont to do. Such a movement will only speed up the revolution and make the knife more difficult to stick.

All the momentum of the throw is established in the section of the arc above your shoulder at the beginning of the forward thrust. Be sure your throwing hand remains in that adjusted position that allowed the knife to align with the forearm. When the weak-side foot has landed and the knife has soared to the target, maintain your balance and cushion your step by bending both legs like a fencer during a thrust with his sword. Your spine should be upright at the throw's end.

## Knife Flight

We will attempt to master the *single-flip throw*, which means one handle-over-blade revolution. The tip of the blade will point (more or less) downrange toward the target at the beginning of the knife's flight. The knife will then flip handle-over-blade until the point once again comes around to contact the target. If the timing, distance, and form are correct, the knife will stick. More than likely, at this point in the lesson, it won't . . . primarily because a proper distance from the target has not yet been established. By going through a series of experimental throws, we will lengthen or shorten the throwing distance to make the knife meet the target at the appropriate angle for sticking.

Advanced throwing includes modifying the grip to slow down or speed up the flip, throwing from a greater distance with two flips, throwing with three flips, throwing on a horizontal plane from the side of the body (at a horizontal log, for example), and throwing underhanded. But the overhead, single-flip throw is the precursor to all these techniques.

**Warning: Be prepared for bounce-backs! Light knives are especially notorious at coming back toward a thrower. Keep spectators well behind the thrower! The thrower must always be alert for "return fire" from the target. If he has bent both legs as recommended, his legs are poised for a quick evasive move.**

### Working Toward Accuracy

By staying true to the form above, your knife should ideally fly forward toward some point on a vertical line that bisects the target. Figuring out elevation is the next objective. By practicing with dozens of throws, find that sweet spot on the arc at which to release the knife. Eventually, you'll get a feel for that proper point of release; your muscles will begin to develop a memory for it. When finally your knife is hitting (but not necessarily sticking into) the target, you are ready to fine-tune your throw to achieve the satisfying "stick" by adjusting your distance from the target.

## A Freeze-Frame Glimpse at Impact

With a single-spin throw, when you release the knife high in the arc, the blade rotates downward, points back at you, and then comes up and over to make the point available to penetrate the target. There is a personalized, ideal distance (for each thrower) that delivers a "stick."

When the knife is *not* sticking, you must concentrate *visually* to ascertain the exact angle at which the knife hits the target. In the early days of throwing, this visual capture may seem elusive. With time you will learn to train your eye to "take a snapshot" of the knife at impact. If you are throwing with good form without unwanted variables (like a changing grip or bending at the waist or overly bending at the elbow), the knife should hit the target in exactly the same orientation every time you throw from a given distance.

Throwing distance varies from person to person because of different strengths, arm and stride lengths, and (sometimes) unconquerable quirks that deviate from the proper technique that affect the RPM of the knife's spin. There are ways to increase or decrease the spin rate, but these are advanced variations. For now, we want to master consistency by learning your perfect distance at which to draw a throwing line in the dirt.

### Finding Your Distance to Make the "Stick"

As an experimental start, stand thirteen to eighteen feet from the target and mark your "throwers' line" in the dirt. A pointed stake serves nicely as a marker. Pay close attention to the knife at impact, for your eye must discern the position of the knife in its revolution at the moment it strikes the target.

There will be times when you simply can't make out the knife's angle at impact. Keep trying until you can. Take a "mental photograph" of this instant. If that mental picture shows the knife point pointed up (say from 60 to 90 degrees from the ground), the knife was not able to complete its full 360-degree spin. In other words, it was not in the air long enough. Therefore, you'll need to step back to make a new throwers' line, giving the thrown knife more air time. Try moving back fourteen inches, re-mark your line, and try again.

If the knife point hits angled downward, the knife was in the air too long, and you'll need to shorten your distance.

If the butt end of the handle hits the target in complete reverse of its intended position, there are two possibilities: 1. The knife has rotated only a half-spin (180 degrees), which means that you are standing much too close; or 2. it has spun one-and-a-half times (540 degrees), in which case you are much too far. Someone will have to watch the flight of the knife to determine this. It may take several throws, because following a knife in the air with the eyes is challenging for a newcomer to the sport.

Once you find your distance, practice making the knife stick time after time, perfecting your form. As you warm up your throwing arm, you may find that your distance changes, so be prepared to adjust. Eventually, your personal distance will become ingrained in your visual memory. When you step before a new target, you will have a feel for where to stand without actually measuring the distance by feet or inches.

---

### Common Errors in Knife Throwing

1. Breaking the glass on the windup.
2. Breaking the glass while hurling forward.
3. At full-cock, pointing the knife to the weak side behind the head.
4. At full-cock, breaking at the wrist to let the knife point downward along the back.
5. At full-cock, bending the elbow sharply so the elbow points forward at the target (thus, reducing the radius of the throwing appendage from the full arm to the forearm).
6. Holding the arm at a right angle out to the side when throwing. (The elbow should be above the shoulder.)
7. Missing the coordination of the step and the throw. (This leg/arm motion should be performed just like throwing a rock.)
8. Breaking the wrist by snapping it forward at the release, thereby spinning the knife faster than wanted. (Pipes should not break!)
9. Changing the proper grip before throwing.
10. Recoiling the wrist at release by jerking it to the rear, i.e., trying to flip the weapon faster. (This is actually an advanced technique for throwing from a closer distance.)
11. Bending forward at the waist when releasing.
12. Stepping forward with a stiffened leg that jolts the body upon touching down. (Often this causes a bend at the waist.)
13. Changing the length of the taken step, which changes your distance from the target at the moment of throwing.
14. Being out of control with body stability at release; i.e., not using those shock-absorber legs for fluidity and balance.

15. Squeezing the handle at any time during the throw, causing the knife to rotate on its long axis like a diver performing twists (along with flips).
16. Releasing too high or low on the arc taken by the throwing hand.
17. Leaning away from the strong side when throwing. (This often indicates a knife too heavy for the thrower.)
18. Torqueing the torso when throwing (rotating the chest away from the target).

## Advanced Expertise

With practice you can learn to accomplish a single flip at varied distances. If you find yourself forced to throw from a closer position (than your preferred distance), you can take your grip farther back on the handle, with more spine showing in front of your hand. This will make the knife spin faster. For extreme closeness, reverse-wrist-flip must be utilized. This is a quick recoiling wrist action at release that accelerates the handle into its spin. But it is a difficult adaptation to perform with consistency. A fast spin is always more difficult to stick simply because its instant of perfect sticking orientation is so brief. Plus, the advanced rate of rotation can cause even a perfectly oriented knife to continue spinning and pry its blade tip out of the target.

If you stand a little farther than your normal one-flip distance, you can slide your loose grip forward on the handle (covering the spine completely) and slightly straighten the index finger and long finger so they are not involved in the grip. At release more of the spine of the handle slides along the palm. This delays the handle's release from your hand and slows the spin.

When you feel ready for considerably longer throws, you can learn your two-flip distance and become adept at this double-revolution throw. It is more difficult to consistently hit the target, let alone make the knife stick, because now you are throwing harder and releasing from a higher point on the arc of the throwing hand's path. (The path of the knife's trajectory in the air also becomes more arced as the throwing distance increases.)

More variables can creep into your form when you throw harder. This is the great difference between knives and archery. When shooting an arrow a longer distance at a target, the archer strives to do nothing different except increase elevation in the aiming. The knife thrower must heave with more force.

## Knife Games

Anytime that multiple throwers are using the same target, establish this rule for the welfare of your knives: "If a knife sticks in a target, before another can be thrown at that same target, the stuck knife must be removed."

### Throwing for Food

On the wooden target, smear a plate-sized circle of dye (from poke berries, charcoal from your campfire, or paint), leaving a softball-size center unmarked. Each thrower makes six throws in a row. A stick into the outer wood rim is worth four points, into the dyed ring seven points, and into the undyed center ten points. If the knife does not stick but hits the center with any part of the knife, award two points to reward accuracy. For a hit on the dyed ring, award one point for a no-stick throw.

If the blade cuts the boundary between two different rings, the higher score is awarded. Keep a tally of scores and let this dictate the throwers' order at snack time.

### The Four Corners

Refer to the *Four Corners Tribe* archery game in Chapter 11. Charcoal can be used to draw the lines on the target. This is another game that can be played by teams.

### Tic-Tac-Bowie

Refer to the archery game *Tic-Tac-Bow* in Chapter 11. Charcoal can be used to draw the lines on the target. Mark successfully struck squares with colored tape to denote ownership. This game can be played with two throwers or two teams.

### Live-Action Throwing

Hang a target in a brand-new setting. Do not allow students to pace off or measure throwing distances other than by eyeballing. Each of your students will test his quick response, his throwing form under duress, and his ability to assess his ideal throwing distance.

While others spectate from a safe distance, position one student sitting with her back to the target ten yards away. A throwing knife is lightly stuck into a log behind her.

As a signal, begin counting down from six. At the sound of your voice ("Six!") the thrower springs into action, takes the knife, moves to her ideal distance, and throws before the countdown reaches zero.

Award five points for a stick anywhere in the target; give one point for a knife that hits the target but does not stick. This is another game that can be fun if played by two teams.

# The Tomahawk

The "hawk" has a more generous edge for sticking, simply due to its blade's size, curvature, and two points. Its leading point is the best portion of the blade for impaling a target. Think of the triangle of metal that defines that point as an arrowhead.

A suspended log disk or slab (like our knife target) is perfect for a tomahawk, too. Set up strict safety rules for this activity.

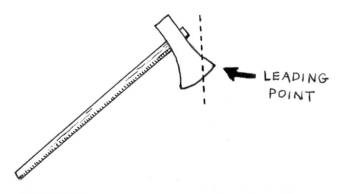

LEADING POINT

The hawk does not bounce from the target as lively as a knife, but it carries a greater momentum and capacity for injury. Even the thrower must be cautious of self-inflicted harm: 1. to a leg while letting the hawk pendulum-swing before windup; 2. to the back at full-cock (should the thrower break form and let the hawk hang downward); and 3. to the head during the initial thrust of the throw (should the thrower break the glass).

**Note: The form taught in these pages is designed not only for efficacy in throwing but also for safety. Using this proper form keeps the tomahawk blade well away from the head. The teacher should give extra attention to the position of the tomahawk at full-cock: high above the shoulder and pointed back at the sky. Never allow a student to let the hawk sag behind the head or back!**

Tomahawk throwing uses a simple grip. Hold it the same way you would grasp a hammer. Thumb position is optional. Rest it on top along the spine of the handle or wrap it around the side of the handle. Compared to the knife the heft of the weapon feels more cumbersome and the spin is more off-center, making the weapon feel less stable at release.

Aligning the thumb on the spine of the handle helps some students to keep the hawk oriented to avoid its twisting during flight. This same grip helps to keep the hawk between the panes of glass, and it eliminates a tendency to let the wrist "break" when the hawk is at full-cock. The tomahawk's head should not hang down at full-cock. Instead, it should be positioned well above the head and pointed back at the sky, just like the knife. Don't bend the arm too much at full-cock. You want good centrifugal force from the nearly extended length of your full arm. Raise the elbow directly above the shoulder. Excluding the grip, the tomahawk throw follows every detail of form covered in the knife throw.

As the hawk reaches the end of the windup at full-cock, **sling** it forward! Don't push it or lob it. Sling it hard!

An ideal position for the hawk at sticking impact is having the butt end of the handle pointing back at the ground at about 45 degrees. In this position the leading point of the hawk's head (where the curve of the cutting edge terminates) enters the target much like the orientation of an arrowhead.

Expect the single-flip throwing distance to be four to six feet longer than for the knife for a given thrower. *Other than throwing*

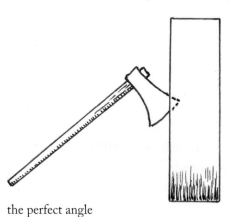

the perfect angle

*distance and grip, follow all the other suggestions for knife throwing:* Use the panes of glass; get the slightly bent elbow above the shoulder at full-cock; point the hawk at the sky behind you at full-cock; float forward with control as you step; use both legs as shock absorbers; release without trying to flip the handle; keep the torso erect and chest facing the target; and don't lean away (to the weak side) from the hawk at release.

The most common errors made in tomahawk throwing are the same as for knives.

**Warning: Always check behind you before throwing, so you'll not harm someone absentmindedly walking by.**

## Tomahawk Games

All games suitable for knife throwing carry over to the tomahawk. Refer to those knife games a few pages back. When your students have become fairly proficient with both knife and tomahawk, set up two targets side by side and give students the challenge of alternating projectiles one right after the other to see if they can make the instant transition from one throwing weapon to another of a different weight and requiring a different throwing distance.

## The Firebird Challenge—A Trilogy of Weaponry

This activity is especially suited for a summer camp or any gathering of adventurers who plan to stay in one area for several days. Before a student may qualify for this adventure, she must demonstrate her proficiency with three weapons: spear, knife, and tomahawk. During each respective lesson, when you, the teacher, deem any student to be sufficiently skilled at throwing, privately present her with a feather (or other token) with this instruction: "Keep this feather. It will help to earn your way toward a special event that I will explain in a few days." After the spear, knife, and hawk lessons have been delivered to all, make a special necklace of inner bark fibers and attach to it a pendant of interest: a bleached animal skull, a feather, an artifact arrowhead. Hang this necklace in a place visible to all, but never let it be handled or worn. When asked about it, explain the challenge.

**The announcement**: "Anyone who has earned at least two feathers in the last few days may attempt the Firebird Challenge. You'll have six weapons with which to demonstrate your throwing skills."

**The challenge arena**: Lay down a ten-foot-wide circle of rope as a common throwing area for all the targets. Within this circle lay upon the ground two spears, two knives, and two hawks. The Firebird Challenger can move around inside this circle at will. In a safe direction fifteen yards from the rope place a three-foot-wide hoop spear target on a sloped bank. Three yards from the rope (in different directions) set up two wooden targets for knives (each with a dyed bull's-eye circle eight inches in diameter). Four yards away hang one hawk target without a bull's-eye. This small arena will possess an alluring mystique for all.

**The challenge:** Within a one-minute time span, the Firebird Challenger must:

1. Throw a spear to stick inside the hoop. She has two tries to accomplish this.
2. Throw one knife into one target and a second knife into the other. Both must stick, unless one sticks in a dyed-circle bull's-eye, in which case that single throw will suffice.
3. Throw the hawks at the remaining target. One must stick.

Arrange the throwing site so an audience of students can watch from a safe place. Any attempt to win the challenge proves to be a great spectator event.

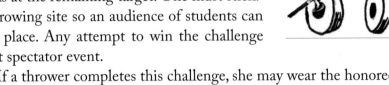

If a thrower completes this challenge, she may wear the honored Firebird Necklace (or display it anywhere she chooses) until another challenger unseats her. In that case, make the transfer of the necklace a formal, public event. The new Firebird champion wears or displays the necklace until any other thrower earns the right to take it from the former champ.

### The Blue Hawk Challenge

Add to the Firebird Challenge the use of the bow and arrow. Anyone who has earned three feathers has the right to attempt this challenge. Increase the time span to one-and-a-half minutes. For the archery portion set a plate-sized target twelve yards from a shooters' circle in a safe direction. Supply two arrows for the challenge. In addition to the Firebird requirements for spear, knife, and hawk, one arrow must hit the bull's-eye.

Determine a new honor for fulfilling the Blue Hawk Challenge—something to be kept by the winner: a miniature animal figure, a string of four blue beads, a crow feather painted blue, etc.

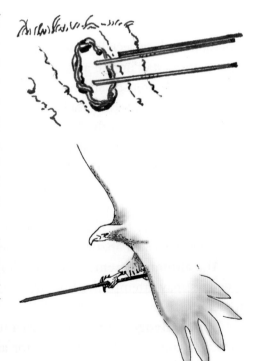

*The blowgun is a most singular weapon powered by a man's breath, of all things, refined to precision by a dainty dart dressed in airy thistle down. It shows the true genius of man. But as to its inception . . . its prototype? I'd put my money on its inventor being a child with time on his hands.*

—Dr. Robert B. Beaver, from *Conversations in the Upper Room*

# CHAPTER 13

# Making the Blowgun and Dart

One of the great adventures of life, in my opinion, is to strike out into the woods to attempt one of the primitive skills without the benefit of any instruction (whether that instruction be from reading or person-to-person). To enter into such a project on one's own is like traveling back in time. I call it the "first man" method of exploring history.

These ventures are full of failures, some heart-breaking, others maddening, and a few humorous. But each failure is a gem in the larger picture of experiential education. For example, when I approached fire-creation, I failed consistently for two months. Finally, I visited a library and saw in a diagram the ingenious notch cut into the hearth of the fire kit. I made fire on my next try. It was a memorable moment and a worthy process.

Every mistake I made in the learning process was important. As a teacher of fire-creation, I can now quickly see a flaw in a student's form simply because I, too, once performed the same departure from what I now know is good form.

But none of my "first man" experiences has really been a pure one. After all, each time I have entered into one of those exploratory adventures to probe the "discovery" of some skill or tool, I was forearmed with the knowledge that it was a feasible project. Simply put, I knew that fire by friction could be done. The real first man went into the project blindly. He couldn't know if he was wasting his time or on the first step of a history-changing event.

In fact, I had probably witnessed the use of such inventions in a magazine, book, or on television. No doubt, I had gazed upon a museum painting of a fire-maker spinning his hand-drill to produce hot ash. Whether I remembered it consciously or not, there is a good chance that I retained some knowledge about design, size, and process . . . maybe even materials.

I realize that the "first man" method is not for everyone. Some would see it as a waste of time. But I love the connection to pre-history and the deeper relationship to Nature that this approach affords. There are, however, areas where the "first man" approach is not appropriate, namely in using wild plants as food and medicine and in hunting. In the former, dedicated study must replace the lost botanical instincts that our ancestors enjoyed. In the latter, we owe it to the wild creatures to be deadly accurate before we enter the hunting arena. A living creature should not be an experimental target.

When I set out to "invent" the blowgun—a weapon that had originated in my homeland (the southeastern United States)—I had no idea how much that unconscious foreknowledge would work against me. My subliminal homework turned the exercise into a farce.

Choosing my material from a prolific stand of bamboo near my home, I selected a stout piece of cane and cut it a foot taller than my height. I know today that a blowgun should be small enough that only the end of the little finger can fit into its opening. But in my youth I chose a cane large enough that I could have stacked US quarters inside its chambers and had room to spare. Why did I select such a large "caliber" cane? I'm almost certain that my subliminal memory was at work recalling a TV special I had seen.

> *There are areas where the "first man" approach is not appropriate, namely in using wild plants as food and medicine . . . and in hunting.*

## Confessions of a Failed Blowgun Inventor

Years after I made my first attempt at crafting a blowgun, I eagerly watched a film about the monkey hunters of the Amazon. Halfway into the documentary, I realized that I had seen this same program when I was a youngster—old enough to be interested but young enough not to have paid strict attention to the details.

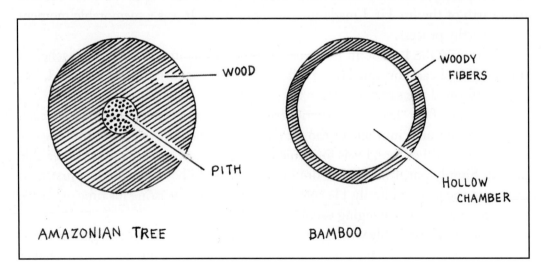

The monkey hunter's blowgun that I had seen had been of a similar exterior size as the cane I had cut, and this proved to be my undoing. The Amazonian's tool had not been made from cane but from a very specific tree. No heating was necessary as the trunk grew arrow-straight. Hidden inside that tree's soft wood was a small, smooth channel filled with soft pith. The Amazonian had simply reamed out the pith material and used the existing smooth channel as the "firing barrel" for his dart. Apparently, that species of tree is very lightweight.

Not knowing I had already doomed my project by its size, I began the straightening process. Like virtually all grass stems, bamboo sections grow in a zigzag pattern and each isolated section shows some curvature. Around past campfires I had learned the trick of reshaping woody tissue with heat, so my efforts at aligning went well—first straightening each banana-curved section and then aligning all the sections into one common line. (See *Heat-Straightening and -Bending* in Chapter 4.)

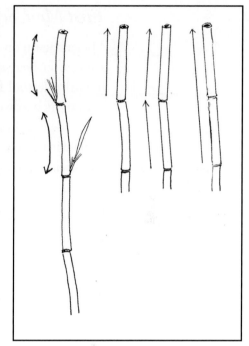

It is possible to overheat and scorch (and thereby ruin) cane, but that was a lesson I had learned making arrows. I heated one end-section over hot coals by constantly turning and thrusting and occasionally testing with thumb and finger. When the section was too hot to touch for more than an instant, I carried the cane from the fire and pried it inside the fork of a nearby tree until that section was bowed slightly beyond straight. I kept it there until it cooled and its glues re-solidified (about a minute). This heating and bending usually took two tries per section, sometimes three, but the end result of straightening wood and seeing it hold its new shape was most satisfying.

Next, I straightened section number two. When I was satisfied with the individual straightness of each of the first two sections, I heated the ringed joint (the node) between them, took the cane to the tree fork, and aligned the two sections as one. This process was continued for the length of the cane—six sections and five joints.

The septa (divider-walls at the nodes) that separated the chambers of my bamboo were easy enough to puncture. I used hardwood "ramrods" to break through them, but the ramrod did little to smooth the erose edges of the broken septa that remained inside. I knew my blowgun would need a smooth bore to work efficiently, so my next challenge was grinding the interior of those jagged rings into smooth areas that matched the rest of the cane's interior.

First I tried more ramrods of different types of wood—all dead, of course, for hardness—but the process backfired. The hard, pointed shards of septa "ate up" every ramrod that I used. So I notched a flake of stone into a shaft of wood, lashed it tightly, and tried to rasp and drill the splinters away by spinning the shaft. The stone repeatedly locked up in the shards like a screwdriver sunk into a screw-slot. I turned to a trusty, tried-and-true tool . . . fire.

I dropped a chunky coal from my fire pit into the mouth of the cane. When the coal lodged at the first broken-through node, smoke began to pour out of the end of the cane like fumes rising from a chimney. To spread out the heat, I turned the cane in my hands to maneuver the coal inside the walls. Within seconds a small stream of smoke escaped from the side of the cane. I quickly dumped out the coal, but it was too late. I had burned a hole through the side wall of the cane.

## First Man, Second Try

I began again on a new day and cut a new cane (unfortunately of the same size). This time, after heat-straightening the cane and punching out the septa, I came up with a workable tool for smoothing out those rough shards inside the joints. I selected a straight hardwood stick whose thicker end fit perfectly inside the cane. An inch from the end I carved a shallow, canoe-shaped bowl into the stick. After filling the bowl with creek sand, I inserted that end into the horizontal cane and carefully slid the stick deeper until I felt the sand engage the rough joint at the first node.

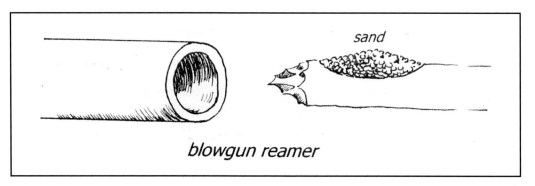

**blowgun reamer**

As I began to grate the sand against the shards, I slowly turned the cane; but the sanding process lasted only fifteen seconds before the sand had scattered down the tube. Extracting the stick, I refilled its bowl. And so it went. I had plenty of time, plenty of sand, and plenty of motivation. I was first man, lost in his work, inventing in a timeless scenario. The rhythm of the sanding was like a percussion instrument underscoring the sounds of the creek. I wondered if this duet had been performed here in this very place beside this creek long before my time.

I don't remember how long I sanded. In the rhapsody of first-man projects, minutes are not counted. But the complete smoothing of five joints with a tool that needed "reloading" with grit every few seconds had to have taken many hours.

The sanding was complete when the interior of the cane was perfectly smooth. Finally, I scraped off the finish from a small oval on the surface of the cane and painted my personal symbol like a badge of ownership.

I had my doubts. It seemed like a Howitzer of a blowgun that would need more firepower than I could ever deliver. But, I thought, once I loaded the channel with a dart whose fletching filled the cavity, perhaps I might be able to propel the dart forward.

I made my first dart from a thin splint of cane from my ruined blowgun. This was easy. I cut and freed up one section from its joints, propped it vertically, set my knife edge on one of its walls, and used a mallet to tap on the blunt side of my blade, forcing the sharp edge down through the cane. I repeated this technique to free up a dart shaft with a square cross section. (This is still my favorite dart shaft. So easy to make.)

I had heard that the Cherokees used thistle down for dart fletching. Their name for the dart was "*tsi–tsi*," which was also their name for thistle. I carefully fletched the dart by wrapping the down to the cane shaft with thread. Then I carried my weapon out to a field with high hopes of seeing my dart fly across the clearing to the edge of the woods. I raised the blowgun to an angle that I thought would offer such a flight, took a deep breath, and blew with all my might. My dart barely made it the length of my blowgun before emerging from the far end and dropping vertically to the ground.

Wanting to know where I had gone wrong, I showed my craft to a Cherokee friend, who was most kind in his assessment. I'll never forget his words.

"Hmm," he said. "I've never seen a blow pipe quite so large."

A blowgun competitor himself, he took me into his basement and showed me an impressive array of blowguns that he used in tournaments. Taking one down from the wall he turned one open end of cane to me.

"You should just be able to get the end of your little finger into the opening. Try rivercane next time. It is stronger and will hold its shape better."

As I examined his blowgun, he continued to study mine, turning it in his hand. He stared for a time at my symbol I had painted on the side of my bloated cane.

"That's nice. Yours?"

I told him it was. We were quiet for a while. Finally I thought to ask him about smoothing the bore . . . about how his ancestors had smoothed the interior of the cane.

Turning toward the window he frowned and finally said, "I don't know."

I was puzzled. "How did you smooth yours?" I said.

Now a smile crept to his face, and he looked back at my symbol and pointed. "Do you know what symbol is on my tools?" When I shook my head he answered his own question. "Black and Decker." He pointed to the power tools hanging on a pegboard above his workbench. Among those tools was an electric drill and a very long bit wrapped with sandpaper.

I shared with him my ramrod-sanding method. He thought about that for a while.

"Could have been the way," he said. "I'm not sure."

(actual size)

And so I decided to revisit the project—this time with rivercane as my blowgun material. For a given diameter of cane, rivercane native to Southern Appalachia has a longer section between joints than does introduced bamboo. That means fewer joints to work to a smooth finish. And rivercane is stronger, less likely to be damaged and better at holding its shape.

## Enlightened Man, Try Number Three

I harvested a proper-sized rivercane and followed the same straightening, hollowing, and sanding techniques from my previous effort, and in this way I produced

a working blowgun that fired a dart with authority. Even so, I held to a nagging suspicion that there had to be a better way to achieve the smooth bore of the blowgun . . . something clever.

Years later I learned how the Cherokees smoothed their dart channels. I can say with certainty that I never would have conceived such a plan, because nothing could have induced me to take a knife to my laboriously straightened cane and split it open lengthwise! With the interior of the two halves so exposed, sanding with a proper-sized stone would be an easy task. After smoothing, the Cherokee craftsmen closed the two halves back together into a perfect channel using glue and cordage lashing.

Blowgun, dart, dart quiver, and cap

### Making a Blowgun

In late summer or autumn, search along the banks of streams for a stand of robust rivercane. Select a cane standing as straight as you can find, with little taper, and, once cut, large enough to insert your little finger just past the outermost knuckle. While historical blowguns of varied cultures ranged from three feet to nine feet long, I suggest you trim a section comparable to your height. Then follow the heat-straightening technique described in Chapter 4.

Punch through the septa inside the cane with a dead and dry hardwood stick or metal rod, and then lay the cane down on a heavy board on the ground. This board will serve as a workbench. Abut the end of the cane to a tree trunk or other brace. Secure the cane on the board by kneeling or sitting on it and split its upper side with the tip of a knife blade and a mallet. Tap carefully and let your knife travel slowly down the length of the cane.

When this split is complete, turn over the cane and repeat on the opposite side. Now you have easy access to the remains of the septa. Carefully remove these spoked shards with a knife and then smooth with the rounded end of an oval stone.

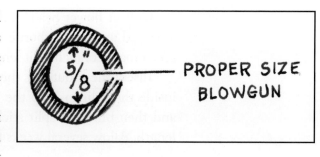

If, like me in my youth, you are reluctant to split open your cane, you can consider the technique I used with sand. Or if you'd like to use modern material, heat the end of a metal rod to bright red and press this end against the shards, being carefully not to burn into the walls of the cane. Finish the bore by reaming the interior with the rod when it's cool. A last high-tech option is the one my Cherokee friend used: an electric drill with a very long bit.

To put the cane halves back together, first make up a batch of hide glue (see *Volume 3*) or use any commercial wood glue and paint the edges that will join, being careful not to allow globs of glue to work their way inside the chamber. Fit the halves together again, bind them with sinew or strips of wet rawhide (or any fine cordage dipped in glue . . . dental floss is a favorite among those who are not purists), and secure this binding by simply pressing the final loose end into the sticky wrapping.

## Making a Dart

The shaft of the Cherokee dart sometimes measured twenty inches. I suggest making one eight to ten inches long. It can be carved from any straight, woody splinter. The Cherokees used yellow locust or white oak. The Muskogee used a splinter of rivercane, heated it, and twisted the shaft into a spiral for strength. For our purposes a straight splinter of bamboo with side walls an eighth-inch thick works nicely and is the easiest to make.

The dart

Use knife and mallet to splinter off dart shafts. Round off the square cross section (the corners) to create a circular cross section. With your knife sharpen a point on the leading end. (A good source of shafts for a group too young for knife-work can be found in grocery stores. Thin bamboo skewers are sold in packages and are ready to be fletched.)

# *Fletching*

There are many different thistle plants. Some flower in spring and others in late summer. It is said that the Cherokees favored the spring thistle for its down (pappus) in fletching the dart, but any pappus that is long enough to be lashed can be used.

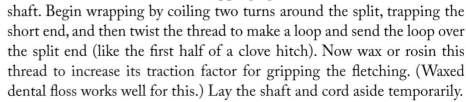

Collect flower heads that have gone to seed but not yet loosened up to go airborne. To dry, pinch the heads inside a green maple branch split lengthwise.

Insert the mouth of the heads in alternating directions inside the split to keep the down from escaping as it dries, and then bind the split stick by spiraling cordage down its length. Allow several weeks to dry.

### Fletching the Dart

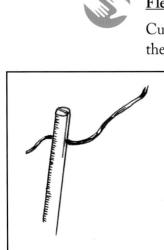

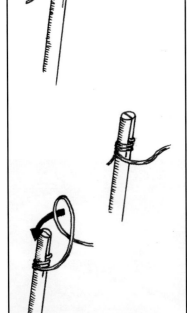

Cut a shallow split in the back end of the dart shaft and insert the end of a twenty-inch-long thread into this split, leaving a fraction of the thread free for trapping against the shaft. Begin wrapping by coiling two turns around the split, trapping the short end, and then twist the thread to make a loop and send the loop over the split end (like the first half of a clove hitch). Now wax or rosin this thread to increase its traction factor for gripping the fletching. (Waxed dental floss works well for this.) Lay the shaft and cord aside temporarily.

Grip the bulbous end of the thistle pod and most of its neck and pluck away all dark, stiff remnants of flower stamens to leave only the white downy pappus for your fletching. Break open the pod and discard its prickly exterior. With the left hand (held thumb-side up, pinky-side down) pinch the white pappus in the angle between the thumb and the ridge of the palm with the seeds on the palm-side and the free ends of filaments toward the back of the hand. Brush away any seeds from the down and clean that seed-end of the pappus of desiccated debris by scraping with a thumbnail.

With the bunch of white down now lined up on the ridge of the left palm (between index fist-knuckle and thumb), clamp the free end of the thread with your teeth and take the dart shaft in the right hand. Insert the threaded end of the shaft deep in the angle of the left thumb and palm, and then, keeping the thread taut, rotate the shaft by overhand turns to wrap the base of the filaments to the shaft as you push the shaft slowly through the left-hand pinch (to your left). Spiral the downy filaments along the shaft as you trap their front end under the thread, leaving their free ends pointing toward the rear of the dart. This method forms the fletching from rear to front, as it must be done (to make it imbricate or "shingle" properly). Add the down evenly as the cordage spirals along the shaft. Cover from a quarter to a third of the shaft with fletching and tie off the cordage in front of the fletching.

Take the shaft between both flattened palms (fingers pointing forward) and spin the shaft briskly back and forth with the same motion you might use to warm your hands on a cold day. The centrifugal force of this motion fluffs the pappus into a broader fletching. Pluck away any dark, stiff material that might remain in the down.

This fletching process is better seen in action rather than read in a book. It does take practice to achieve an even application of down along the shaft. A skilled practitioner can wrap this fletching in what seems an effortless exercise that takes seconds. If you can locate a blowgun maker in your area, by all means arrange a visit and see the art performed in person. Otherwise, look for examples on the Internet. Your first wrapping of fletching will undoubtedly take minutes, but you'll get better at it as you craft more darts.

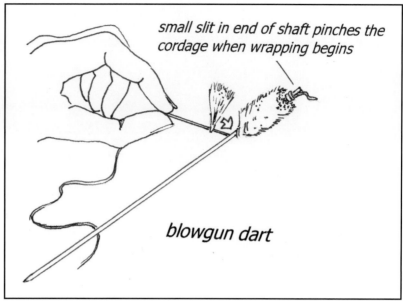

*small slit in end of shaft pinches the cordage when wrapping begins*

*blowgun dart*

### Shooting the Blowgun

Load the dart into the larger end of the cane and insert it deeply enough so you will not have contact with the fletching when you blow. Raise the blowgun and support it with both hands.

There are varied methods of holding the cane. Many present-day Cherokees hold with two hands palms-up, both near the mouth . . . or with the hand closest to the mouth palm-down in order to seal the lips manually to the cane (using the clamp of thumb and index). Experiment with wide and close grips to see what you prefer.

Aim and blow into the tube with a quickly building force. Blow powerfully but not explosively all at once. The entire exhalation is brief, coming from the chest (rather than ballooned cheeks) with the climax of pressure coming at the end. If you have trouble sending an entire burst of breath exclusively into the channel, orient the closer hand palm-down and use it to lock your lips to the cane.

Because the cane lies directly below both eyes, the left/right aim is naturally built into the shooting form. Elevation aiming, as in archery, comes with experience.

Cardboard boxes work nicely as targets. Draw a silhouette of a rabbit, bird, or squirrel (or simply a bull's-eye) on the side of a box and practice shooting with the box on the ground and up in a tree. Shoot from varying distances to learn your angles of cane-elevation. Occasionally, the point end might need to be resharpened. Do this sparingly so as not to dramatically shorten the dart.

# PART 2

## The Blessed Path of Water

## Lake to Whitewater Canoeing

# Author's Note

**Note to the reader who is not in a teaching scenario with students: This canoeing section is formatted heavily toward instructing a class of beginners, perhaps more so than any other portion of the four volumes of these books. But I have written the details of these lessons with the non-teacher in mind as well. If you are an individual seeking to learn or improve paddling skills, take these exercises to heart by going through the drills on your own. Buried inside each group activity are jewels of expertise that an individual might not otherwise discover on his own.**

A person's first experience stepping into a canoe, kneeling, and drifting off on the surface of a lake is, on some level, a magical departure from the norm. Buoyancy alone—so effortless and complete—is a spectacular phenomenon to the young. Replicating the same act on a river is a transcendental moment. The current transports the canoeist into a new dimension: a nonstop conveyor-belt medium that is rife with hydraulic complications not to be found in other areas of life. Navigating the complex dynamics of moving water would seem to be adventure enough for any outdoor enthusiast, but there is also the constantly changing panorama of the land on either side, as well as the riverbed beneath, both of which are worthy of one's attention.

Ironically, canoeing is one of the better methods for exploring a land. Thanks to the wide swath of the river itself, a canoeist is released from the oxymoron of "not being able to see the forest for the trees." Indeed, the river traveler is privy to all the changing faces of the woodlands through which he travels by having a constant cross section of forest to admire. Aesthetically, river running is a front row seat in the theater that features the masterpieces of Nature. With a little practice, one can be so quiet in a canoe that the opportunities for seeing wildlife are greatly increased over foot travel. The river can provide an ideal path for animal photographers and observers.

As a quiet canoeist I have come around each bend of a river full of expectations. The results of that preferred approach have given me treasured moments with otter, bobcat, bear, beaver, and dozens of other animal species in Georgia. In Idaho the reward was mountain sheep. In West Virginia it was deer swimming alongside my boat. In Colorado it was a curious coyote. Regal moose in Wisconsin. Eagles and porcupines in Minnesota. Giant snapping turtles and alligators in Florida. In Texas and Mexico I drifted into a herd of wild mustangs as they stood belly-deep in the Rio Grande to cool off and drink their fill. (Their splashy exit from the scene was spectacular.)

You never know what you'll encounter. Once on the Amicalola River as I drifted soundlessly, I heard a fast-paced rustling in the leaves on the eight-foot-high floodplain on my left. In the next instant a cottontail rabbit launched off the bank, making an impressive fifteen-foot-long leap into the river and splashing down just in front of the bow of my boat. Its dramatic dive was followed by frenetic strokes as it swam to the other side of the river. As soon as those little paws gained purchase on sand, the rabbit scrambled up the right bank and disappeared into the forest. Curious, I turned my boat around to hover in place. The daredevil diving rabbit vignette was a complete mystery to me for twenty seconds.

Then three hounds appeared on the rim of the same bank from which the rabbit had jumped, and those dogs began baying a wailing *a cappella* rendition of desperation. None was willing to wet its paws, much less make that mighty leap.

Once smitten by this medium of travel, you have choices for your experiences in riding rivers: making your way through thundering whitewater or gliding through pastoral quiet. There is much to commend about either approach, and so the best practice would be to include both and everything in between. But no matter where one chooses to travel by water, he needs to learn how to maneuver his boat in order to maintain his safety.

Besides the pure joy and excitement of running rivers . . . besides the inspiring scenery . . . something unique seeps into the soul of a river paddler. It is a gift both mentally nurturing and physically healthy. A relationship with rivers brings you closer to the heart of the world—literally. Some broad thinkers in the scientific community consider our planet a viable organism in itself. The streams comprise its circulatory system. And so river runners, it could be said, float the veins and arteries of the Earth and in so doing connect to a sculpting power that has been at work shaping the very face of this planet since its first rains.

The actions of rivers can be dramatic. Huge volumes of water can twist, fold, foam, crash, and roar in a thundering and formidable rapid. In other places the surface of the water is so glassy that it reflects an inverted image of the world with a resolution that rivals reality. Wherever one finds himself on a river, he is immersed in the universal solvent from which, many scientists believe, we originally came—the ocean.

All these streams we travel are making their way to the sea. Are we river runners continuously making our way home?

The river is a place to recapture our youth. We are at play on the river. In fact, every person I know who has spent a lifetime on rivers seems, in physical appearance alone, to defy the aging process.

As coaches like to say about their sports, there is a metaphor for life here. On the sports field an athlete learns to shoulder responsibility, to perform under pressure, to synchronize with teammates, and to accept defeat as well as victory.

On the river, the metaphor melds into reality. A paddler's welfare—his very survival—depends upon his execution and discretion. No rules can be bent. We have no say in it. The river has already made the rules and enacted them inside the laws of physics. The best we can do is react to them based on our acquired knowledge of the medium. Sometimes this means picking up our boats and walking around a rapid.

Standing on a boulder above a river's turbulence, making up her mind about how to "run a rapid," and then delivering her best in the white dash and splash of a formidable power that has been given a name—rapids like "Edge of the World," "Sock-em-Dog," or "Bus Stop"—a paddler will come to know herself as few athletes can. The scope is grand. The consequences are immediate and absolute.

The malleable form of water fits intimately into the human soul. Talk to any lifelong river runner and you will hear something about an impassioned connection to moving water. We humans are made up mostly of water. As paddlers, perhaps we can feel its current as it runs through us. One friend of mine likens the phenomenon to a lightning rod in reverse: "We dip our paddles into the water and feel its electrical charge travel up the shaft into our souls." There it sets our nerve endings into a glorious vibration. The river, it would seem, makes us more alive.

The fact is—no matter how poetically or how prosaically we try to explain it—we paddlers do form relationships with all rivers . . . and special ties with individual rivers. We develop bonds of love or brotherhood or sisterhood with moving water. We keep going back to rivers simply because we have expanded our lives to include them. We are like horsemen traveling the countryside to meet all the legendary equines of song and fable. So smitten, we are destined to ride the backs of these great steeds forever. It seems that the rivers have deemed it so.

*The Cherokee canoe is hewn from a poplar log and is too heavy to be carried about like the bark canoe of the northern tribes.*

—James Mooney, *History, Myths, and Sacred Formulas of the Cherokees*

# CHAPTER 14

# Headwaters—Lessons of the Creek

When I was a young boy, I loved making things of wood. For hours at a time I could get lost in such projects. Wherever I found scraps of lumber piled up as trash, I saw a treasure of building materials. (Very early in life I discovered scavenging to be a most noble occupation.) On the large scale I made forts and tree houses and gravity-powered, four-wheeled "hot rods." Smaller works included bowie knives, swords, shields, and many models of multi-masted ships.

In this nautical category I favored pirate ships with matchstick cannons (which could fire . . . once), furled sails cut from discarded bed sheets tied to the yards, tall masts, and complicated riggings that I strung from a ball of twine out of pure imagination. When I first tried floating one of these models in a creek, my ship proved top-heavy and capsized in the first few seconds of its maiden voyage. It was a beginning lesson for one who would one day become a canoeist.

Because I wanted to see my boats properly float, I abandoned the elaborate rigging and opted for a simpler, sea-worthy craft: a boat with a spare deck and a simple hull design. The result was a model of the Civil War battleship *Monitor*. All the construction material that was needed was a small flat board tapered at both ends as bow and stern and a short section of an inch-thick wood dowel to serve as the turret. A finishing nail partially hammered into the side of the turret represented a cannon. Another nail driven down the center of the dowel allowed the turret to rotate on the deck. What could be simpler? Two pieces of wood and two nails.

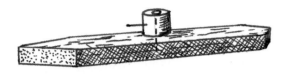

The finished product was about nine inches long. It sat on the water's surface with unquestioned stability. As soon as my *Monitor* had established itself as sea-worthy on the still waters of a backyard pool, I nudged it toward the challenges of moving water.

A good-sized stream—Camp Creek—was a half-mile from my home. From that day on it served as the Missouri River for my Lewis-and-Clark ambitions to drive deeper into wilderness.

I had no idea that this crude, self-made toy was about to serve as a teaching guide for my future career as a canoeist. The *Monitor* presented a good facsimile of the weight distribution of canoe and paddler. Not only did this craft pull me into depths of the forest where I had never before traveled, but this little boat instructed me in the physics of moving water. I was a dedicated student simply because I imagined myself inside this model boat that met adventure after adventure in the creek's rapids. I was personally invested.

A decade later this love of water travel would expand to a grander scale—using a vessel about twenty times longer than my hand-crafted *Monitor*. In this one I knelt, wielded a paddle, and experienced the adventure of river travel firsthand. In many ways, it was a *déjà vu*.

Those rapt creek journeys of my youth tutored me in the ways of whitewater and lay down a matrix of instincts that would become invaluable to me. During this time (and unknown to me) I absorbed unnamed principles of hydraulic science demonstrated by my toy boat in the complexity of the creek's eddies, waves, and rapids. All this information served me well when I stepped into a canoe for the first time.

For example, in my youthful creek days I knew by experience and repetition that each time my boat broached (sideways) above a small waterfall, my *Monitor* was going to fall into the bubbling pillow of foam immediately below the falls and tumble there for a while, until it was somehow spat free by the fickle will of the water. This hydraulic phenomenon was a literal depression in the surface of the creek, a perpetual pocket of froth that never floated downstream but remained in place. Into this "hole" (the common name given this depression by paddlers) water plummets down from the waterfall and also recycles back into the hole from the downstream side, creating a kind of watery trap.

On the other hand, if my toy boat happened to line up bow- or stern-first above the drop, there was a good chance it would punch right through the foam or span the hole to continue its journey without delay. This turned out to be an important lesson.

My *Monitor* and I logged a lot of creek miles—I, barefooted, full of exploratory excitement, and leaping from rock to rock or slogging through silted pools as my boat caught its breath between dramatic rapids. My boat was mindless yet made nimble by the miracle of buoyancy and the water's unceasing hunger to pursue a downhill course. It's a whole different story when you are inside a canoe and maneuvering to get your boat in the right place at the right time. One of the worst things a canoeist can do in whitewater is wait and see what happens. A successful paddler must be proactive.

Scouting water from a canoe on a never-before-seen river is much like sight-reading in music; that is, opening up sheet music that you have never before laid eyes on and getting through it without any practice whatsoever. As a canoeist reads the river he makes instantaneous decisions based upon what he sees the currents doing immediately before him as well as at a distance.

This has become my favorite part of canoeing and the reason why my list of rivers paddled has grown into the hundreds. This is all a part of the adventure of exploring. One friend of mine even named this a "Casanova Syndrome," claiming its insatiable need to woo as many lovers as possible. But I can place no connotation of immoderation to a love of rivers in general. An infatuation with all rivers, in my opinion, is a worthy and enriching way to live. After all, rivers do not, as far as I know, experience jealousy.

"Reading water" inside the thunder of a rapid is the very definition of living in the moment. It is virtually impossible to think of anything else. All the humdrum details of life are cast aside and concentration is pared down to the series of strokes needed to keep the boat upright, dry, and "on line." (Staying "on line" means navigating a proposed route that the eye constructs on the spot. This route is somewhat like a lightning bolt: built backwards in segments from the destination point—the place a canoeist wants to be at the end of the rapid—to his present position.)

One of the most important lessons my boyhood creek experiences taught me was that a boat does not naturally find its way along the best path. In a rapid if a paddler does nothing at all, his chances of a successful run are greatly diminished. A canoeist learns that the route chosen to *enter* a rapid is all-important. Not only does he act to counter what the currents will do to his boat, but also he learns to make use of those existing currents to achieve the "unnatural" route that means success.

By this I mean that the canoeist's route is rarely the route that a floating log would take. It is a route assembled in the mind. Part B of the route is successful only if part A is achieved. Part C works only if part B goes as planned, etc. But all this planning begins with part Z, because if you don't plan ahead, trouble awaits.

The difference between a whitewater canoeist and a light, floating log lies in three learned categories: strokes, body/boat-leans, and route-planning. But before a canoeist can begin the education of that triumvirate of river savvy, he must understand the many personalities of moving water.

# *Creek Currents*

All the dynamics of the storied rivers—the Colorado, the Salmon, the Chattooga—can be found in any piedmont or mountain creek, only on a smaller scale. You can instantly transform the magnitude of the perceived drama of a creek by imagining yourself as a two-inch-tall paddler traveling in a six-inch-long canoe. What was once a babbling squirt of water between two fist-sized stones now becomes a thundering waterfall between boulders. Just downstream of this, what was once a riffle is now a giant standing wave.

A *standing wave* differs from the waves that you see marching repetitively to the shores of all the oceans and expansive lakes. Riverine standing waves remain in place—like a buckle in a rug—while the water flows through them, following their contour like a rollercoaster rising then falling over an abrupt peak in the track. They remain in place because the objects that make the waves are underwater and stationary.

Wherever some object at the water's surface cannot be moved by the river's current—a jammed log, a protruding boulder, an island—you'll see the water deflect away or part around it. When water parts, because it possesses momentum, its divided streams meet again at some distance below the downstream end of the deflecting object. That is, the downstream current cannot change its direction to encapsulate the object on its downstream side. You can see this wherever a fast current parts around any boulder. Behind this rock there would be a vacuum if it were not for gravity pulling water from downstream to fill in the vacant space. This backward running water is called an "*eddy*."

Wherever a creek does not find an obvious downhill route, water backs up to the point of finally spilling over a relatively low spot. This backed-up water is called a "*pool*."

When enough volume of water falls over a ledge so it depresses the water level below, this forms a *hydraulic* or *souse hole*—basically a depression. Here, again

because of gravity, water from downstream pours upstream into the depression. The waterfall's main current plunges down into the pool and runs downstream rather low in the creek's depth. Since water near the surface is filling up the hole from downstream, this creates a sucking phenomenon. If you could view the waterfall/pool interface from the side and just below the water's surface, you'd see a large, recycling, swirling motion.

There are some objects through which a current can flow—like a multi-branched tree that has fallen into the water. Such hindrances are called "***strainers***" because they act like a colander allowing water to pass but not solid objects that can get hung up in the branching. In a river, strainers create one of the most dangerous hazards in canoeing. As I often tell my students, "The strainer is the colander; we would be the pasta. But unlike the kitchen scenario, the water never drains out. It keeps coming with no end. And unlike pasta, we need to breathe."

When multiple standing waves span a majority of the creek's width, you can see a well-defined ***trough*** between any two neighboring ***wave crests***. These troughs provide watery "valleys," which, when combined with its two framing crests, are often referred to as ***surfing waves***. Using such a wave, a skilled canoeist can defy the current by *not* continuing downstream. This can be accomplished by hardly taking a stroke once the canoe is positioned correctly in the trough. In effect the canoe is continuously falling down the upstream side of a wave into the trough just upstream of it and being stopped by the next wave immediately upstream. In effect, the canoe is purposely "stuck" in a ditch sculpted out of the water.

### Visiting a Creek

Take your students to a nearby creek. In choosing your creek, let your ears be your guide. The more noise the water makes, the more rocks are present to create an instructive surface terrain. Locate a large rock (protruding above the surface) that forces the water to part around it (without going over the top of it). Just downstream of this rock you will see a somewhat shield-shaped triangle of water where the current is flowing "the wrong way." This is an ***eddy***, which is usually marked on its sides by ***eddy lines***. These lines are literally etched into the surface of the water by the current differential. Break a two-inch-long, dry, dead stick and place it in the middle of the eddy to watch it travel upstream toward the rock.

To understand this phenomenon, imagine the creek bed dry due to a closed dam somewhere upstream. When the water is suddenly released from the dam, a rush of water comes down the bed and the water parts around the rock. Because of the momentum of the water, it does not hug the rock and converge again at the downstream edge of the rock. Depending upon the speed of the current the water does not converge for several inches or feet downstream of the rock. That would seem to leave an empty dry space just behind the rock. But Nature fills a vacuum. Just as it is in the main downstream current, gravity is the driving force of this diametric current. Water pours into that empty space.

Where does the water come from? The water speeding past the rock is too fast to be pulled in, so the water downstream at the convergence of the parted currents is pulled back.

Explore the water surface to find standing waves and hydraulics. Send a floating stick through each and see how it is affected by the water.

## Making a Boat

From a three-inch-wide board that is a half-inch thick, cut nine-inch lengths and give each student one blank to be used as a hull. Using pocketknives they can carve points on each end for a pointed bow and stern. Using pipe-cleaner wires each student can construct a one-inch-high, simplistic "canoeist" to kneel in the boat.

Staple this "canoeist's" lower legs to the wood just behind the midpoint of the deck.

Provide bright paints so that each boat-maker can make identifying marks on her ship. By choosing a name for her boat, the builder instills some ownership and personality into her craft. These boats soon become recognizable to all.

## Creek Lessons

Choose a section of creek that has a navigable rapid; that is, not impossible for a model boat to get through. The terrain of the creek bed may require some rearranging of rocks to open channels. Let the students have some free-play time watching their boats float through the rapids. Your best role at this juncture is to serve as the boat catcher below the rapid. Watch the joy in the eyes of each boat-maker as he sees his little alter-ego paddler and canoe fend for themselves in the "wild" currents.

When all are ready for a big voyage, launch boats one at a time from a common starting spot and see how each boat performs. Talk about why certain boats encountered different experiences. In so doing, you will be discussing specific currents and eddies and waves. Let names evolve for these places, for example: "Tidal Wave" and "Bubble Bath" and "the Magnetic Eddy" and "Roller Coaster" and "Dead Man's Curve."

After many trial runs, allow each student to choose his own launch spot (lateral to the original launch spot) that might afford the boat the most successful run through the rapid. You can hold contests to see which boats can make it to a finish line without getting held up at any one spot for more than thirty seconds. (At the thirty-second mark, remove that stalled boat and call it a "disqualified run.")

### Navigation Forecasts

In a different rapid area, ask each student to draw a map of the surface of the water. Have some fun as a group as all help to name "landmarks" on the course so they can be labeled on the maps.

Point out a common launch spot where each boat will begin a run of the rapid. Let your students predict the routes their own boats will take by marking them on the map with a colored pencil. Repeat this exercise several times using different starting places. Then move to another rapid and repeat again.

### Boat Race

You might be surprised how much enthusiasm can be stirred up by a simple boat race. String up a finish line above the water and name a common launch spot. Run the race in heats of two boats. (If you spread out too many boats at the start, you will have some boats beginning in slack water while others start with a jolt in fast current.) Run the same two boats in a best-out-of-four-runs trial. Each time you run a heat, switch the two boats' starting positions. With a two-two tie, both boats qualify for the next heat.

The boat that first crosses the finish line upright is the winner. If no boats finish upright, the first to cross upside down wins. Any boat snagged in the same place for thirty seconds is disqualified and loses that heat. Set aside each heat-winner on a Throne of Champions—a large rock you have chosen for this place of honor.

When all first heats are done and semifinalists are established, start heats again, racing only those boats from the Throne of Champions. Continue until you have a winner. After the race, discuss the merits of the winning boat. Is there some feature of this boat's design that might have given it an advantage?

### Catching an Eddy

By positioning a boat just upstream of and a few inches away from a well-formed eddy, demonstrate how, by giving a push, the boat can travel diagonally across the current and penetrate the eddy line. With a good push the boat can enter the eddy and turn quickly toward the rock that makes the eddy. This is called an "*eddy turn*." (If the boat is not pushed with authority or if the current is too strong, the eddy will merely catch the bow and turn the boat so it continues downstream backward. Choose a site with a less strong current that allows a successful turn.)

Give each student a try at making an eddy turn, discovering how hard a push is required to make the boat fully penetrate the eddy. This

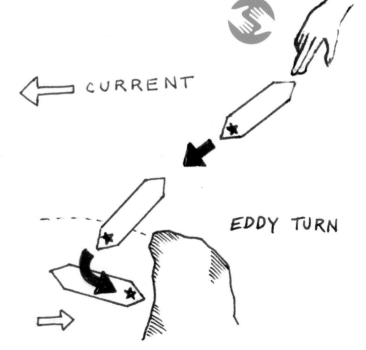

CURRENT

EDDY TURN

lesson will go a long way in helping future paddlers to understand the importance of the diagonal sprint required to successfully get a full-sized canoe into an eddy.

### Peeling Out of an Eddy

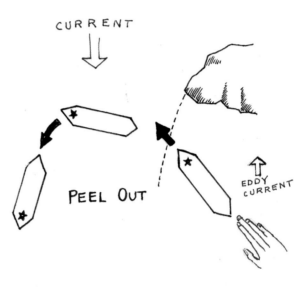

Repeat the above exercise in reverse by pushing the boat from the eddy into the current. When the boat leaves the eddy and enters the current with the bow turning downstream, this is called *"peeling out."* Point out the angle that successfully takes a boat into the current. An angle too close to perpendicular to the current will quickly spin a boat and push it back into the eddy. A boat that approaches the current parallel to that current (bow pointed too upstream) will be pushed back into the eddy. An angle close to parallel but canted toward the current affords a wider arc in the peel out. The faster the current, the closer to parallel the peel out angle needs to be.

### Surfing a Wave

Push a tack or hammer a small nail onto the deck of the bow of a model boat and tie a six-foot-length of twine to this to serve as a leash for your boat. Find a nicely shaped wave that stands three to four inches high. Standing upstream of these waves, position your boat in the water a few feet above the first wave. Let out the line slowly until your boat's stern is lifted up by the largest wave and then hold it steady. The boat will surf from side to side and you will feel the pressure on the

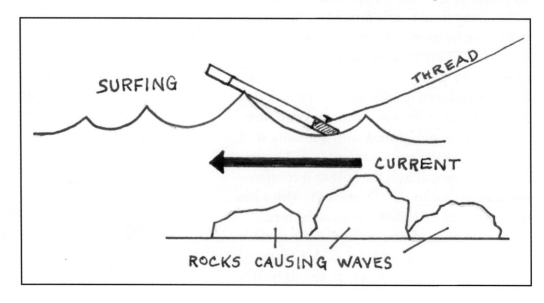

thread disappear from time to time when the boat is aligned perfectly. Try positioning the boat to let the thread go slack while the boat remains surfing on the wave.

### Ferrying

With the twine still attached to the bow, stand in a wide part of the creek where the current is not obstructed by rocks above the water's surface. Set your boat on the water and feed out several feet of line. While holding the boat in place, apply a gentle tug to one side to angle the bow so the boat is no longer parallel with the current. If you walk laterally and keep a light pull on the line to maintain this new angle, the boat will effortlessly glide laterally, perpendicular to the current without drifting backward. Then angle the boat the other way and traverse back to the original starting point. This lateral movement of the boat from one side of the creek to the other (without losing "ground") is called a *"ferry."* Ferrying comes in very handy to a whitewater canoeist who spots

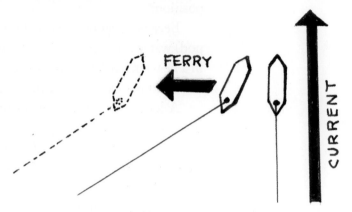

a problem downstream. By ferrying she can move safely to one side of the river without getting closer to the problem. Then she can get out, walk the shore to scout, assess the danger, and perhaps identify a safe route around it.

## Canoeing versus Kayaking

There is no denying that the sleek lines of a kayak have captured many a beginner paddler's fancy over the bulkier design of a canoe. Today, however, many new kayak designs (very popular, I might add, for the sake of "playing" in whitewater) are anything but sleek. They appear so truncated that one wonders where the paddler's legs could possibly be. Nevertheless, the kayak has become associated with the hip trend of "on the edge" toys—along with skateboards, snowboards, and dirt bikes.

Kayaks are highly maneuverable. The advantages of having a double-bladed paddle include more stroke symmetry, faster stroke rate, and less need for correction. Kayaks can go where canoes can't go. In the right hands, they can do things canoes can't do. Kayaks are light. They look cool—like a missile. In the water they are nimble and quick to respond.

Comparatively speaking, the canoe is deemed by many to be heavy and cumbersome. Of course, the lines of a canoe can be sleek, too. It's all in the eye of the beholder. And canoes can be light—surprisingly so. But there are some profound differences that, in my opinion, make the canoe the ultimate choice for a self-propelled watercraft for a beginner class.

In no way do I mean to belittle kayaks. Each type of boat is wonderful simply because it allows us to "walk" on water, and kayaks (and other decked boats like

C-1s and C-2s) perform this nimbly when commandeered by seasoned paddlers. Here are some practical considerations and safety points to keep in mind when choosing canoe vs. kayak.

1. **Pinning**—Pinning a boat is the most feared of whitewater scenarios. When submerged upstream of a rock or tree and exposed to current on their broadest sides, any small watercraft can close up like laundry folded over a line. In the process, the cavity of the vessel is crushed flat. How does a canoe or kayak get into this vulnerable position?

Because a canoe is basically a shell (that is, open at the top like half of a split pea pod) water can splash or pour into the shell when going through rapids. This results in a heavier, harder-to-handle craft. A water-laden canoe rides deeper in the current and becomes extremely difficult to maneuver, making it more available to obstacles.

A kayak is a closed vessel (unless it is a "sit-on-top" kayak that is often supplied to inexperienced tourists by outfitters on gentle rivers) with a relatively small cockpit for entry and exit. Once the paddler is seated, this cockpit is covered by a stretched spray-skirt or apron worn around the paddler's waist. Water cannot fill the boat unless the spray-skirt fails or the boat cracks. This makes the kayak less likely to take on water and become sluggish.

When a canoe capsizes in moving water, its openness becomes a liability. The shell of the boat becomes like a windsock in a hurricane and fills with a massive amount of water pressure (tons). If it hits an obstacle underwater, the boat might pin and fold. If this happens a canoeist can quickly escape by bodily pushing out of the boat and out of harm's way. This is one of the most critical safety assets of the canoe, and one main reason I choose canoes for teaching children.

When a kayak capsizes the ideal solution is to roll the kayak upright with a specialized stroke of the paddle, but if the paddler fails to roll, he must exit his boat. Because his legs are deeply buried in a tight space under the deck, an ejection is more difficult than from a canoe. If the kayak pins on a rock and folds before a successful underwater escape, the deck and hull can sandwich the kayaker's legs in a permanent, flattened clamp. If the kayak folds like a jackknife around the paddler, the situation is especially desperate. Even if several strong people can get to a pinned boat, pulling the boat free in time to rescue the paddler might be impossible. The power of moving water is nothing short of overwhelming.

Most whitewater solo canoeists strap large inflatable airbags under the thwarts (crossbars) of their boats in the bow and stern, leaving only the paddler's position free of flotation. Tandem boats usually make use of one large bag at the center of the boat and, possibly, a small bag at each end. These are form-fit bags made just for canoes, and they render the boat more buoyant when capsized. Kayakers use similar bags in bow and stern.

2. **Maneuverability**—The kayak, because it is lighter, shorter, and more buoyant (it does not float as deeply in the water; that is, it has less "draft"), is a more maneuverable craft; however, this same ease of turning can be frustrating to a beginner, who finds that each forward stroke takes him quickly off his intended course.

The canoe lies deeper in the water, making it more difficult to turn, but this same factor allows a paddler to more easily paddle forward without dramatically changing the boat's direction.

3. **Forcing the Paddler to Read Water Accurately**—The very openness of a canoe forces the canoeist to be more mindful in reading currents and mentally charting the way through rapids by the "driest route." Riding on top of the water along a well-planned route is more demanding than simply bulldozing through a rapid, as a kayak can do. Though the kayaker might also perform such a refined route with equal finesse, he doesn't necessarily need to.

Beginner kayakers often choose to float through a rapid in a kind of defensive mode, trying to prevent a capsize. Such an idle floater may come out of the experience wet from the waist up, but no worse for the wear.

A canoeist must be meticulous about reading water, about planning and executing a "dry route," and about hitting certain spots in the rapid with his boat turned at specific angles. He does not have the luxury of barging through waves, because every ounce of water added to the weight of the canoe works against the canoeist.

4. **Body Position**—A kayaker sits with his legs out in front. A whitewater canoeist kneels. A paddler must decide which of these two positions is most appealing to him while working with arms and torso.

In the kneeling position a canoeist's shoulders are higher, allowing more body weight to be applied to a stroke. He also has greater reach from the boat compared to a paddler sitting in a boat. These two points translate into more force per stroke. Paddling on one's knees takes a great deal of strain off the lumbar spine.

5. **The Paddle**—A kayaker uses a double-bladed paddle, one blade at either end of the shaft. Two blades allow him to counterbalance one stroke with the next, which, theoretically, means that fewer correction strokes are needed.

A canoeist uses a single-bladed paddle with a handle at the other end of the shaft. This simple T-shaped handle is aligned with the blade and gives a paddler more control, more strength in each stroke, and instant orientation of the blade at any moment. More body strength can be applied to a turn and more body weight (which transfers as strength) can be applied to a stroke. In short, a single canoe stroke is more powerful than a single kayak stroke.

A double-bladed paddle is more cumbersome to a young beginner than a single-blade. While one kayaker's blade is working in the water, the other is above her, where it can tangle in tree branches extending from the banks. A canoeist's paddle lies completely below his top hand grip.

6. **Space**—For carrying gear, whether it is first-aid or camping gear, or a passenger, the canoe is superior to a kayak, if both are considered with their airbags removed. A canoe is very useful for hauling firewood.

Because kayaks have very limited space at bow and stern (or no space available due to the presence of airbags), any extra bulky gear must be stored between the paddler's legs, which becomes a liability that makes a fast exit more difficult.

However, it should be noted that overloading either craft will impair its maneuverability, which is another liability.

7. **Ease in Entering and Exiting**—Though this consideration may seem a minor one, I consider it to be germane. Adventurers ought to make many stops on a river trip to examine more closely all the things spotted on the banks or beyond. A canoeist can simply park his boat at the bank, stand up, and step out.

A kayaker must unfasten his spray-skirt, extract himself from the cockpit, and then stand with a big, floppy apron still attached to his waist.

8. **Capsizing**—When a kayak turns over, if the paddler has mastered the paddle-sweep and hip-thrust necessary to right his craft, this watertight boat can be "rolled" upright, and the paddler can continue on his way as though nothing had happened (other than a quick and chilly baptism of the upper body). However, in teaching a class of young beginners, you may have only one or two who can accomplish the kayak roll in a pond or swimming pool. Even then, to roll in the thick of action on a river is always more difficult.

When a canoe capsizes, the situation is more problematic. Before continuing the journey it is necessary that a tandem team get their boat ashore to empty it of water. A swimming team finds that a canoe with airbags can be pushed or pulled much more easily than a bare canoe. The latter is very heavy. With young students it usually takes a group effort, though a competent adult paddler can achieve this boat-rescue alone. (This maneuver will be covered soon.)

9. **Class size and manageability**—Because canoes can be paddled tandem, twelve students can occupy six boats. Those same twelve students in a kayaking class would occupy twelve boats. A smaller number of boats makes for a more manageable class.

## Making a Model Open Canoe

Choose a five-inch-thick, dead trunk of soft hardwood like tulip magnolia, basswood, or buckeye and cut a one-foot-long section for each student.

Trim the rounded cross section of each piece to a triangular one by setting the cylinder of wood upright on a workbench (a log or stump). Draw an equilateral triangle on the upper end, with each triangle point touching the round circumference. Position a sturdy blade on one line and carefully hammer the back of the blade with a mallet. Move the blade all the way down the length of the block. Repeat on the other two lines.

If the cross section did not result in an equilateral triangle, choose the broadest surface for the hull (bottom) of the canoe. Carve away the four corners of the hull's rectangle and in so doing sharpen each end (the boat's bow and stern) from the sides, much in the same way you sharpened the ends of your *Monitor*. Carve away wood on top of the boat into a hammock shape to establish the height of the canoe's gunnels (tops of the side walls) until the boat looks like a canoe without a cavity.

Allow a quarter-inch for the thickness of your canoe walls at the gunnels. Draw a line to establish that thickness and then use a fixed-blade (non-folding) knife to

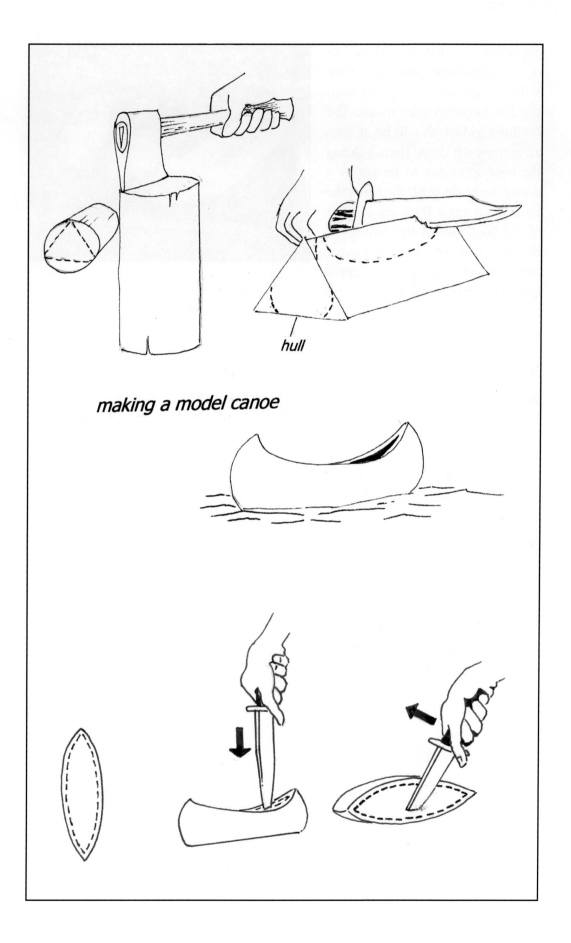

hull

making a model canoe

dig down into that line. Make lots of straight-down punctures (like a line of dashes on a page) until the line becomes continuous. The resulting groove should be at least a quarter-inch deep. Then, holding the boat so as not to be cut by a slip of the blade, push the tip of the knife at an angle from the interior of the boat toward the bottom of the just-cut groove. Do this a number of times until you can apply leverage upward with the knife blade to chip out chunks of wood. Once you have established a shallow bowl inside the canoe, repeat the line of punctures and chip out the desired cavity.

### Burning Out a Model Dugout

Make a fire using hardwood fuel and let it burn down to coals. Prepare the same cylinder of wood used above and again reduce its cross section to a triangle. From this blank, because there is no need for a hammock-shaped profile at the top of the boat, simply carve a flat surface for the deck. (Because dugouts were too heavy to be used in rapids, Cherokee canoes were flatter on top. They needed no high bow to fend off splashing water.) After chipping out the first quarter-inch of the cavity, reenact history by burning out the unwanted wood inside your canoe, just as the Cherokees used fire to hollow out a dugout canoe made from a tulip tree. Using homemade tongs (See *Volume 1*, chapter 16) simply lay down small hot coals to burn out a cavity.

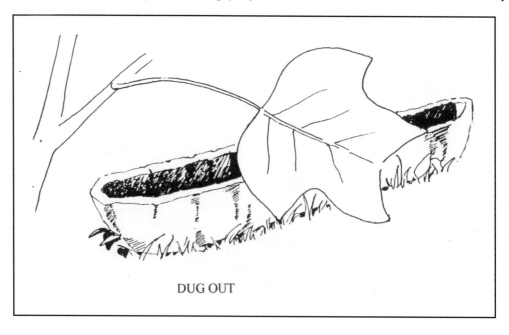

DUG OUT

Protect the walls of the canoe by applying mud on their inside surface. Place a hot coal inside the canoe and hold it down with a stick of green wood. Blow through a blow tube (half-inch-thick cane, three-eighths-inch Joe Pye weed, or a drinking straw) to superheat the coal and scorch the wood wherever you desire. Once the wood is charred, it can be more easily chipped out using the tip of a knife blade. Work patiently. Don't burn through a wall.

### Running Dry

Repeat all the creek exercises performed with your *Monitor*, this time paying attention to how much water splashes or pours into the boat. You can devise competitions using the twine as a leash (such as ferrying and eddy turns) or without the twine (races that are run individually and timed by a watch) by measuring the quantity of water poured from boats after the contest and factoring this into the scoring. For example, one fluid ounce of water adds one second to race time.

*A Chief Half Pania [Pawnee] . . . crossed the river in the Buffalow Skin Canoo and the Squar [squaw] took the boat (on her back) and proceeded on to the Town 3 miles.*

—William Clark, *The Definitive Journals of Lewis and Clark*

## CHAPTER 15

# Walking on Water—On the Lake

Throughout history small watercraft has proved invaluable in any number of ways: for crossing streams in a dry fashion, for transporting burdensome weights of goods and gear, for hunting (either for the aquatic animals swimming under the boat or the land creatures that a canoeist so silently drifts past), food-gathering (wapato, cattail, and wild rice), and, of course, for making long journeys.

All of these tasks were made easier with a canoe by the virtual absence of friction between a hull and water (compared to a travois or a sled). A boat also spared a beast of burden the onerous duty of lugging heavy loads overland.

Said simply, the canoe's great contribution in any task is its buoyancy. Though we take it for granted, a floating canoe should seem like a magical gift of transportation to a place that is otherwise not so accessible. A boat gives us "wings" so that we can enter the medium of water much like birds take to the air.

## The Gator at the Gate

On my self-imposed survival trips I spent most of my food-gathering time walking floodplains and scouting stream banks—some of them quite steep. Often I resorted to stripping down, getting down in the water, and harvesting from the river. Wherever the water was too deep to stand, I invariably found myself longing for a boat.

Ordinarily, we do not expect to find a boat out in the wild, but on this occasion it happened to me. It was a homemade johnboat—crudely put together with few boat-making skills—but for me it was a blessing and a bridge to all the food that I could want.

For this particular trip I had hitched a ride in a private boat over to an island off Georgia's coast and made arrangements to be picked up in nine days. In my initial exploration I had located a long freshwater slough just behind the tertiary dunes. This was an important find for two reasons—one being a source of fresh water, the other being a massive stand of cattails forming a thick wall at the inland side of the channel.

I wanted to get to those edible cattails, but there was a deterrent. Floating lazily out in the still water was at least one alligator—a six-footer. I could see its eyes and nostrils just above the water line like bumps on a gnarly log that was mostly submerged.

I weighed my options. Separating the slough from the inland forest was a swamp and then a dense thicket of saw palmetto, which I wanted to avoid, because that vegetation provides a prime habitat for rattlesnakes. In addition, the serrate stalks of the palmetto fronds are unfriendly to human flesh.

The cattails were only thirty feet away from me, but the alligator—now alert to my presence—had begun cruising the length of the stand like the guardian of the grove. Every previous in-the-water encounter I'd had with gators had been the same: immediate flight on the gator's part. But there are no laws governing animal behavior, and I could not afford an exception to the "rule." I decided to walk beside the slough in the hope of finding another stand of cattails where I might swim to a food source unimpeded by reptiles with large jaws and impressive rows of teeth.

On that walk I found the johnboat hiding in tall grass and partially obscured by a shifting dune. It was a simple concoction of nailed-up, sun-bleached plywood and two-by-fours, filled with dead leaves and sand, and filigreed by a lacy fan of pepper vine. At first I thought I had stumbled across a pile of washed-up lumber, but when I made out gunnels and a flat bow angled slightly upward like the closed ramp of a D-Day landing craft, I realized I had been blessed by Saint Serendipity of the Lost Boats. After excavating the boat from the sand, I dragged it to the water and found only minor leaks. All I needed was a paddle.

From a thicket of shrubs between dunes, I broke a dead trunk of myrtle and fashioned its multi-forked end like a rake. Through these tines I wove a length of split grapevines tightly enough to serve as a crude paddle blade. With holey paddle in hand I returned to the boat and set off on my mission.

The johnboat is the antithesis of aquatic nimbleness. Moving it forward with my skeleton of a paddle seemed less an excursion and more an exercise in roiling up froth from tannic water. It was enough to send the disgruntled gator to a quieter spot. Everything about this escapade was clunky and cumbersome, but the simple gift of buoyancy was liberating. It allowed me to "stand" in a place that just minutes before had seemed forbidding. The experience filled me with a profound appreciation for all boats that float . . . no matter how primitive their design.

Not only did the johnboat serve as a bridge for me to get to the place I needed to go, but it was also my freight-hauling receptacle. Into the shell of the boat I stacked sheaves of leaves and a pile of pale orange rhizomes. Here was the very definition of happiness at living in the moment. My mission was complete; my plate was full; and I still had all my body parts. If I thought he would have eaten it, I would have offered some of my booty to Mr. Gator. I was cattail-rich.

That critical journey of thirty feet across still water remains a memorable chapter in a lifetime of paddling all kinds of waters. There was nothing graceful or elegant in this passage to the cattails. My makeshift paddle perfectly matched the awkwardness of the boat that it pushed along. Each time I lifted that woven blade from the water to take a new stroke, I felt as if I were dredging up a pitchfork-ful of soaked seaweed. But the concept of floating—walking on water, if you will—revealed itself to me for the magic that it truly is. Since that day I have felt the wonder of buoyancy each time I step into my canoe at the beginning of a whitewater trip. I doubt the appreciation will ever leave me.

## Still Waters

There are some good reasons for starting your whitewater sessions on a lake—the main one being that, barring troublesome winds, you can keep all your students together for the class. Beginners can't be expected to contend with river current before they learn the strokes that help them go where they want to go. And you, the teacher, cannot afford to let someone get separated from the group. On the river, a student out of sight is an especially troubling liability.

Wind currents on a lake can be challenging to both student and teacher, for the side of the canoe acts like a sail. The larger the lake, the more a boat can be affected by wind. If you have the latitude of choice, wait for a mild day to begin your lessons.

## *Nomenclature*

Beginners need to know three parts of the paddle and three (of the many) parts of the canoe. The rest can come later. I help my youngest students remember these names by using word associations.

The **forward** end of a boat is the *bow*. (When we take a **bow**, we bend **forward**.) The back end of a boat is the **stern**. (When I was a young boy, whenever I broke some parental rule, my father got **stern** with *my* **back end**.) The **gunwales** (or **gunnels**) are the tops of the sides of the canoe—the edge that water pours over and into the boat should the canoe be tipped too far to one side. These side walls were that part of a ship where the **whale guns** (harpoon cannons) were mounted. Whale **guns** were positioned at **gunwales**. It has become common to refer to an individual **gunnel** (in the singular form of the word) on either side (right or left) of the canoe.

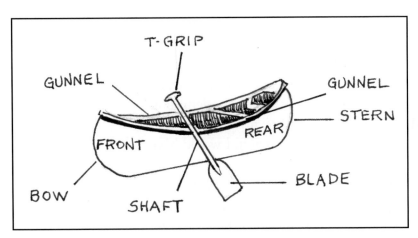

The **paddle**, which looks somewhat like a blunt arrow, shares a common name with that projectile in its long slender *shaft*. The flattened *blade* is designed to push water or slice through water (on its thin edge) . . . like a knife **blade**. The end grip—if it is shaped like a "T"—is aptly named the **T-grip**. (There are also flared grips roughly shaped as triangles.)

## *Choosing the Correct Paddle*

To know which length paddle to use, stand with a paddle blade touching the ground before your toes. If the T-grip comes up to the "jugular notch" (suprasternal hollow at the base of the throat) but no higher than your chin, this is the correct paddle for you. For a student under five feet tall, use the higher end of that parameter (chin height).

## *Choosing a Proper-Fitting Lifejacket*

A practical lifejacket or PFD (personal flotation device) needs to be worn like a vest, not like a belt. It should be loose enough to allow comfortable movement—including swimming—but snug enough so it does not slip over the face when the wearer is floating upright in the water.

Once the jacket is on, have someone take hold of the material above each shoulder and give a sharp tug upward. If the jacket rides up and covers the face, this awkward shift will probably occur in the water and be disorienting and constricting. If the jacket does not have adjustment straps to tighten the fit, try a smaller-sized jacket.

# Earth-Friendly Portage

In getting our boats to the lake's edge, we confront an ecology lesson about point source pollution. Erosion is a major and ever-growing factor in the poor health of our streams. Our overcrowded areas of the world make life very hard for surface water. Poorly thought-out development has created countless point sources of erosion. Many children have now grown up with brown, silt-laden streams as the norm. They need to know that dirt pollutes water just like smoke and exhaust pollute air. To an aquatic plant or animal, life in a dirty river is comparable to a non-smoker inhabiting a smoke-filled room.

As canoeists, who will eventually frequent rivers, we need to set examples, to teach other canoeists (whom we will encounter) by carrying (not dragging) boats over land to the water. There is a second reason not to drag a boat. It adds to the deterioration of the boat's hull, where stream rocks already take their toll on the canoe. Plant this seed of respect for land and for the canoe in your students' minds.

Partners may carry their canoe to the water by any means they can. The easiest way, by far, is to team up with four carriers spaced at the four "corners" of the gunnels,

ready to paddle with life jacket, paddle, and knee pads

lifting one-handedly by the gunnels in a balanced way. Stress the correct way to lift—not with a bent back but with erect torso and bent legs.

Most modern canoes have at each end of the boat a handle to grip, usually constructed as part of the bow and stern plates. Two partners can carry by these end-handles, but below is another method they might prefer.

### Carrying a Canoe a Short Distance to the Water

Two paddlers stand on opposite sides of their boat facing one another at mid-ship. Bend with the legs (keeping the spine erect) and take a wide two-handed grip on the gunnel. Lift the boat by standing and pulling away from each other. Sidle toward the water until almost half the boat is over water. At that point set down the canoe, partly in water, partly on land.

# Getting the Canoe Stable for Entry

When a canoe is partially on water and partially on land, this presents a precarious position for getting into the boat. Because of the V-shape of the end of the canoe on land, the boat can easily rock to either side. To make the boat stable for entering, both partners should walk to the landward end of the boat and lift. The canoe can now glide

out effortlessly as you walk it toward the lake, until the entire boat can be lowered into the water. Now swing the boat parallel to the shoreline and hold on to the gunnel.

## Choosing Ends, Choosing Sides

Before getting into the canoe one partner commits to the bow, one to the stern. It doesn't matter which person takes which position unless one is significantly heavier than the other—in which case, the lighter person should go to the bow. As a gift to your students, I suggest that throughout these lessons you instruct them to alternate positions on a daily basis. This versatility will serve them well throughout their paddling careers.

The paddlers must also commit to using paddles <u>on opposite sides</u> for the entire day—one on the right, one on the left. It doesn't matter who takes which side (even if one is right-handed and the other left-handed), but once the commitment is made, there should be no switching for that day. Again, for the sake of your students' versatility, I recommend having individuals change their allegiance to right or left every few days of instruction. A complete course of lessons on one side is good. A series of lessons on alternating sides is far better.

It is generally a bad habit to rely on switching sides to solve an immediate navigation problem. Yet it is to the paddler's benefit to be ambidextrous with her paddle. Later in the paddler's career, she will learn that it is most prudent to enter a rapid knowing she will never switch her hands on the paddle shaft. This is the preferred approach. But to have the luxury of choosing on which side she will paddle (because she has that ambidextrous ability) is ideal.

Note: <u>Not switching</u> does not mean that the paddle blade cannot be lifted over to the other side of the boat. It can, but only for a bow paddler or the solo paddler. In this case, the canoeist maintains her original grips on the shaft and T-grip. Such a maneuver is called a "***cross-over stroke***" or "***cross stroke***" and will be covered in the next chapter. For now, tell your students that the paddle should remain on the committed side.

# *Entering the Canoe*

Place paddles inside the boat at their assigned ends. Wearing his lifejacket, one paddler holds the boat steady by a mid-ship gunnel while his partner—wearing her lifejacket—steps onto the imaginary centerline (like the centerline of a highway) on the hull (floor of the boat). Keeping most of her weight on the land and her center of gravity low, she crouches as she extends one leg into the boat.

Gripping her hands on the gunnels for balance, she now slowly shifts her body weight over the boat, steps in with the other leg, and kneels on the bottom so she can lean her rear end against the edge of the seat. (If the bottom of the boat is not padded for knee comfort, paddlers should wear strap-on kneepads.)

**A rule: During team-entry and exit and all paddling lessons, paddlers should kneel! Call for occasional rest periods to sit in canoes or stand on shore.**

The first paddler situated in the boat then holds on to something reliable on the land . . . to keep the canoe from drifting toward open water. If nothing reliable is available, she props her paddle on land or on the bottom of the lake to hold the canoe steady while her partner steps in using the same technique. At this point both should be kneeling. Exiting is the same process but in reverse.

In this first lake lesson, watch your students' faces as they take in the miracle of "walking on water." For some, it's a first-time buoyancy experience outside of a swimming pool. This is a good time for them to experiment and listen to their instincts in figuring out how to maneuver the boat. Watch them and see how they solve problems of physics as their boats drift randomly. Lessons in Newton's Laws await them in the water.

All beginners are immediately tempted to switch sides. Remind them of their side-commitments and challenge them to go the rest of the day without switching.

## <u>Instinctive Paddling</u>

Without the benefit of any on-the-water instruction give each team a mission to complete—such as: "Paddle your boat to that low tree branch, touch it, turn around, and come back." Let them experiment with inventing strokes. It will make the proficiency of the strokes you teach later all the more appreciated.

trial and error on the lake

## *Exiting the Canoe*

At the end of the day or at a lunch break, when you are ready for your class to return to land, give them the simple instructions to reverse the entering-the-boat process. Watch them to see how well they perform this. Remind them, when necessary, that only one paddler in a team should be moving at any one time.

Many impetuous young ones have a tendency to toss their paddles onto land while they are still in the boat. Inevitably, a comic scene results. The first paddler to step out of the boat, in his hurry to get to lunch, pushes off too hard. If the second paddler has not secured the boat to land, the boat drifts from shore, stranding the one in the boat without a paddle. This is a grand moment of accountability. Let them devise a rescue solution.

*A canoe can be as nimble as a beaver in water. I should know. All it takes is understanding how to use your tail and webbed feet . . . meaning, of course, your paddle.*

—Dr. Robert B. Beaver, from *Conversations in the Upper Room*

# CHAPTER 16

# Taming the Canoe—Strokes

A canoe does not act of its own accord to please its paddlers. It will not, for example, progress in a given direction simply because it has been pointed that way. Even on a lake a canoe will not automatically cruise in a straight line with two equally strong paddlers stroking on opposite sides. Why? Because the stern paddler has a mechanical advantage over the bow paddler, causing the boat to veer away from the stern person's paddling side. (This law is true only when the canoe is moving forward. If going backward, the advantage goes to the bow paddler.)

In a river the skein of cross-currents constantly bombarding a boat can make for a complicated medium on which to travel. It takes skill to coax a boat along the predetermined route that a paddler plots in her mind. Knowing which strokes to use is essential to navigating, but just as important is knowing at what moment to employ these strokes.

There are only a half-dozen strokes to learn . . . and then some minor variations on each of these. None of the basic strokes is very difficult to learn, but the timing of when to use them is an acquired skill that comes from experience. For example, consider the task of paddling your boat in a straight line. In time, you will learn to feel that moment when the boat is about to veer from the desired course. The subtle stroke needed is then anticipatory. This is what makes a veteran's run of a difficult rapid look easy. No desperate moves are made. Corrections are performed even before a deviation is detectable to someone watching from a distance.

# Gathering for the Lesson

Now that your beginners are spread out on the lake, it might seem overly optimistic to call out to them to make their way to you for the lesson. But expect it of them. Most will make it. By this time almost everyone will have learned that pushing water to the rear moves the boat forward and pushing water to the front puts on the "brakes" and then moves the boat backward.

You'll probably have to help some with "primitive strokes," which means telling one tandem team member to "push water to the front" and the other to "push water to the back" until their boat turns toward you. Then both paddlers can push water to the back until they start to veer again and the instructions are repeated. (Such maneuvering is considered "primitive" because this turning technique involves slowing or stopping the boat. This is due to the use of that reverse stroke that pushes water to the front. Soon these paddlers will learn to spin their boat without losing speed.)

# The Power Position

Once everyone is within hearing range, lay out the steps to show each paddler how to position himself in the *pre-stroke pose* called the "***power position***." This is a pose that beginners are not likely to invent on their own. It is one of the key factors that separates an efficient, graceful paddler from one who is self-taught, without benefit of instruction.

### <u>Assuming the Power Position</u>

After all students are gathered within the sound of your voice, take them through this progression:

**Step 1:** "Everyone kneel and prop your rear end against the edge of the seat."

**Step 2:** "For those of you paddling on the left: Hold the paddle in your left hand only, grasping it on the shaft two feet down from the T-grip. Now, keeping your torso upright, reach forward with that arm, the shaft _vertical_ at arm's length, the blade in the water right next to the boat. Position the blade so that one flat side faces forward toward the bow, the other toward the stern."

**Step 3:** "Those paddling on the right side, do the same with your right hand."

"From now on we will no longer use the terms "left" and "right" sides. Your paddle-side is called the "**on-side**." Your paddle-less side is called the "**off-side**."

**Step 4:** "While keeping your rear end on the edge of the seat, bend forward at the waist to extend your arm and paddle toward the front of the canoe as far as you can reach _while keeping the shaft vertical and close to the gunnel . . . and keeping the blade positioned perpendicular to the boat._ To do this you'll have to lean your body slightly to your on-side, even to the point that would slightly tilt the boat." (When both partners perform the same lean on opposite sides, the counter-balance results in no boat tilt.) "To achieve optimum reach, rotate your torso around your spine enough to slightly turn your back to the on-side. In this pose your _on-side shoulder should now be lower than your off-side shoulder and forward of your face. Your off-side shoulder should be higher and behind._"

**Step 5:** "While holding that position, take the T-grip with your free hand by having that arm reach virtually _over your head._ The on-side arm should be straight. The off-side arm should be slightly bent. Keep the shaft as vertical as you can. If you open the fingers of both hands at this point, all fingers should point to the front."

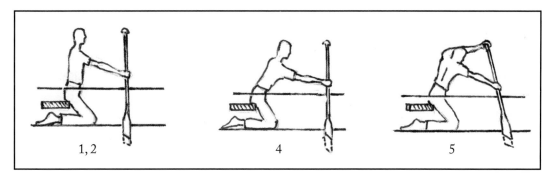

You have now put your students into the **power position**—the most enabling pose for performing the forward stroke (pushing water to the back, propelling the boat forward). We will cover the forward stroke soon. But now is the time to get familiar with this pre-stroke pose. After giving everyone a few seconds to relax, ask them to assume the power position again. Throughout the first day's lesson, ask the students to assume this pose frequently, simply to help the body position sink into muscle memory. Check their form and coach them on the perfect pose.

*power position*

## *The Stroke That Leads to Fatigue*

Few people, if left to their own devices without instruction, would learn the power position. The more common propensity of beginners for moving the boat forward is to sit upright (with no tilt) for the security of keeping the boat and body safe from capsize. To take an uninformed forward stroke, novices and untrained canoeists tend to reach forward with only the lower arm, keeping the upper arm much too bent. Then the lower arm generally pulls the paddle with the biceps to push water to the stern and propel the boat forward. Because the biceps is a relatively small muscle, this stroking form is a recipe for fatigue.

The more one uses the power position, its requisite lean, and the proper muscles for the forward stroke (these instructions are coming up soon), the sooner the paddler achieves an alliance with paddle and water. When the power position is fully realized for its efficiency with the forward stroke, the sensation can best be described as the paddler working over his paddle, propelling *himself* across the water *while coincidentally dragging the boat underside him.*

During the next lesson on feathering, interrupt your instruction from time to time and call out, "Assume the power position!" as if it's a game. Get this form inculcated into your students early in their canoe schooling.

## *Feathering*

Ironically, the first stroke we shall learn should have no effect on the boat. The **feather** demonstrates how the blade got its name. In feathering, the blade slices through the water, its thin edge leading with virtually no resistance from the water, much like a bird's wing feathers cutting through the air.

### Feathering the Paddle Blade

To set up for the feather, hold the paddle horizontally (on-side) over the water, parallel to and right next to the gunnel, making sure that the entire paddle is completely hovering above the water. (That is, if you suddenly dropped your paddle there would be a "splash" but no "clunk" from banging the gunnel.) The plane of the blade should be parallel to the side of the canoe; therefore, the prongs of the T-grip should be pointing up and down.

Slip the blade down into and through the water, letting it follow the arc of a pendulum, the bottom hand

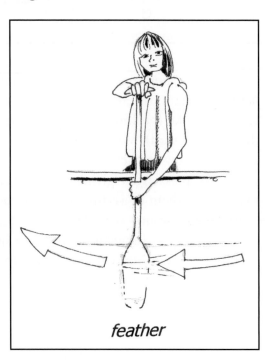

*feather*

moving forward, the top hand moving up and back and its arm bending until the elbow is pointing forward. The blade should rise out of the water in front and point forward. Now send it backward along the same arc until the paddle has returned to its starting position. Repeat this. Halfway through each arc, make sure the paddle is perfectly vertical. (Do not allow the T-grip to lean over the canoe). The top arm must reach out perpendicularly from the boat in order to achieve paddle verticality.

### Testing the Feather Stroke

After the students have practiced the feather, appraise each team one at a time. Ask them to synchronize their feather strokes at your command—feathering forward, then back. Give them a countdown: "Three, two, one, feather!" Watch for verticality of shafts, clean slices through the water, and performing the stroke in unison. If the boat makes a sudden lurch in any direction, one or both paddlers used an improper angle of the blade. Repeat the exercise. When a boat does not move appreciably, that team has passed the test.

### The Speed Feather

Test them again, but this time they must perform the forward and back strokes with brisk slices through the water. The speed feather will show off any incorrect angle of the blade by turning the boat. If the boat moves, the paddler who erred will have felt the pressure on his blade. You, the instructor, can detect which end of the boat reacted to the misaligned stroke. That paddler can make the correction by changing the cant of the blade—a simple, slight rotation of the T-grip to position the blade parallel with the path of the blade. Repeat the test until the boat shows no lurch.

## *The Draw Stroke*

When a person *draws* water from a well using a rope and bucket, the water is pulled *toward* him. The same is true with the **draw stroke**. Water will be pulled by the blade toward the paddler's hip along a path *perpendicular to the canoe*. During this stroke the paddle shaft should remain as vertical as possible and the arms should remain virtually straight. The only way to achieve such a position is for the paddler to bend at the waist sideways with the off-side arm over the head as she leans out over the water. It is difficult for a beginner to give herself over entirely to this lean, but gradually she will get comfortable with it when she learns that the draw stroke supports her body weight over the water.

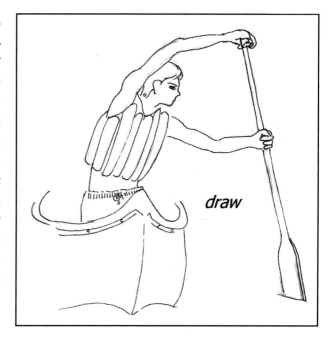

draw

### Learning the Draw Stroke

While facing the front of the canoe with no paddle in hand, stretch your arms out to your sides like wings. In this position your on-side arm points in the direction where you should reach with your paddle for the draw stroke—directly out from your hip . . . *not in front of your hip*. (There seems to be a universal tendency for beginners to reach to a spot beside their knees rather than their hips.)

To begin the draw stroke, grip the paddle with both hands and reach out to the on-side by bending at the waist to slip the blade straight down into the water as far from the boat as you can manage while keeping the paddle shaft as near-vertical as you can. The blade should be positioned parallel to the side of the boat. Keep both arms almost straight, top arm over your head, and turn your face to the paddle blade.

Still keeping your arms almost straight, force the blade toward your hip (perpendicular to the canoe) *by straightening up at your waist.* By doing this you are actually pulling the boat underneath you. *Just before the paddle touches the boat*, feather it out of the water toward the rear.

If the shaft hits the boat during a draw stroke, momentum tries to carry the blade under the boat and the resulting leverage might pull the T-grip from your hand. (I have seen students hang on to the T-grip when the shaft hits the boat, only to be pulled over the gunnel into the lake.)

The paddle should be vertical at this instantaneous stopping point. By immediately feathering the blade out the rear, the blade makes two distinct paths in the water following a perfect L shape (or backwards L, depending upon your paddle-side).

If both paddlers in a team draw at the same time, one end of the canoe is being pulled to the right while the other end is being pulled to the left; thus, the canoe

---

**The Most Common Mistakes in Attempting the Draw Stroke**

1. Reaching out only with the bottom arm, making a vertical paddle an impossibility.
2. Pulling in the blade with the bottom arm and pushing the T-grip out with the top arm, rather than keeping both arms nearly straight and using the torso muscles to straighten up the spine.
3. Entering the blade beside the knee instead of the hip. From this incorrect start, by pulling the blade toward the hip, the stroke converts into a hybrid forward/draw stroke, which causes the boat not only to spin but also to move forward and thereby carve a big circle (much slower than a true draw spin).
4. Drawing the shaft too far, hitting the boat with the paddle. In retrieving the paddle from this position, water might be inadvertently pushed away from the boat, which would negate the original stroke.
5. Cutting the corner on the L pattern, making it a J.
6. Feathering out the front rather than the back.

spins on a vertical axis at its center. Whether a boat spins clockwise or counter-clockwise depends upon which partner paddles on the left and which on the right. This maneuver is called a "***draw spin***."

### Draw-Spinning on a Dime

Ask each pair of partners to perform a draw spin, being sure to synchronize strokes. As they draw, imagine an axle running vertically down through the center of the boat and planted firmly into the mud at the bottom of the lake. Watch to see if the boat stays on that axle or drifts away from it. If the latter, one (or both) of the paddlers did not reach out on the perpendicular to begin the stroke.

(If one paddler is much heavier than his partner, the boat will spin lopsidedly.)

## *The Pry Stroke*

In a sense, the ***pry stroke*** is the draw stroke performed in reverse. It begins with the paddle held alongside the gunnel, blade to the rear, because the first part of the pry stroke requires a feather. But this time the feather should carry the blade not just underwater but **underneath the boat** with the shaft at an angle, so the blade disappears from the paddler's view at the end of the feather.

The blade should feather *directly* to this position (under the boat beneath the paddler's on-side leg) rather than feathering to a vertical position and then being forced under the boat. (Such a flaw would technically be a small draw stroke.) To direct the paddle blade to its proper place, angle the blade with its leading edge turned slightly toward the boat. Then *reach out with the top arm during this feather stroke* until the top arm is straight and considerably stretched out over the water. Once the feather portion of the pry stroke is complete, there is hardly a pause before the prying part of the stroke is applied.

*side of boat begins as fulcrum*

*pry*

*gunnel becomes primary fulcrum*

Only when the shaft is angled under the boat like this can the pry stroke be powerful. Using the side of the boat and the gunnel as a fulcrum, pull the T-grip across the boat right in front of your torso. This motion brings the T-grip hinging down and lowering in front of you. (Don't pinch your lower hand between paddle shaft and gunnel! Raise that hand above the gunnel and use it to keep the shaft from sliding on the gunnel.) Above all, do not push the shaft outward away from the boat! Let the leverage of shaft on boat provide all the power.

Have the students learn to do this last phase of the pry with one hand only (on the T-grip) to make sure they understand how the fulcrum works.

### Pry-Spinning on a Dime

Repeat the previous spinning-on-a-dime exercise—this time using the pry stroke. If the boat does not remain on the imaginary vertical axle, one or both paddlers are not prying water perpendicularly from the boat. Either that or the feather part of the stroke is pushing water to the front rather than slicing through the water.

---

### The Most Common Mistakes in Attempting the Pry Stroke

1. Feathering with the paddle shaft at the wrong angle, so the blade never goes out of sight. (Demonstrate this inferior feather and show how the second phase of the stroke pulls water upward, contributing very little lateral force.)
2. Feathering the shaft to a vertical position then correcting with a small draw to get the blade to its proper position underneath the boat. Such a draw initiates a boat movement in the wrong direction.
3. Feathering with the blade at the wrong angle, so the attempt at feathering pushes water to the front, moving the boat in reverse. Remember, feathering should not move the boat at all.
4. Prying water forward instead of laterally, in effect rendering a stroke that moves the boat backward.
5. Pushing the shaft outward with the lower hand rather than using the hull and then the gunnel as a fulcrum.

---

### The Spin Olympics

Now that tandem teams can spin in both directions, have the boats space out on the lake around you so each boat has plenty of working room. Ask all the students to point their boats at you, the teacher. When all are in position, call out either "Draw spin!" or "Pry spin!" The first boat to spin 360 degrees and point at you again is the winner. Keep your eyes on the boats and point to the finishers as you call out each place earned: "First! . . . second! . . . third!" Repeat several times and critique your students. Watch the order of finishing change as teams improve. Here are some Olympic tips to share that can allow new champions to emerge:

1. Synchronize: Both paddlers in a team should stroke at the same time. It is the stern paddler's duty to synchronize because he can see the bow paddler. If he can't keep up, he should tell his partner to slow down her stroke rate. Synchronization is more effective at moving the boat than alternating strokes.
2. Maintain form: Don't let the competition encourage abandoning the precision of the stroke. For example, when a draw spin is called, if one (or both) paddler(s) reaches forward of the perpendicular line (from the hip) to begin the stroke, that boat will circle instead of spinning in place. Carving a circle is much slower than spinning on a dime.
3. Confusion of terms: Inevitably there are students who mix up the names of the two strokes and perform the wrong one. Think up a helpful reminder, such as an alliterative association: "Draw at a distance. Pry pretty close." Such a trope can help a confused paddler to get started correctly.

## *Stopping a Spin*

Stopping a draw spin is done by prying. Stopping a pry spin is done by drawing. These two strokes are opposites.

### Loch Ness!

I save this exercise as the last before lunch, so paddlers can earn their meal. "You can go in for lunch when you snap a clear photo of the Loch Ness Monster!"

We pretend that each boat is equipped with a camera mounted on the bow. The goal of each team is to capture that elusive, unblurred photo of Nessie. If the Loch Ness monster surfaces for only eight seconds at any one time before diving under again, then photo time is limited. A team must spin a boat quickly to aim its "camera" at the monster and then suddenly be still to take the picture.

Testing one boat at a time, point to some object along the shoreline and tell a tandem team that this same object (say, a clump of grass on the shoreline) is Nessie and she has just surfaced. Immediately count down from eight. The assigned team must spin its boat (being sure to use the shortest spin, draw or pry) and then stop it when pointed at the target, all before "zero."

Each assigned spin should require a 90-degree to 170-degree adjustment. When you name a target, the crew must first communicate to decide which spin to use. Teamwork—an absolute must for a successful tandem team on the river—begins here. The team performs the spin toward the named target and then stops the boat's spin. It must be perfectly still to "take the picture." You, the teacher, be the judge.

How do you stop a spinning boat to make it perfectly still? By performing the opposite stroke with moderation. When a boat successfully makes the camera shot, let the tandem partners go in for lunch.

# *The Forward Stroke*

Return to *The Power Position* section and read over the details on body position. From this pose the shoulders can rotate around the axis of the spine, pushing with the top (off-side) shoulder, pulling with the bottom . . . *all with hardly any bending of the arms!* By leaning your body weight *down* on the paddle (during the stroke) and using the muscles of the rotating torso rather than the arms, the forward stroke is made more powerful; and, because this form uses the larger muscles of the torso, the paddler will not tire out through the day.

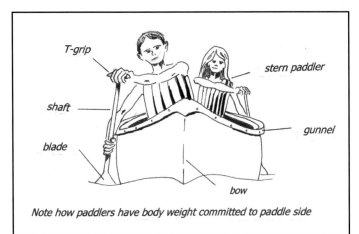

*Note how paddlers have body weight committed to paddle side*

During the backward movement of the blade in the forward stroke, when the blade reaches a position lateral to the thigh, the paddler should start lifting the blade out of the water. A stroke done behind the body does not contribute to the forward thrust of the boat.

Lean out to the on-side so the paddle shaft can remain in a near-vertical plane throughout the stroke. At its entry into the water, for example, the blade is ahead of the T-grip because of the extreme forward reach of the on-side shoulder. But the T-grip should remain directly above water, not leaning over the boat.

## Practicing the Forward Stroke

First of all, prepare your students by telling them they will be traveling in circles in this exercise. (Soon we will cover the correction strokes that produce a straight line of travel.) Send boats out into their own private spaces on the water and have them do twenty forward strokes that are synchronized. Do this four times, alternating which team member counts the strokes out loud. While they are performing each set, they will naturally paddle in circles. Their main goals are: 1. lean toward the on-side, 2. keep the arms almost straight throughout the stroking, 3. keep the paddles 100 percent over the water (not angled over the boat), 4. use the rotation of the torso to create the stroke, and 5. synchronize.

## Proof of Power

One boat at a time, test each team's forward stroke efficiency. Have a boat sit motionless in the water with the paddlers poised in the power position. At the signal "Stroke!" each paddler should perform one synchronized forward stroke and then immediately lift his or her paddle out of the water to let the boat cruise on the power of that one stroke. You can make this a contest by setting up a starting place and a goal to reach in a certain lapse of time.

## *The Reverse Stroke*

One of the most common mix-ups among young students is the use of the words forward and reverse in stroking; because in performing the forward stroke, the paddle moves backward. And vice versa. Reinforce the idea that stroke names indicate *direction of travel*, not *direction of paddle*.

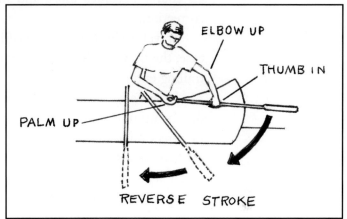

To execute the **reverse stroke** (to make the boat travel in reverse) lean over the gunnel and lay your entire paddle on the surface of the water to float there by itself, shaft parallel to the boat, T-grip toward the bow, blade toward the stern. The paddle, of course, floats with the blade flat on the surface. Place your proper hands on the shaft and the T-grip. The T-grip hand should be palm-up as you grasp the handle. The back hand should have the thumb closer to the boat, large knuckles of the fist farther from the boat. Now raise the paddle upward to a height just below the gunnel, and then reach back with the paddle blade until the T-grip is beside your hip.

Start with the back elbow pointed up, then straighten both arms as you push the blade forward through the water, moving as much water as possible with the blade. Keeping the arms straight, push water toward the bow using shoulder rotation, *moving the paddle through a vertical plane throughout the stroke.*

Once a student has learned the stroke this way, she should not, of course, float the paddle each time she wants to use a reverse stroke. She should reach back immediately to the T-grip-beside-the-hip position, paddle horizontal above the water.

Each time a paddler begins a reverse stroke, she should look back over her onside shoulder to see where she is headed.

### Practicing the Reverse Stroke

Repeat the earlier exercise *Practicing the Forward Stroke*, this time using the reverse stroke. The students should concentrate on the same five points of form.

### Proof of Power in Reverse

Repeat the earlier exercise *Proof of Power*, now using the reverse stroke. Again, if desired, set up a competition for distance covered in a set time.

## *Paddling a Straight Line*

As everyone will have discovered by now, a canoe does not travel in a straight line by itself. Some canoes are made with a deep keel (a fin that runs the length of the hull) to make a straight-line journey more likely, but such keels reduce the boat's ability to spin and that is a liability in whitewater. As both team members perform the forward stroke, the boat will usually veer toward the bow person's paddle-side. This happens because the stern paddler has a mechanical advantage with her paddle working at the trailing end of the boat. Once the boat *begins* to stray off course, a turning-momentum is established and will only get worse, so straightening back on course becomes more and more difficult the longer a team waits to make a correction.

Traveling in reverse, the veering principle repeats but the roles flip-flop. In this case, the bow paddler has the mechanical advantage because now he works in the trailing end of the boat.

A canoe can just as well veer the other way for other reasons, such as one paddler being much stronger than her partner . . . or one paddler performing a stroke incorrectly. No matter which way the boat starts to veer, the paddlers—at this point in their training—have the ability to spin the canoe back on course with synchronized pry strokes or draw strokes. This need for correction provides an opportunity for each team to understand and practice the two hallmarks of tandem canoeing: teamwork and communication.

There is a secret to paddling a straight line: *Learn to feel when the boat is starting its veer and correct that veer <u>early</u> with a tiny spinning stroke* . . . rather than waiting for a blatant misalignment and having to correct with big, multiple strokes in a more exaggerated spin.

## Who's in Charge?

A common misconception about tandem paddling is the notion that the stern paddler is the captain of the boat. If this were true, a docile experience is in store for the bow paddler, who would learn to take no initiative and, therefore, have no reason to pay attention to the needs of the boat. In all my classes I teach equal sovereignty over command of the craft. Bow and stern paddlers share the captaincy of the canoe.

Because the stern paddler has a better view of his partner, it is he who can best accomplish the synchronization of strokes by simply matching the timing of the bow paddler's strokes. And this stern paddler can better determine the boat's heading at any given moment, because she has a longer view of the boat. (Compare, for example, aiming an arrow by looking down the length of the arrow from its feathered end rather than looking out from its point to appraise its flight path.) For this reason, the stern paddler has the better vantage for calling out the need for a certain stroke to correct boat alignment.

But beginners make mistakes—both with terminology and directional needs. So, when someone calls a command, teams should consider that command up for discussion and subject to change.

The bow paddler has the better view of the "terrain" of the river just ahead (when your teams finally do get on moving water), and so he should make the more immediate calls concerning the route of passage. For example, the bow paddler might see a barely submerged rock five yards ahead that the stern paddler cannot see at all. It is the bow paddler's job to call out the direction the boat needs to travel to avoid the rock.

### The Straight-Line Paddle

Give each team a different destination on the far side of the pond and challenge the paddlers to travel to it along a straight route without letting their boat ever turn perpendicular to their proposed course. Encourage them to talk about which stroke is needed at any given moment.

### Sharing the Captaincy

Repeat the previous exercise with these new instructions: "Only the bow paddler can give stroke commands."

Then repeat again with this condition: "Only the stern paddler can give commands."

Practice this half-mute scenario with all the team exercises that follow to ensure that both paddlers absorb an understanding of maneuvering the boat . . . and to establish a balance of power in the canoe's captaincy.

### Perfecting the Straight-Line

Repeat the straight-line paddle exercise giving smaller and smaller increments of acceptable error. For example, complete that journey across the pond by never letting the boat angle off course more than 45 degrees, then 20 degrees, etc.

### Straight-Line Paddling in Reverse

Repeat the above exercises as the boats travel in reverse. Each paddler must be sure to look back over the on-side shoulder each time she positions for a new reverse stroke. Now the idea of a shared captaincy cements.

## *Side-Slipping*

As your class sits idly in canoes on the lake around you, present this riddle to your students: "What happens if the bow paddler performs a draw stroke and the stern paddler performs a pry?"

Every time I have thrown this riddle out to a class of youth, I invariably get these two answers: 1. "Nothing!" (as if the two strokes negate each other) and 2. "We'd turn over!"

Then, inevitably, someone thinks it through: "We'd move sideways!"

(Correct!)

In every instance of determining how to maneuver a canoe, it is often helpful to use a visual exercise from a bird's-eye view. Consider each half of the canoe as independent from the other. What effect will a certain stroke have on that half of the boat?

For example, if the stern paddler is paddling on the left and she performs a draw stroke, how does the stern-half of the boat respond? (It moves to the left.) If the bow paddler—paddling on the right side—also performs a draw, how does the bow-half of the boat respond? (It moves to the right.) Observing from a bird's-eye view, now imagine the stern moving left and the bow moving right. How does the boat react? (It spins clockwise.)

Now back to the side-slip: Point to a tandem team and ask them to visualize your questions. "If Daniel (paddling on the left) performs a draw, which direction will his half of the boat travel?" (*Left!*) "And if Becca (paddling on the right) performs a pry, which direction is her half of the boat going to travel?" (*Left!*) "Therefore, if both halves of the boat are moving to the left, what happens to the entire canoe?" (*It moves sideways—or sideslips—to the left!*)

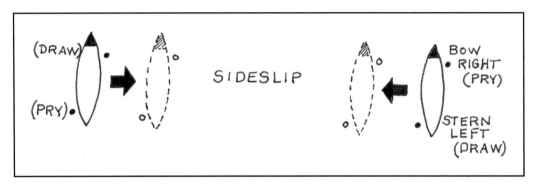

Few beginner tandem teams initially perform the side-slip with equal forces applied to the draw and the pry. (One paddler usually gets ahead of the other and the boat does not maintain a true lateral movement. In fact, it spins slightly.) There is only one recourse to solve this disparity of stroking. The one who is overpowering must slow down to let his teammate catch up. How is this problem identified and rectified? By exercising teamwork. By communicating. Remember to stroke in unison. Once again, this unison factor is the stern paddler's responsibility.

### Side-Slipping Exercise

Have each team position its boat parallel to the shore (twenty yards away) where there is a landmark that can be named (a rock, a root, a sedge, etc.) Side-slip the boat toward that landmark until the side of the boat (but not the bow or stern) touches the shore. After accomplishing this, return to the starting position, spin 180 degrees, and repeat the exercise from this new orientation. Now each boat has side-slipped in both directions.

# *Stopping*

No matter what maneuver a team is performing, in order to stop the boat's movement each paddler should perform the *opposite stroke* from the one powering the original maneuver. When stroking forward, stop the boat by stroking in reverse. When draw-spinning, both paddlers perform a moderate pry to stop the spin. When pry-spinning, they draw. When side-slipping, the paddler who was drawing now pries, and the paddler who was prying now draws. To stop traveling in reverse, each paddler uses a forward stroke.

*Those people left us and crossed the river through the highest waves I ever saw a small vestles [sic] ride. Those Indians are certainly the best Canoe navigators I ever saw.*

—William Clark, *The Definitive Journals of Lewis and Clark*

# CHAPTER 17

# A Dance on Water—Moving across the Glassy Surface with Grace

There is a natural tendency for a beginner in any sport to enter the endeavor tentatively. It's always difficult to be aggressive before you have developed the skills that build confidence. In river canoeing this often translates as a paddler riding through a rapid in the wait-and-see-what-happens mode.

In fact, floating through a rapid like a log, more or less, is seldom successful in rapids of higher difficulty. Being proactive with strokes is more than an asset. It is the only way to successfully negotiate certain rapids without a mishap. Generally speaking, the faster a canoe moves (relative to the speed of the current), the more easily it can maneuver with turns and diagonal sprints across the current. When current speed overwhelms canoe speed, maneuverability is lost.

Whitewater competition is comprised of three categories: *wildwater* (racing downriver for a number of miles against the clock); *slalom* (running through a series of manmade gates strung over a rapid-infested section of river, racing against the clock while maneuvering sequentially through pairs of hanging poles); and *rodeo* (performing tricks in a rapid to impress a judge). The benefits of racing are especially plentiful in that part of the sport known as "slalom." Nothing improves the expertise of a river paddler like whitewater slalom.

When a canoeist stands on the shore of a river and scouts an upcoming rapid, the process is generally one of selecting the most prudent route—one that the paddler feels he can successfully negotiate. Sometimes the decision is one of eliminating the most impractical routes and settling upon the "lesser of evils." If this remaining choice contains too much risk, the wise paddler chooses the dry route of *portaging* (carrying the boat around and bypassing the rapid entirely).

In slalom racing, the course designers position some gates in rapids in such a way that running through the gate without touching it is a distinct challenge. In other words, the choice of where to run the rapid has been taken away from the paddler. He is forced to run a route that he might not have willingly selected. In this way, the paddler is broadening his experience, stretching his capabilities, performing maneuvers in a rapid that perhaps he would never have dreamed of doing by his own volition.

Over time, such demands make one a much-improved paddler. In fact, those improvements might have been unreachable without the demands of slalom racing. Such enrichment of paddling skills inevitably endows a paddler with a certain degree of balletic finesse. The racers who perform best inevitably become the most graceful. Watching such a paddler cobble an unfaltering path through complicated cross-currents and hydraulic turbulence is a thing of beauty indeed. As in all sports, the skilled practitioner makes a difficult feat look easier than it really is.

But to the accomplished paddler, the maneuver actually *is* easier. His time in the slalom arena has given him experiences outside the norm. He has been pushed to experiment in complicated currents. And because he spends time in the racing arena, time and again he sees logic-defying maneuvers performed by the veterans who precede him. He sees what is possible, and that knowledge gives him a reason to work on a particular individual "move" that he might have considered unattainable.

On a milder, friendlier scale, this same "push" toward improvement can be introduced on the lake by creating a slalom course. On still waters, where there is no current with which to contend, it is difficult to encourage some students toward aggressive paddling. After all, what is the need?

All that can change with a slalom course and a stopwatch.

## *The Slalom Course*

To establish a fixed point on the surface of the water, tie an anchor (a five-pound rock, a brick, or a piece of metal) to an empty, capped milk jug with a length of rope that allows the anchor to reach the lake bed. Position another buoy two yards away. With just these two jugs, you have all you'll need for a rudimentary slalom course. Around these points a tandem team must navigate a predetermined route, trying to avoid touching the jugs with boat, paddle, or body. There are many courses that can be designed around these two jugs. A sample beginner course is offered below in the next exercise.

Perhaps the best way to introduce a course to your students is to use a scale model canoe on land. Pin two markers into the ground to serve as the milk jugs, and then run the model through the maneuvers you wish your students to accomplish.

This "dry" demonstration provides a chance for team members to discuss strategy. After the students have had a chance to make practice runs on the lake, provide an inspiration by allowing two teachers to run a canoe through the course.

### Beginning Slalom

(Refer to the diagrams below.) We'll start by asking teams to run a slalom course without being timed by a watch. Their job is to perform the maneuvers accurately at a leisurely pace <u>without touching the milk jugs</u>. Establish a start-/finish-line parallel with and twenty yards from the pair of jugs. What follows are the instructions to give your paddlers:

"Get settled behind the starting-line with your boat pointed just to the right of the jugs. To start the course paddle to the right side of both jugs. When your boat is just past the line of jugs, stop without letting the boat spin either way (keep it aligned with your entrance route). From this stopped position, side-slip to the left beyond the far left jug. Stop. Make a full spin clockwise. Stop. Paddle in reverse in a straight line toward the starting-line with the jugs on your right side.

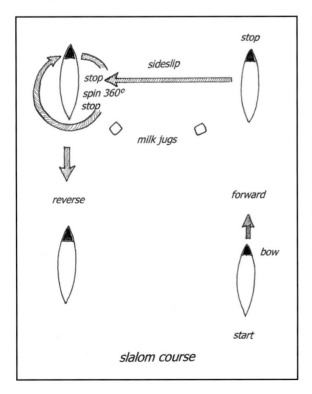

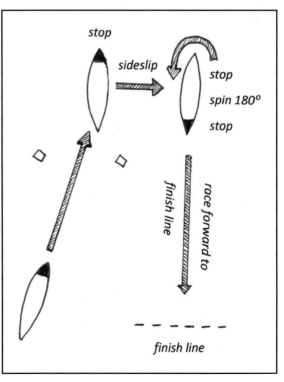

"At some point when the boat is past the jugs, stop, spin slightly to angle the bow so that it points between the jugs. Paddle forward through the jugs (don't touch!) and then stop. Side-slip to the right, past the jugs. Make a half-spin counterclockwise to point at the start/finish line. Paddle forward to the line to finish."

## Running Clean

After all students have run the course two or three times, you may wish to initiate an unhurried (still untimed) competition to see which team can complete the course with the fewest touches on the jugs. To run though the course without touching a jug is called "running clean."

## Slalom for Form

My students love to perform the previous slalom course like a gymnastics meet, in which I award points for every maneuver done correctly. Runs are not timed but assessed for execution. I assign points like this and total them after a run:

*Straight line paddle (never more than 20 degrees off course): **+2 points**
*Stopping completely: **+1 point**
*Side-slip without losing a boat angle by more than 20 degrees: **+3 points**
*Spin with synchronized strokes: **+2 points**
*Alignment corrections after stopping or spinning: **+1 point**
*Penalty for touching a jug with boat, paddle, or body: **−3 points** (Touching the same jug more than once during a pass-through does not multiply the penalty. The maximum penalty that can be invoked on a pass-through is **−6** . . . one or more touches on each jug.)

Students are always anxious to repeat the course and better their score.

## Slalom Under the Clock

Once students have had adequate experience in the slalom course, challenge them with a timed race. One tandem team performs at a time, positioning their boat behind the starting-line and awaiting your signal. Give each team a starting countdown and start a stopwatch at zero. Stop the watch when the team's stern crosses the finish-line. During the run, if a boat, paddle, or paddler touches a jug, a penalty is invoked. Add five seconds to the score for each jug touched. (Repetitive bumps on the same jug within the same maneuver count as only one penalty. This means that, when a canoe is attempting to go past or through the jugs, a boat cannot be penalized more than ten seconds . . . five seconds for each jug.)

## Advanced Slalom

There is no limit to the number of slalom courses you can create. By adding additional pairs of jugs, you can make a course more challenging. The increased difficulty comes not only from the advanced maneuvering required but also from the task of remembering the sequence of the course.

For example, add two more jugs—again two yards apart—this pair making a rectangle with the original pair. The distance from one pair of jugs to another should be two yards longer than the length of the longest canoe being used. The pair closest to the starting place is called the "home gate" and the other is the "far gate."

Here is a sample Advanced Course (refer to the diagrams):

"Start by running forward through the home gate. Stop. Spin in the direction of choice to run through the far gate in reverse.

"Once outside the rectangle, stop, side-slip right, and then run a figure 8 around pairs of jugs (not individual jugs) by cutting left between the two gates, bearing right to go around the home gate, then cutting between both pairs again and then bearing left.

"When the boat has returned to the place where it began the figure 8, race past both pairs (jugs on the left), stop, side-slip left, stop, run reverse through both gates, stop, side-slip left, stop, and race to the finish."

Again, add to the time any touches on the jugs as five-second penalties.

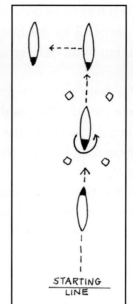
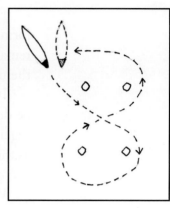
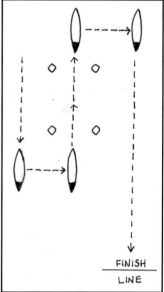

# The Power Cruise

The most abused stroke in canoeing is the forward stroke. To make your paddlers a cut above the average, help them perfect this most important of strokes. By using the proper form, the forward stroke becomes more efficient with less energy. It begins with the power position and is executed with nearly straight arms and a torqueing motion from the torso. If the stroke is performed well, a single stroke can move a boat an appreciable distance on still water, assuming there is no headwind.

## Exploding with the Forward Stroke

Position two anchored milk jugs four feet apart and eighty feet from shore. In the starting position a boat must have its stern touching shore, its bow pointing out in the general direction of the jugs.

Because starting a boat from a standstill is one of the most frustrating moments for beginners (this is when boats most quickly veer off course), it is smart to angle the boat away from the jugs at the starting line. (Angle the canoe 30 degrees away from the bow person's on-side.) That way the initial strokes will veer the boat toward the jugs and save the team the trouble of performing correction strokes after one or two forward strokes. You, the teacher, should be positioned out of the way exactly halfway between jugs and shore.

Each team may use only four <u>synchronized</u> forward strokes, and they must perform them all in the first 40 feet. To start them, call out "One!" Announce the remaining numbered, synchronized strokes as quickly as they are able to perform them.

If a team needs to draw or pry between forward strokes, such strokes must be done quickly. The paddlers should talk to one another and perform the strokes together. Allow them that brief time to align the boat and then resume your count as they make a forward stroke again. But *all four strokes must be completed in the first half of this trip.*

When they reach your position—even if they have not used all their allotted strokes—you should call out, "No more forward strokes!" If either or both perform a forward stroke after this announcement, they are disqualified from that run and must return to shore to get back in line to try again.

After four strokes, no more forward strokes can be used, but a team can employ all the draws and pries they care to use, as long as none of those correction strokes provides any forward thrust. The performing team attempts to cruise on the power of the completed four forward strokes and to glide between the jugs without touching them. It takes power (from the former four strokes), patience, and <u>efficient</u> draws and pries.

I've found no better exercise for appreciating the fine touch of alignment. If a team allows its boat to veer off course too much, the drastic correction strokes needed will kill their forward momentum.

### Proof of More Power

Once a team has accomplished the above feat, it's time for them to try it with three strokes. Then two. Then the "awesome" one-stroke challenge! It becomes a self-instructive exercise on getting the most out of a forward stroke.

**Notes to the teacher:** During the cruising part of this challenge, be sure that students do not reach forward for a draw stroke, which would convert it into an illegal, extra forward stroke. Likewise, watch for a pry stroke that pushes water toward the bow rather than to the side. Such a flawed pry will kill the boat's momentum.

### Canoe Tag

Use a soft foam ball, volleyball-size or smaller. The "it" team carries the ball, chases others, and attempts to throw the ball into another boat without it bouncing out. If the thrown ball remains in the target boat, a new team is "it."

If the ball is first thrown by the bow paddler, it must be thrown by the stern paddler on the second occasion of a throw. Team members always alternate throwing.

Any team being thrown at cannot swat at the ball or deflect it in any way. They must let the ball go wherever it is going to go. If it misses or bounces out, they make their getaway, and the same "it" team must retrieve the ball and try again for any team at all.

If the ball successfully stays inside the target boat, the new "it" team cannot throw back at the former "it" team until the new "it" has first thrown at another boat. (In other words: no "tag-backs.")

When any team has been "it" three times (this does not count the first team's time of being "it" when the game started), the game ends.

### The (Infamous) Banana Race

Lined up in a flank at one end of the pond, tandem teams await your "go" signal. They are simply going to race from one side of the pond to the other. (Or if the pond is not large, they can race around a buoy and back.) Along the course of the race, lots of action is packed into the event. Racing teams are listening for your whistle. (Unless you can perform a shrill, loud whistle with your mouth, a coach's whistle will be needed.) Each time you blow the whistle, they must stop, close their mouths, and lift their paddles out of the water to hear from you one of the following commands (all of which have been explained in detail during instructions):

1. **"Draw spin!"** Each boat must perform a 360-degree spin before continuing the race.
2. **"Pry spin!"** (Same as above, but spinning the other direction.)
3. **"Submarine!"** Each paddler must scoot his paddle beneath the boat from one side to another and pluck it out of the water. (Two important hints for your students before the race begins: First, stop the boat! Then send the paddle's T-grip first.)
4. **"Do-si-do!"** Paddlers must switch places inside the boat. (One paddler travels to mid-ship and crouches. Then, staying low, the partner carefully moves to the other's former place. Finally the one crouching takes her partner's former place.)
5. **"Whirling Dervishes!"** After stopping the boat, each paddler must stand up and bodily turn around in a 360-degree spin. (Safety hints: 1.) Stop the boat. 2.) Only one paddler should spin at a time.)
6. **"Switchblade!"** Paddlers must exchange paddles. Later, call it again to return paddles to owners.
7. **"Upsy-Daisy!"** All paddlers must invert paddles, holding the blade in the top hand and stroking the T-grip through the water.
8. **"Daisy-Downsy!"** Return those paddles to normal position.
9. **"Bobbing bottoms!"** This dreaded (or highly anticipated) command should be used only in favorable weather when a capsize would not be unwanted. Paddlers move to mid-ship, face one another, sit on opposite gunnels, hold tight to the center thwart and hang their bottoms over the edge. By carefully rocking the boat, both paddlers must wet their bottoms.

# *The Low Brace*

This defensive stroke can prevent a capsize. If both paddlers become adept at the low brace, the chances that their boat will turn over in whitewater are greatly reduced.

To perform the stroke place the paddle carefully on the surface of the water, perpendicular to the canoe, T-grip close to the boat, blade pointing away. Now let go of it. As the paddle floats on its own, reach with your off-side hand, palm-up, fingers underneath the T-grip, and take a firm grasp with your fingertips visible at the surface. Grasp the shaft with the on-side hand at the normal place, palm-down, thumb closer to the boat. Bend that arm so the elbow is bent upward directly above the shaft. **Safety note: This arm orientation protects the on-side shoulder from injury.** At this point you are necessarily leaning out over the paddle. With the T-grip still in the water, lean out enough to push down on the shaft and feel the pressure that can be applied to push your weight back into the boat.

We began this exercise by floating the paddle on top of the water. We did this to get you and your paddle in the proper position to initiate the low brace. Now that you understand how to begin the stroke, never let go of your paddle to position it. Simply lean out over the gunnel and assume this position to begin the low brace.

low brace

### Learning the Low Brace

Float your paddle out to the side as described above. Take the prescribed grip and gently lean out and push yourself back into the boat. Now repeat the exercise without floating the paddle. Simply slap it into place. Do this until you can lean out so much that it appears you will fall into the water before saving yourself with a well-timed slap of the paddle flat on the surface.

### Perfecting the Low Brace

When you have practiced this push enough to feel confident that the paddle will help you stay above water, it is time to modify the exercise so it works even better to keep your boat upright. This involves keeping your head low and thrusting your hip toward the paddle to *pull the boat underneath you* (rather than pushing yourself up on top of the boat).

For the sake of breathing, there is a natural instinct for people to raise their heads high whenever they suspect they are falling into water. This is one instinct that must be changed in righting a tilted boat. Keep your head low throughout the low brace and pull the boat underneath your torso.

As you improve your low brace, increase the lean and push and hip thrust until you can actually *fall* toward the paddle and slap the water with the blade to right yourself. Remember, to do this effectively, keep your head low until the boat is righted.

If a first low brace does not satisfy your needs, to perform a second you must first feather the blade out of the water to begin anew. This feather is directed forward and up, the forward edge of the blade surfacing. Just angle the blade with a twist of the T-grip and lift quickly.

## A Captain and His Blind Crew

This is an especially good exercise (actually eight exercises) for a pair that is challenged by the "teamwork" aspect of paddling; in particular, where one paddler keeps calling out the wrong stroke for the other to perform. This exercise helps each paddler to appreciate what his partner experiences at the other end of the boat.

Erect a long "fishing pole" that leans out high over the water from the shore. A bamboo cane works nicely. Jam the heavy end into a slanted post hole and support the leaning cane by a Y-shaped prop. Lash the pole into the crotch. From the high end of the cane suspend a string that hangs down to within two feet above the surface of the water. Secure a single grape or other small fruit in a small lasso and let the prize hang over the lake at a height that a paddler can reach with his mouth.

(Exercise 1) A canoe team should position their boat ten yards away. The bow paddler is blindfolded and the stern paddler (the captain for this first exercise) is not. Both team members use paddles. During a one-minute window, the captain gives all the commands and attempts to maneuver the boat by paddling and telling the blind crewman which strokes to do. The goal is for the blind crewman to successfully eat the grape without using his arms or hands.

(Exercise 2) Repeat the exercise with the paddlers changing the sides on which they paddle.

(Exercise 3) Repeat the exercise again with the paddlers in the same boat position but their roles reversed. Now the stern paddler is blindfolded. The bow paddler is captain. The stern paddler attempts to eat the grape.

(Exercise 4) Then repeat the previous exercise with changed paddling sides.

(Exercises 5, 6, 7, and 8) Next, have the paddlers switch positions in the boat. Repeat all of the above variations of the challenge.

Now it is time to face the inevitable: Sooner or later any paddler is sure to capsize in a river. It is better to practice for that reality in the lake than to wait for such a surprise in a cold, quick, river current. By gaining some experience with capsizing in calm waters, your students will likely handle a river capsize with better results.

### Man/Woman Overboard!

When the weather is reasonable for swimming, challenge a team to purposely capsize their boat. Because they are wearing flotation devices, they will have no trouble remaining buoyant. Teach them to avoid being trapped under the canoe but to stay close to their boat to facilitate their lake rescue. They must hold on to their paddles, a habit that will serve them well on the river.

Other boats in the water can be positioned nearby to alleviate any feelings of panic in the two "swimmers."

Challenge the team in the water to swim their boat to shore. This can best be accomplished by both gripping the same end of the canoe (using the hand that is holding a paddle) and stroking together with the free arm. And so the teamwork builds.

If the swimmers cannot move their boat to shore, other canoe teams can give assistance like tugboats in a harbor.

### Righting the Boat on Shore

When the canoe is close enough to shore that the swimmers can stand, ask them to position the canoe perpendicular to the shoreline, they themselves at mid-ship on opposite sides of the boat. If the canoe is right-side-up, position it upside-down. Lift and walk the canoe onto land until at least half the boat is out of the water. Then both team members walk back into the water to the submerged end of the canoe, lift that end high to drain the boat, and finally carefully flip it upright.

## Lake Rescue

For an adventure in righting a boat on the lake, instruct two canoe teams to approach the capsized canoe and its two swimmers. Rescue boat #1 should position itself perpendicular to and touching its mid-ship to one end of the capsized canoe. Rescue boat #2 should park parallel to #1 (on #1's free side) and lock gunnels together by #2's paddlers clasping both gunnels with all four hands. This will provide stability for the rescuers in boat #1.

The two swimmers should turn their swamped canoe upside down, move toward the end of their boat farthest from the rescuers, and push that end deeper into the water to help elevate the end nearer the rescuers.

Stabilized by the paddlers in boat #2, the boat #1 rescuers should lean over their gunnel to lift the end of the capsized boat over that gunnel. Together they must slide this boat over both rescue boats, being sure to keep this canoe upside down and perpendicular to the two upright boats. When the rescued canoe is more than halfway out of the water, the paddlers in boat #2 can help with the sliding.

When the rescued canoe is completely out of the water and drained, the four paddlers of both rescue boats can carefully flip the boat upright and slide it back into the water. The paddlers of rescue boat #1 now position the emptied boat parallel to theirs and lock gunnels to stabilize it. Boat #2's paddlers lock gunnels with boat #1. At this point, all three boats are connected in a flank.

Now the swimmers can climb over the gunnel on the free side of the rescued boat. If a student is physically unable to do this, a third rescue boat must enter the process. One strong paddler from that boat must enter the rescued boat and help the water-treading student into his boat by pulling on the lower border of his life jacket.

*"I have been living here all my life," said the river fish to the muskrat. "My world is always in motion. But when I drift with the current, it seems to be your world that is in motion. Which way is it?"*

—from a long-forgotten campfire story

## CHAPTER 18

# Within the Whisper of the River—
# Lessons in the Sand and in the Shallows

A river never stops moving. That's the most challenging principle of river canoeing that any beginner must accept. All thoughts of maneuvering and all planning of routes must include the conveyor-belt-syndrome: that things are not going to slow

down or stop, no matter how much you might want them to. A paddler must be weaned into that reality.

For an instructor this poses a new problem. While gathering your class around you on the lake was relatively easy, students can get strung out all along the river. For this reason, you'll want to start out on a slow river that does not feel "pushy." There should be many calm sections and only a smattering of rapids or shoals. You'll want sections with boulders, small standing waves, well-defined eddies, and rapids that demand more than a straight line for passage. Choose a river known for its beauty. A large part of this education is about appreciating the river and seeing the way a river should look.

I always paddle solo with my river classes. This allows me quick mobility in getting to whatever team needs help at any given moment. I recommend taking along one other strong, canoe-savvy adult (either solo or as part of a tandem team with the weakest student) and no more than six student boats.

Because the river is a perpetually moving medium, it is another world. Instead of us holding sway over our immediate surroundings, the river has us; and this is what presents an inimitable arena for accountability in education—whether we are considering environmental education or not. Accountability in a canoeing experience is inevitable.

As a teacher and expedition leader for a fleet of river students, your first priority is safety.

---

**Here are some points of safety to consider:**
1. Two adult members of your party (of six student boats) must be accomplished paddlers who can quickly get to any team needing assistance.
2. Carry first-aid gear, dry matches, a throw-rope, and a few wool sweaters.
3. Know the geographic area where you will be paddling, so that if an emergency arises you can, if necessary, make your way overland for help.
4. Carry extra paddles in case one breaks in use or is lost.
5. Plan your trips for friendly weather.

---

Your second priority is to equip your students with the skills necessary to navigate the complexities of a river. Never expose your group to a level of difficulty for which they are not prepared.

---

**Your primary jobs in teaching are:**
1. Help the students develop a skill level in their teamwork that enables them to be autonomous—captains of their own ship—so they can make a sound plan for negotiating a certain rapid and then execute that plan.
2. Foresee what could go wrong. Identify where a mishap might likely occur; place a rescuer in that vicinity so he can provide immediate physical help should the need arise.

3. Help the students to recognize dangers on the river and to know how to avoid them and extricate themselves from them.
4. Engender respect for the river and its surrounding land.

On the river a student must learn <u>to make things happen</u>. He has to think, make quick decisions, and carry them out without delay. Teamwork between partners is a must.

Many times through the years I have seen the partners of a tandem canoe argue and blame and fume and sulk as they encounter one "disaster" after another. They capsize, get wet and chilled, get angrier, and climb back into their boat only to repeat the scenario. They yell at each other. They yell at the river. They verbally fight a battle that cannot be won with words and neglect. The river can't hear them. The river can't change its nature. Only the students can change.

Eventually, the consequences of such lack of harmony overrides the students' will to be antagonistic toward one another. They are forced to work together, and so they do. It never fails. By the second or third river trip experience, such problem-teams always come around and perform well. Their success at negotiating rocks and eddies and rapids brings laughter and feelings of success. It is a most gratifying process to witness. The boost to self-esteem inherent in successful paddling is worth all the teacher's efforts of providing the canoeing venue.

Returning to the same stretch of river for a canoe trip is always a good idea. This gives the students the advantage of familiarity and a better way to gauge their skills. If they were unable to make a specific maneuver in a specific rapid on a previous visit, they now have another chance at success. Plus, they have had time to think about it, ask questions, make a better plan, and correct their methods.

There is always a degree of nervousness about entering the unknown. By repeating a river, the unknown factor is removed, making the day more fun. And that is exactly what we want students to carry away from their early days on the river. If they remember the fun, they will come back to Nature. If they come back, they will learn and grow with Nature, see it through matured eyes, and nurture their own unique relationship with the natural world. In so doing, they will have reason to treat the river with respect, to speak on its behalf, to become stewards.

## *A New Instinct*

The southeastern United States is blessed with many fine rivers, and so there is a variety of river difficulties from which to choose for students. I invariably elect to use a mild mountain stream for a beginner experience. But such a river must have enough eddies and rapids to practice everything the students will need on more difficult rivers. So often, people prefer to leap forward into higher difficulty just for the thrill of the ride. In this way they miss the opportunity for grace and the refinement of skills.

The "been-there-done-that" mentality of the fast ride misses the most valuable lessons that a river has to offer. These more difficult rivers certainly have their place in the evolution of a paddler's skills, but—in my opinion—these experiences should come much later.

Moving water presents profound, new challenges to the lake-trained paddler. It takes time to adjust to the new demands; namely, making decisions and executing moves early enough not to be swept into unexpected situations. The river is a conveyor belt that does not suffer indecision. Expect a period of adjustment as the students search for a new sense of timing on moving water.

At the river, before we get into canoes, my students gather around a picnic table, whose tabletop I use as a model for the river itself. The cracks between the table's boards serve as vectors of current. On those boards I can situate rocks and sticks to serve as boulders and logs.

More often, wherever I am teaching a canoeing class, picnic tables are not handy. In that case, for my model river I use a sandy beach near the water and draw vectors of current into the sand with a stick. This is a common practice among paddlers, especially at rapids where they scout and talk about the options available for a successful run. The visual model is always worthwhile, because with beginners there are too many ways to miscommunicate with words alone.

Making a model of the river in sand on the very morning of embarking on that first whitewater trip turns out to be more effective than presenting these river principles in any other place or time.

Students are feeling the excitement and apprehensions of the trip because it is at hand. Last-minute lessons take on new importance and relevance to them.

Arrange "boulders" (rocks), upright trees (a branched stick jammed into the ground), and a downed tree or strainer (a branched stick laid down). Use the model canoe you made in Chapter 14 to demonstrate the maneuvers that follow in this chapter.

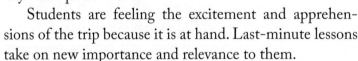

---

**Lean Downstream! The First Law of Whitewater Paddling**
Whenever in doubt . . . or whenever your boat has stopped in the current due to an obstruction or a dynamic of the water . . . lean downstream! Lean enough so the boat tilts downstream.

## Modeling the River

Gather your students around a cleared space on a sandy beach and draw lines (or build walls) to define the riverbanks. Center a heavy stone between banks to serve as a "boulder" in mid-current. Draw an arrow to define the downstream direction of your model river. Demonstrate the First Law of Whitewater Paddling (see above) by placing the model canoe upstream moving toward the boulder.

Share this tenet with your wards: "You never want to run into an obstacle with your boat turned sideways."

As you drift the boat toward the boulder, turn it sideways. When the canoe is in contact with the rock and stalled, place your hand flat on the sand with your fingertips touching the upstream side of the canoe.

" . . . And here's why," you explain. "My hand represents the current."

Run your hand beneath the canoe to demonstrate how the current will try to capsize the boat, tilting it upstream. (Slip your fingertips under the stationary boat and keep pushing toward the rock, letting the traction of the tops of your fingers and knuckles roll the boat until it capsizes.)

## Laying Down the Law

Take along with you to the river two thumbtacks. Press one partway into the curve of the bow and the other into the curve of the stern of your model boat, positioning each just slightly above mid-curve. Attach a six-inch-long string to each tack.

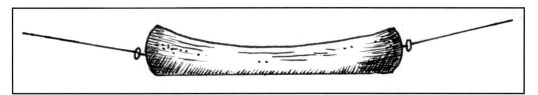

Ask each student, one at a time, to step out into a shallow but swift current. As she faces upstream and holds the boat by the two short strings, ask her to lower the model slowly into the water until it touches the surface. Then she should lower her hands until the strings are horizontal. Watch the current grab the boat enough to roll it upstream and capsize.

# Understanding the First Law of Whitewater

The natural instinct of most people—as gleaned from their experiences on land—is to lean away from the object they are about to crash into. This instinct must be purged from the beginner canoeist.

Actually, the physics for previous land experience and this new water concept is the same. When I was a boy, whenever I found a large cardboard box left at someone's curb, my buddies and I confiscated it, flattened it into a sled, and hauled it off to a big grassy hill for a swift ride, carrying as many bodies as we could fit onto it.

As we zoomed down the hill, all of us naturally leaned back, away from the fast approaching possibilities of disaster. Should we see an unexpected obstacle in our path—a grass-less patch of dirt and gravel, a boulder, a tree stump—our good instincts instructed us to lean away from the pending collision. After all, anyone leaning forward would be the first to be catapulted from the sled when it came to a sudden stop or slow-down.

Consider a bird's-eye view of my friends and me zooming down the hill. You are the bird sailing at a fixed height above us on our descent as you carry in your talons a video camera pointed straight down at us. You move exactly at our speed. When this footage is played back on a screen, the lesson would become clear. We, the intrepid cardboard crew, appear stationary on the screen while the grass "flows" beneath us to our rear. The "moving" grass is the river. We were, correctly, leaning downstream.

## *The Correct Lean on Moving Water*

In the last exercise we used strings to keep the boat from moving with the current. If a rock or log stops a sideways canoe, the same principle applies. The boat flips upstream.

### Stuck Between a Rock and a Current

On your dry model of a river in the sand, allow your model canoe to "drift" toward the rock (simulating a boulder). But this time at the point of impact tilt the boat decidedly toward the boulder. This shows how the current has a much harder time upsetting the boat.

By maintaining such a lean into the rock, a team of paddlers can remain kneeling in the boat, prod the canoe around the boulder using their hands on the rock, and emerge safely from a potentially dangerous situation.

## *Whitewater Dangers*

Although your beginning river should in no way blatantly offer river phenomena that might breed disasters—such as rapids with infamous reputations for spilling boats—the first trip down the river is the time to introduce your students to the causes of whitewater accidents. This is one of the key reasons for using the dry model on land—to introduce dangers without actually experiencing them. But we can also use shallow places in the river itself to demonstrate dangerous canoeing scenarios on a smaller scale.

### The Strainer

Hold a multi-branched tree limb laid horizontally in the current, with water scouring through the "colander" of branches. Release the model canoe upstream and let it drift into the strainer. Ask your students to imagine themselves inside the canoe.

The best solution to the danger of a strainer is prevention. Keep your class away from strainers. Wherever such a fallen tree exists, shepherd your class to the far side of the river, where there is no chance of contact or entrapment.

There is no firm, tried and true escape plan for someone caught in a strainer, other than keeping the head above water at all cost, no matter what that takes. Capsized paddlers have been known to wash under and safely away from a strainer, but who is to say how complicated a strainer might be below the surface? The branching of a strainer can be difficult to negotiate by the stranded paddler or by a rescuer. But the unfortunate paddler must try to climb to keep his head above the water. It might be necessary to discard a lifejacket to crawl through the branching.

A rope thrown from upstream to such a trapped paddler is not a perfect solution, because the stranded person must be pulled upstream, which often causes the swimmer to bob under at times. All the current pushing on this person might be too much, causing him to lose his grip. Tying the rope around the paddler carries risk, too. I don't recommend it.

Though I never had a team capsize in the vicinity of a strainer, I did have a plan for such a scenario: To climb out on the strainer and help a paddler(s) work his way through the limbs to get to the downstream side. From there, rescue by rope could easily be performed by the other adult from shore. (You'll read about throw-rope rescues later.)

## *Being Proactive in a Strainer*

The best advice regarding strainers is, of course, to avoid them. Know your river. Scout ahead for changes in the banks and collapsed trees. Attentiveness to this can keep you from harm's way.

But . . . if caught in a strainer, a team should keep the boat from capsizing by leaning into the tree, holding onto branches by hand. Staying afloat is all-important. If the canoeists cannot work their boat around the obstruction (with complicated branching, this might be impossible), the paddlers will need to climb higher into the branches to be aided by adult rescuers who approach from the downstream side of the tree and help them climb to the safer side of the strainer.

### The Hydraulic

Find a small hydraulic or souse hole (typically referred to as a "hole") in the river, one large enough to stop a model boat that is turned sideways in the current. Demonstrate how the hole can hold a boat in place for an unpredictable length of time.

## *Solutions*

Just like with a strainer, there is no single statement that can guarantee anyone a safe escape from a hole. But there are general suggestions that might be of value.

An upright canoe caught sideways in a substantial hole has only two exits: paddlers must keep the boat tilted downstream as they stroke toward one of the two sides of the hole. If they find themselves capsized, bodily tumbling in a hydraulic that won't let them go, they may have to swim down to find the escaping current. (This would require removing the personal flotation device.)

Like with the strainer, the best advice for this predicament is to avoid it entirely. Do not put a class on a river that contains a strainer or a large hole unless the obstacle is easily avoided.

## Capsizing and Pinning

If a broached canoe capsizes just above a rock and then has its open side exposed to the current, depending upon how swift the current is, the pressure inside the canoe can be measured in tons! Such a pinned canoe can flatten and wrap around the rock. If paddlers are inside the boat, there is a possibility of being trapped as the hull and thwarts (crossbars from gunnel to gunnel) press together. All of this could have been avoided by leaning downstream onto the rock to prevent the boat from capsizing.

Another dangerous obstacle in current is most often encountered during a flood, when water rises over the banks to wash through the forested floodplain. (A teacher should never put a class on a flood-swollen stream.) A standing tree offers an immovable, narrow point around which a boat can wrap. In this case, the fulcrum point (the tree trunk) at which the boat bends is so narrow that the bending can be severe. There is virtually no "cushion" of water pillowing off the tree, as it can with a broad boulder. Relatively speaking, the tree is like a knife-edge, and, though a dull one, it is unrelenting at remaining in place.

## The Dangers That Everyone Needs to Understand About a Hydraulic or Hole

As water plummets over stone to create a waterfall—no matter how high or low—the weight of that falling water depresses the pool of water below—thus the name: "hole." Water from the downstream pool rushes back by gravity to try to fill the depression. In this case, when the volume of falling water is heavy, the adage about water finding its level is not true, for a hole remains depressed. The combination of the falling water (from upstream) and the backward-traveling water (from downstream) creates a powerful dynamic. A hole sucks objects down much like the action of rollers on an old-fashioned, crank clothes wringer. If the object is very buoyant, it bounces and lurches in the hole, trapped there by its own buoyancy.

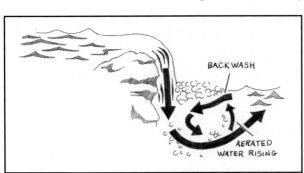

At a waterfall-rapid like this, the main current goes deep, following the path of the plunging water. A canoeist who capsizes in a perfectly formed hole might be in a very precarious situation. He can't swim out downstream because of the upward slope and the backwash current that he faces at the surface. He sometimes can't swim out the sides because those are also uphill climbs from the deepest depression of the hole. Of course, swimming like a trout up the falls is out of the question. On the surface, there appears to be no escape—unless, that is, a safety rope is thrown to him from the shore. In that case, the swimmer can best be pulled out laterally at one side of the hole.

Often the white froth in a hole is so aerated that the buoyancy factor is poor at the surface. For one caught in such a hole, this makes breathing difficult. Such a quandary has one last option: to swim downward with the main current of the plunging water from the waterfall. To accomplish this a capsized paddler would have to abandon his lifejacket and dive deep in order to resurface well downstream of the hole.

Holes and rapids are fickle entities. They pulse and explode and ebb in ways that are difficult to predict. Sometimes a trapped swimmer gets spit out by some erratic spasm of the water. Each time I have witnessed such a tense scene, the swimmer in a hole did a lot of bobbing and recycling and sputtering for breath before getting washed out. "Swimming in a hole" is almost always a bad experience. I have known it to affect survivors in profound ways. Holes have also drowned people.

If a boat hits a small- to medium-sized hole straight-on, there is a good chance the canoe can knife its way through or across it. But if the hole is large enough or if the drop is substantial, even hitting the hole head-on cannot guarantee a successful exit from the hydraulic. The buoyancy in the froth can be so reduced that the bow could plunge under and the boat fill with water immediately. Or the slope leading out of the hole downstream may be too much to overcome. In this latter case, even a canoe running a true line could be pulled backward into the hole.

Even if a canoe makes a dry run, when it gets pulled back into a large enough hole, the falling water from above and behind fills the canoe. Then the two forces of current—from upstream and from downstream—trap the canoe in place where it can tumble violently.

Running over a hydraulic in perfect alignment looks easy.

If the hole is small enough, a skilled, still-upright canoeist can "surf" the hole by leaning the boat downstream and bracing his paddle downstream like an outrigger. He can keep the canoe afloat if the falling water (from upstream) strikes that side of the boat that is tilted up. This pounding keeps the boat pushed away from the waterfall. There is a stability that can be achieved in this situation. It all depends upon the finesse of leaning the boat at the proper angle—an angle that changes from one hole to another.

To get out of a hole intact and upright, canoeists usually succeed by stroking aggressively to slip out of one side of the hole to let the nearby current (just outside the hole) take them downstream. But such a self-rescue is not reasonable for a youth or beginner.

A hole can be a lonely place to be. A paddler might be stuck in one, while—twenty feet away—people watch from the banks. If they don't have a safety rope, they might as well be in another time zone. Your beginners will not be dealing with such dangers, but they will be dealing with lesser degrees of the same physics.

*From the edge of the water I step and glide myself free . . . gone like a leaf as I weave through the stream.*

—from the song *Amicalola* by M. Warren

# CHAPTER 19

# On the River's Back— The Never-Ending Current

## *River Trip Agenda*

Choose your river journey's beginning place (the "put-in") carefully. You don't want a swift current to take your students away immediately. You'll want to gather with your class in their boats in a gentle section of river before the group actually encounters any challenges of note.

## *Embarking*

Tandem teams can enter their canoes by the lake-system: one paddler holding the boat parallel to the bank while the other steps in and kneels. With current added to the equation, always orient the canoe's bow pointed upstream. Be sure that the bow cannot swing away from the bank before both paddlers are situated. If the bow paddler enters first—and this is recommended—she must have a reliable handhold on land (a root, a tree branch, a rock) to use as her partner steps into the canoe behind her.

For that first half-mile, let your students simply try out their lake-learned skills in this new world of unrelenting current. A new sense of timing must sink into them—a timing not accessible on the lake.

All paddlers should begin the journey in the kneeling position on kneepads. Later in the day, when many of the lessons have sunk in, they may sit in the seats during the quiet stretches, but remind them to kneel during all sections of the river that require definitive action on their part.

### Straight Line Paddling in Current

As leader, get out in front of your class and paddle your boat downstream in reverse so you can watch your students paddle forward. Instruct them to maintain straight courses with the current, never letting their boats veer more than a few degrees to either side.

### Follow the Leader

Have your class form a single file line of canoes as you continue downstream. Maintain a three-boat-length space between canoes. As the leader, you should zigzag down the river in front—beginning with easy zigs and zags—choosing targets (that stand out visually) to aim for with each leg of the zigzag. Touch that target (say, a boulder) with your paddle and blow a whistle, signaling those behind you that you have identified an object that they too must touch.

The target might be a low-hanging tree branch, a log in the water, a rock, a vine, etc. The boat behind you must duplicate your route. One of the paddlers in that boat must also touch the target and yell a signal to the next boat behind them, making sure the team following understands what the target is. The third boat follows them and does the same. Meanwhile, continue to signal new targets (allow long spaces between the targets) with your whistle.

Inevitably, a team will get their boat stuck at a target and a traffic jam follows. Expect this. Unravel the knot and start anew.

When you can see that your students are acclimating to the nonstop nature of the river, teach them their first technique for stopping in current: hovering.

## *Hovering*

To hover a canoe is to keep the boat in the current without drifting downstream or powering upstream. The hover can be performed pointed down- or upstream, but facing upstream is much easier. Such a maneuver requires teamwork by the paddlers to maintain the upstream angle (by partial draw and pry spins) and to counter the force of the current with forward strokes. Hovering is one technique for stopping to scout downstream (over a shoulder) and one of the first feats to be accomplished after a class gathers on the river.

## Hovering on the River

After all have practiced paddling downstream in a straight line for a time, choose a rock-free section of river where teams can spread out and spin 180 degrees to point upstream. Learn to match the power of forward strokes with the power of the current in order to remain in place relative to the shoreline. Each team should pick out a marker on one bank and attempt to remain beside it.

Because canoes do not naturally travel in a straight line, expect the need for corrections while hovering. When the boat begins to veer, react immediately with a measured, partial spin to counter the veer. Corrections are needed almost constantly, but hovering can be easy if a team reacts to a deviation early rather than late.

The most common mistake in hovering is to use a sloppy pry stroke that pushes water toward the bow. Such a flaw forces the boat downstream. In such a case, paddle upstream to regain the original marker, continue hovering, and perfect that pry.

# *The Ferry*

Ferrying is a technique for moving laterally from one side of the river to the other without losing "ground." It comes in handy for safety. Imagine spotting a danger downstream, spinning 180 degrees to hover, and then deciding to get safely to shore. A ferry can transport you laterally without getting you closer to the danger downstream. It can carry you to a feasible place to get out and begin a portage.

You can demonstrate the ferry in the sand with your model boat (see *Ferrying* on page 173), but the lesson is best seen on the water.

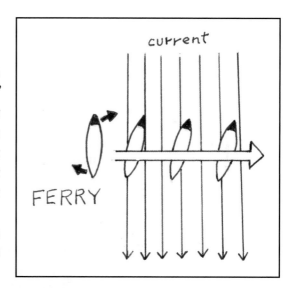

## Ferrying on the River

To ferry in the current, first spin your boat 180 degrees to face upstream. Angle the bow toward the direction you desire to ferry. This angle varies according to current speed. In very fast current, the angle is slight, say 5 to 15 degrees. In slow water, the angle is closer to 45 degrees. Keeping the boat so angled, paddle forward as you travel laterally in a path perpendicular to the current. Between forward strokes, frequent small corrections are necessary to maintain the proper angle. These correction strokes should be performed simultaneously by both paddlers, a teamwork requiring communication. In order to prevent downstream drift while ferrying, make your forward strokes match the current's force, and, above all, do not allow any phase of the pry stroke to resemble a reverse stroke.

### Ferrying from an Eddy

Choose a large eddy on one side of the river where all the boats can gather for a lesson. One boat at a time, ask a team to leave the eddy, ferry to the other side of the river (or some other eddy), and return by ferrying.

Ferrying from an eddy is trickier than ferrying from a hover out in current. The moment of breaking over the eddy line (from eddy to current) is a critical one. The paddlers need to charge out of the eddy aggressively and counter the current's immediate attempt to turn the boat downstream. The angle of entry from eddy to current is also crucial. If a boat spins right away as it leaves the eddy, the exit angle should be lessened on the next attempt so the boat is pointed more upstream. The faster the current, the less the angle of entry.

### Feeling the Hydraulic

In a safe place where you, the teacher, can stand in the water with a paddling team inside their canoe, position their boat sideways in a small hole. This will allow them to feel the tug of the water as it tries to roll the boat upstream. Ask them to tilt the canoe downstream by leaning their bodies and boat in that direction. This lean keeps them afloat. This experience is a good teaching tool to inculcate into students two important principles: lean downstream whenever a boat is stopped in current, and always enter a hydraulic with the boat aligned straight downstream.

# Boat Alignment

There is one simple rule about aligning a canoe in a river: Unless performing a specific maneuver—like ferrying, catching an eddy, peeling out, etc.—the safest position for a boat is to be aligned parallel with the current. In fact, it would be better to ram a rock head-on in a canoe rather than to hit it broadside.

An attentive tandem team aligns the boat with the current by performing a draw spin.

## *Eddy*

When a river current encounters an immovable object (like a boulder, bridge abutment, or a point of land jutting from the stream bank) and parts around it on one or both sides, a flow of backward-moving water forms on the down-stream side of the obstruction. This area of water moving backward is called an "eddy." The physics of its inception is described on pages 168 to 169.

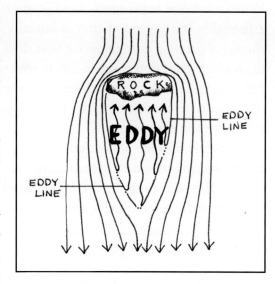

Seen from a bird's-eye view, an eddy usually shows a clearly defined border or "eddy lines" etched into the surface of the water. If an eddy is formed by a projection of land from one bank, there is a single eddy line that arcs from the point of land back toward the riverbank some distance downstream. If the eddy is large, this eddy line often fades and disappears altogether. It is this type of eddy on one side of the river that provides more room and a better practice arena for students learning to turn into an eddy.

## *The Eddy Turn*

On the river the need for a place to pull over and stop is more than a rest time. It can be a place from which to scout whatever whitewater challenge is waiting down-stream. An eddy provides such a refuge and can save a canoeist from accidentally washing into a dangerous situation. "**Catching an eddy**" (as the vernacular goes) is also a significant part of the fun of canoeing. Executed correctly, it is a most satisfy-ing piece of the dance on water and often the safest way to make one's way down a rapid-infested section of river. Continuous use of eddies is called "**eddy-hopping.**"

### A First Look at an Eddy Turn

Draw a wide riverbed in the sand and allow a six-inch jut of land to project into the current from one side. Draw vector lines in the sand to demonstrate how water is pushed away from the projection to form an eddy. Draw the eddy large enough so your model boat will fit inside it.

From well upstream of the eddy and from two boat-lengths away laterally, scoot your model boat downstream over the sand as shown in the illustration below. Though this scale model performance on sand cannot include the influence of cur-rent, it will give your students a simple preview of a maneuver they will be perform-ing countless times in their river training.

## *Fine Points of the Eddy Turn*

When a tandem team spots an eddy to catch, they must first position their boat at a favorable starting point that is laterally distant from the eddy; that is, the boat should begin on a current vector that does not run close to the eddy. This gives the team ample time and space to create ***cross-current momentum***, which will allow the canoe to penetrate the eddy line and enter the eddy. During the establishment of this important momentum, the boat's approach to the eddy takes a diagonal route relative to the current.

A classic mistake of beginners is getting too close to the eddy at the start. It's a common error, because it would seem to a novice that starting on a vector that runs close to the eddy might be helpful in reaching the eddy. But without <u>cross-current</u> momentum, a canoe usually does not succeed in entering the eddy.

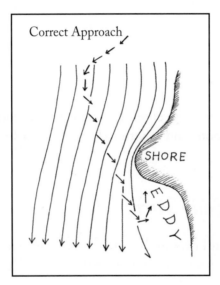
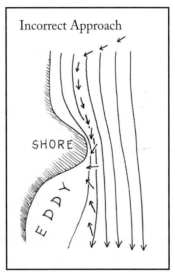

## *A Flawed Eddy Turn Scenario: Too Close to the Eddy*

Imagine a hundred Ping-Pong balls spaced one foot apart across the surface of a real river—all released at the same moment. The paths they travel as they are carried by the current serve as visual lines that represent the vectors of current force. When water parts around both sides of a boulder, the deflected Ping-Pong balls come back together gradually some distance downstream of the boulder. The paths of these balls roughly form a long isosceles triangle or teardrop shape as they reconvene below the rock. Inside the triangle is the eddy. (See the illustration on the previous page.)

If a canoe *approaches* the eddy turn maneuver (well upstream of the eddy) on one of the lines (Ping-Pong balls) that eventually runs very near the rock, that boat is starting off too close to the eddy. Such a placement will force the boat to remain pointed straight downstream on the approach, because turning the boat to aim toward the rock/eddy would cause the bow to hit the rock as the boat drifts downstream. Even if the bow barely misses the rock, there may not be adequate time to turn the boat and pick up diagonal speed to leave the main current and enter the eddy.

A canoe will not automatically enter an eddy simply because it is nearby and pointed in that direction. The paddlers must create the force that propels the boat into the eddy. If a team does not establish cross-current momentum, they may get their bow into the eddy at the last moment, but the canoe then merely responds to the two opposing currents by spinning 180 degrees while still mostly in the main current. The result is both disconcerting and possibly dangerous, for the boat continues backward downstream. If a dangerous situation awaits there, the paddlers will drift into it blindly.

## The Perfect Approach to an Eddy Turn

Ironically, your best chance at a successful eddy turn involves getting lateral distance *away from the eddy* before you begin your approach. This calls for planning ahead.

1. Locate and name out loud the eddy you wish to catch. Both team members need to be focused on the same mission.
2. While still well upstream of the eddy, position your boat on a current vector-line that eventually runs about three to ten yards from the eddy. (In very fast current, use the lower number; in a lazy river use the higher.)
3. In slow to moderate current, angle the canoe 45 degrees to the current by a partial draw or pry spin that points the canoe in the general direction of the rock/eddy.
4. When the timing is deemed appropriate, begin the **sprint** to establish a new momentum diagonally across the current. In slow current, the sprint can begin only about five to eight yards upstream of the rock. In faster current, the sprint must be initiated much earlier. This distance varies with every current speed.
5. Sprint aggressively with strong forward strokes. For maximum effect, synchronize these strokes. This timing is the job of the stern paddler.
6. While sprinting, maintain that 45-degree angle. This is the job of both paddlers, who must constantly make correction strokes between forward strokes. As a team gets more experienced, the stern paddler can take over more of the directional work while the bow paddler concentrates on creating forward momentum.

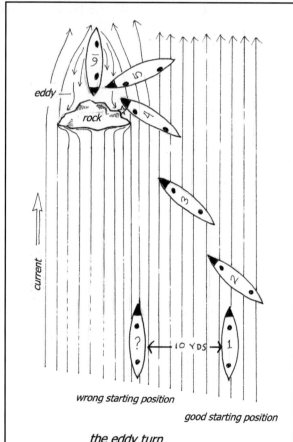

*wrong starting position*

*good starting position*

**the eddy turn**
1 Starting position away from rock
2 Approach angle; note bow pointing upstream of rock
2, 3, 4 Sprint
4 Eddy turn; star denotes placement of bow paddle
5 Turning
6 Turned; at rest

7. Adjust speed as needed. If you see that you are going to hit the rock, slow down the sprint. If you see that you are going to hit the eddy too low, speed up.

8. Just before the boat reaches the eddy, the stern paddler can help initiate the turn by a quick draw or pry, whichever is appropriate.

9. When the bow paddler can reach into the eddy over the eddy line with her paddle blade, she performs the turning stroke that serves as the "hinge" around which the canoe swings like a door.

10. At this same moment, both paddlers should lean toward the rock to tilt the boat. This lean is upstream relative to the river, but it is downstream relative to the eddy current, and this is what makes that tilt stabile.

## The Eddy Turning Strokes

The turning stroke planted into the eddy by the bow paddler is a specialized static stroke; that is, unlike all the other strokes covered up to this point, it is held in place without actually moving the paddle relative to the boat. It does require strength to hold the blade in place, for all the weight of the canoe swings around the bow paddle. The stern paddler simply leans into the turn with his paddle ready for a defensive low brace or a proactive forward stroke—whichever may be needed. The bow paddler holds the turning stroke until the boat points upstream at the boulder. Once in the eddy, a forward stroke by both paddlers will ensure that the boat stays in the eddy without drifting downstream.

The turning stroke requires that the bow paddler set the blade at a specific angle in the water by rotating the shaft with both hands. It seems easy enough, but the paddler must rotate the shaft and blade in a direction that does not feel natural to a beginner. This rotation must be practiced until it becomes a rote response. If the paddle is rotated in the wrong direction, such a turning stroke simply does not work.

Have your students—while standing on land—practice the stroke first on the side to which they are assigned to paddle for that day.

### The On-Side Eddy Turn Stroke

Gather those who will paddle in the bow for a given day's lesson. Ask the stern paddlers to spectate, for they need to know what to expect of their partners. (Furthermore, in the best of canoe classes, stern paddlers will also learn to be bow paddlers, and vice versa.) This exercise will teach the eddy turn stroke (which is used by bow paddlers only) both for righties and lefties. Righties will first address an eddy turn to the right; lefties will address an eddy turn to the left. In other words, both are learning their *on-side eddy turn stroke.*

Space your students on land in a flank, standing shoulder to shoulder but with three feet between neighbors. Ask them to go through the motions of a forward stroke, as if they are kneeling in a canoe. Each student should note which side of the blade actually pushes water. (It does not matter which physical side of the blade is used. Paddles work just fine no matter which way the blade faces are oriented, but each student must define both sides of the blade *as he is holding it at the moment.)* No matter how the paddle is held, the side of a blade that pushes water toward the stern during a forward stroke is always considered the "**power side.**" The other is called the "**reverse side**" and is used primarily to push water in pries, reverse strokes, and low braces.

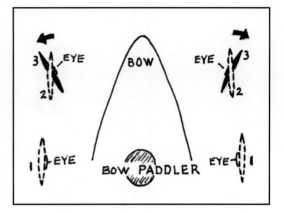

As an ideal teaching prop for this lesson, use a marker or paint to draw an eyeball on the power side of the blade. This drawing now defines the power side and, therefore, how the paddle must be held. (If using a marker is not feasible, look for a brand name, a scratch, or some other mark on the blade to serve as a label for the power side.)

Now instruct all paddlers to simulate the <u>beginning of a draw stroke</u> by reaching out with both arms to the on-side. In this position the *power side* of the blade (the eyeball) should be facing each paddler. With the students poised to begin the draw stroke, ask them to reposition the blade bow-ward by feathering one to two feet (depending on how tall a student is). The blade should not approach the tip end (front) of the bow but instead move forward parallel to the boat.

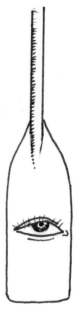

Now the eyeball appears to "look at" the boat just behind the curve of the bow. Rotate the shaft (turning the T-grip with the top hand and twisting the shaft with the bottom hand) just a few degrees to allow the eyeball a direct look at the bow's curve.

---

### On-Side Right and Wrong

If done correctly, this slight rotation causes the thumb of the top hand to point back toward the paddler's face (if that thumb were opened up from its grip). The bottom hand tries to bend backward at the wrist, as if the big knuckles are trying to get closer to the back of the wrist.

If done incorrectly—rotated to make the eyeball look downstream and then turn away from the bow—the top-hand thumb will point forward toward the bow, and the lower wrist would bend as if the fingertips are trying to touch the inside of the wrist. Though it may appear that the paddle is in the same position as the correct version of this stroke, the pressure applied by the arms is very different. This incorrect version acts like a reverse stroke, keeping the boat out of the eddy.

---

To perform the turning stroke effectively, both arms should be extended, almost straight. Tense the arms in this turning position. In the river, during an actual eddy turn, the paddle should be inserted into the water already positioned in this turning angle and remain static throughout the turn, the blade maintaining the same distance from the boat.

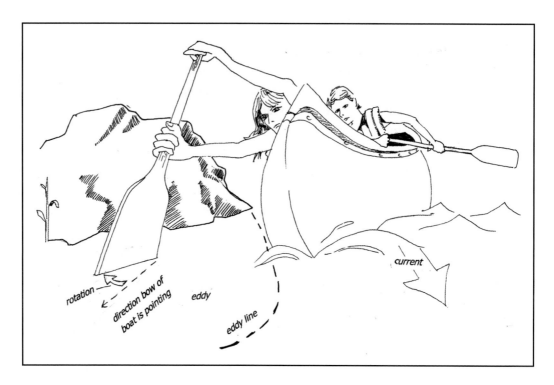

Instruct each student to kneel in a canoe on land and demonstrate this eddy turn stroke on the on-side. If a student finds the position confusing, take his hands and help him perform the proper rotation of the shaft.

### The Off-Side Eddy Turning Stroke

This is the stroke that is most vexing to beginners. It is easy to get it wrong in the excitement of whitewater action, because, again, the rotation of the shaft feels unnatural.

With your bow paddlers again standing in a flank, ask them to pose in the power position as though ready for a forward stroke, the eyeball showing on the power side and facing the stern. Now instruct them to lift their paddles high (as if out of the water and over their bows) from their on-side and carry it to the other side of the boat without surrendering the grip on the paddle with either hand. This movement is called "**crossing over.**" In this new position the same "eyeball" side of the paddle serves as the power side. There should be no turning of the paddle within the hands when crossing over. On this off-side of the boat the eyeball should now be looking back at the paddler.

Note: This cross-over is not considered "changing sides" because the hands never let go of their original grip. (Changing sides is defined not only as switching paddling sides but also reversing which hand is on the T-grip and

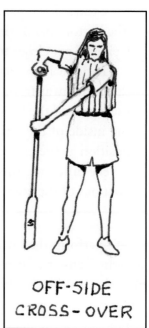

OFF-SIDE
CROSS-OVER

which on the shaft.) The off-side eddy turn stroke requires crossing over—different from "changing sides"—even though the paddle moves from one side of the boat to the other.

During the cross-over, the eyeball (power side of the blade) should constantly face the paddler. If the blade is lowered into the water on the off-side, directly out to the side (this requires twisting at the waist), the blade could be pulled toward the paddler to perform a *"cross draw"*—an advanced stroke that we will get to in time. But instead of drawing, move the blade bow-ward exactly as you did in the on-side eddy turn, and rotate the blade slightly so the eyeball appears to look at the bow end of the boat. It is this rotation that feels counter-intuitive to beginners. It must be inculcated into each paddler by lots of practice.

---

### Off-Side Right and Wrong
If done correctly, the rotation causes the thumb of the top hand to point forward. If done incorrectly, the top hand's thumb points back at the paddler.

---

Once again, both arms should be extended—almost straight. The blade should remain static throughout the turn. Once a student has properly demonstrated the stroke, have her then practice it while kneeling in a canoe on land.

"So, what am I doing during the eddy turn?" asks the stern paddler.

After sprinting and initiating the turn with a last-second draw or pry, the stern paddler has only one active job: to lean into the turn. But he should always be prepared to perform a low brace in case the boat tries to capsize to his on-side. (The bow paddler has the same responsibility for the other side of the boat.) The stern paddler must also be prepared to perform forward strokes if, after turning, the canoe tries to drift downstream out of the eddy.

## Practice, Practice

Sometimes, after so much inculcation to lean downstream, a student forgets which way to lean inside an eddy. Leaning the wrong way is almost certainly a recipe for a capsize. To help students with this confusion, compare this leaning to their habit on a bicycle.

No matter how many times your students practice these turning strokes on land, be prepared for incorrect shaft rotations on the river. Reinforce the "eyeball" imagery.

# Capsizing

"What happens if we do turn over?" someone asks. The students laugh, but—more than likely—everyone secretly wants to ask this question. First of all, assure your wards that everyone capsizes while learning whitewater. Because you have chosen a safe river, the consequences of capsizing are minimized. But this is the time to instill in your budding canoeists an attention to safety after turning over.

If the water is swift and more than mid-shin-deep, do not try to stand up! With a foot jammed between rocks, people have drowned in two feet of fast water. Instead of standing, assume the whitewater survival float position as described below.

## The Whitewater Survival Float

If a canoe capsizes, students are abruptly introduced to the turbulence and cold shock of a mountain stream. Because a capsized canoe is heavy, beginners should move away from the boat and assume the safest body position: body horizontal, belly-up, feet downstream. Teachers can maneuver their boats so as to be nearby should a floater need assistance. It should be the job of other teams to help retrieve paddles or other gear loose in the water. The floaters should wait until they reach calmer waters, flop onto their bellies, and swim perpendicularly for the closer shore. Once the students are safe, teachers and other students can work together to push the boat toward the same shore. All participants should wear a lifejacket.

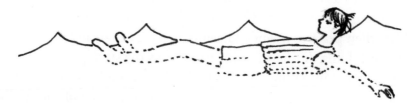

 ## Dry Whitewater Survival Float

Learn this position on land first. Sit down on the ground next to the river as you face downstream. Lie back, and extend your arms like a human cross. In the river, stroking with these outstretched arms will help to keep your feet downstream. By maintaining this position, a floater will hit obstacles first with his feet.

In the river it's not as easy to keep the hips high, but doing so will prevent hitting a rock with a tail bone. Legs should be slightly bent, prepared for fending off obstacles. When you do hit something with your feet, push around it, and then by using your arms get back into the feet-downstream position to be ready for the next obstacle.

### Wet Whitewater Survival Float

It is best to practice the actual survival float voluntarily in the river before it becomes a necessity. Choose a reasonable current for your students to perform this float in water. Ten to twenty yards downstream a teacher should stand with a throw-rope, to be used only if the student has trouble swimming. Ten to fifteen yards below that teacher, place another adult with a throw-rope to serve as a backup.

From a defined starting place, only one student should float at a time. At the teacher's signal, a student should get into the current, stretch out on his back, feet downstream, and arms out to his side, keeping all his body near the surface.

After floating for ten to twenty yards, as soon as the water slows or when common sense dictates, the floater should flop onto his belly and swim for shore in a line perpendicular to the current (the fastest route out of the current). Or, if the river is sufficiently shallow at that point (below mid-shin), stand up and walk out.

### Throw-Rope Practice

Now repeat the float with instructions to be "rescued" by a rope. When the rope is thrown just downstream of a floater, she should grab it with both hands, flop onto her belly, and take a deep breath. When the rope straightens, the floater might dip underwater momentarily. Then she gets a free ride as the teacher hauls her in.

## Canoe Rescue

On beginner whitewater trips, the leader should be responsible for retrieving any capsized boat, paddles, and other gear floating in the water. As the students become more experienced, they will learn to hold onto their paddles, swim their capsized boat to shore, and secure all their gear inside the boat so it will not scatter. The leader's first priority is to ensure that both paddlers safely get out of the current. Some students (who are showing competency in their strokes) can help by picking up floating articles that have spilled. As soon as the two floating paddlers are safe, the leader should go after their swamped canoe.

### Boat Rescue

Moving a boat filled with water is a Herculean task, so it is best to deal with an empty boat. The easiest boat rescue is performed on top of another canoe (solo or tandem), just as it is done on the lake. Turn the swamped boat completely upside-down and then lift one end of the inverted canoe over both gunnels of the rescuing boat. While doing this, position the capsized boat perpendicular to the rescuing boat. Slide the boat on top of the rescuing boat until it is balanced out of the water. Then carefully flip it upright on top of the rescuers' gunnels and slide the canoe back into the water. This task does require strength. If you, the leader, cannot perform this feat, here is your reason to paddle tandem with an experienced canoeist strong enough to accomplish the task.

This rescue technique is more easily done if gear is not strapped into the swamped boat, which is why I have not suggested any concerted tie-downs inside students' boats.

*Quickened by the white splash and dash, my life is the moment . . . the roar is my fear.*

*—First Hymn for Warwoman Creek* by M. Warren

## CHAPTER 20

# Discretion—Keeping the Journey Safe

The teamwork of tandem paddlers becomes all-important on the river, and each member of the team has unique responsibilities. The bow paddler is better positioned to scout a path ahead on the water. He initiates a change of course to avoid an obstacle, and the stern paddler follows his lead. The stern paddler is better positioned to time her stroke with her partner's, this synchronization resulting in more effective maneuvering of the canoe. The better a team paddles, the safer their river trip.

Of course, no one can guarantee complete safety on any river, but a trip leader can greatly reduce the possibility of accident by being attentive to six factors:

1. Choose a familiar section of river with rapids that are appropriate for the skill level of your students. This section should contain no strainers or large hydraulics unless both are easily avoided.
2. Learn the surrounding area in the event of an emergency (how to hike out; where to find help).
3. Carry drinking water, first aid, and safety equipment (listed below).
4. Be physically adept at getting yourself to any place on the river where help might be needed. If not you, find a strong, experienced, adult paddler to accompany your class.
5. Have an adult in your group who is experienced enough with whitewater to foresee what could go wrong in any given rapid.
6. Communicate with your students, so they know what to expect at any given point on the trip.

## Safety Equipment

For you, the leader, I recommend a list of gear to carry faithfully, either in a dry bag or secured in your boat. As history has taught us, it is best to be prepared not for what you *expect* to happen . . . but for what *could* happen.

1. Matches/lighter in a waterproof container. Include with this a small bundle of reliable kindling, such as lighter wood (strips of Virginia pine). A wet student is susceptible to hypothermia even in spring and summer on an overcast day.
2. Injector for insect sting, hyper-allergic reaction. Adult and child sizes.
3. Extra wool sweaters and caps, even in summer.
4. First-aid kit and the knowledge of how to use its components.
5. A throw-rope and the skill to use it. An adjunct to the rope includes a few carabiners (rock climber's metal clips) and the knowledge of how to use these to rescue a pinned boat. River rescue seminars and books are available at outfitters' stores.
6. Flotation airbag inside each canoe to make a capsized canoe easier to rescue.
7. Plenty of drinking water in case someone depletes his supply.
8. Spare paddles (one spare per every other boat).
9. A map and compass (or knowledge of the area) so you know in which direction to travel for help should the trip be forced into an evacuation by land.
10. A knowledge of your students' medical conditions so you know what you are dealing with should someone fall prey to his malady.
11. A flashlight.
12. Duct tape.
13. Sangfroid.

The last item above is an intangible . . . but important. I suppose only a wealth of wilderness experience grooms this in leaders. It is the ability to think rationally and instill calmness in a challenging situation. The students will look to the teacher for that timbre of calm and confidence that dispels panic.

## Looking for Danger

Early in my career of teaching canoeing, I led a group of twelve-year-old summer campers who had never taken a river trip. After two weeks of training on a lake, they were eager to embark on moving water. Halfway through that journey we came to the only rapid of note that we would encounter that day. It was a wide shelf of rock with a five-foot drop. It offered two possible routes—one on each extreme side of the river. I had run both sides on previous visits and knew that the steep right side required a quick turn too demanding for my beginners, so I instructed the class to beach their canoes on the left shore, where we got out of our boats to scout the more reasonable side where the rapid was sloped.

To all the campers the rapid appeared harmless. It involved a left turn at its entrance, but the water was slow there, putting the needed maneuver well within the capability of my young paddlers. From there, the rapid was full of standing waves but straightforward. There the water tumbled down a rollercoaster chute of swift water that everyone was anxious to run.

I looked at the rapid through the eyes of my twelve-year-old wards and decided that the entrance was the most problematic part. After passing through a "gateway" of two rocks, if a team did not turn their boat left, their canoe would drift sideways in the faster water of the chute. Partway down this flume the first standing waves were large enough to capsize a boat if the paddlers leaned the wrong way. I decided that if a canoe was going to turn over, it would probably be there.

I had run this rapid dozens of times prior to this trip. But on that day, because of my responsibility for the campers, I looked more intently at the riverbed to see what caused those waves. Beneath the blur of moving water and just upstream of the waves, something caught my eye . . . something I had not noticed before this day. Two feet below the surface, a wide flat rock slanted upstream. Deep shadow showed on its upstream side, revealing that it was undercut—like the partially opened door of a storm cellar. The shadowed pocket that it made appeared to be a perfect size to hold a body.

As my assistant shepherded the campers back into their boats, I made my way out into the river and stood in hip-deep water next to that shadow. Five boats came through and cruised passed me, each team screaming the requisite cries of victory after making the needed maneuver for a successful run. It was the sixth canoe that fulfilled the prophecy of my what-could-go-wrong theory. These paddlers reacted sluggishly in the rapid's entrance and found themselves turned sideways in the chute. Seeing the big waves waiting for them, they followed their older instinct to lean away from a problem (they leaned upstream) and quickly capsized. The last thing I saw as they turned over was the wide-open flash of surprised eyes. The boat rode up the waves upside down and tumbled down the chute. Behind it a single head bobbed up, and the rapid washed both boat and swimmer through and out of the turbulence.

Downstream where the others waited, my assistant waded into the current to retrieve boat and swimmer. I waited a long two seconds for the other camper's head to surface. I knew that he might be under the canoe, but when the assistant flipped over the boat no one appeared.

I looked into the shadow underwater and saw a small patch of bright orange. Here, perhaps, was one of the reasons that manufacturers made brightly colored lifejackets!

Taking two long steps, I reached down through the rushing current, grabbed a handful of lifejacket and pulled against the current. Up came the missing paddler.

When I looked into the young boy's fearful eyes, I thanked God I had been standing right there in the river beside the undercut ledge.

It's easy to imagine another version of this story: I am waiting below in my boat, ready to recover anyone who takes a spill . . . perhaps chasing the canoe to help the second paddler get out from under it. I can see myself flipping the boat upright, finding it empty, and quickly scanning a very desolate surface of the river. From that perspective I would never have been able to see the boy pinned under the rock.

That near tragedy happened over forty years ago. I recently received a phone call from the camper who had been wedged under that rock with all that water pressure holding him in place. He's now a chef in a restaurant, his only pressure getting the food orders out in time from the kitchen.

Plan your beginner river trip with this strict stipulation: The place you choose as a put-in (the beginning of your river trip) should be based upon an absence of river complications for the first half-mile of the journey. Give your students ample time to get accustomed to the never-ending current before any demands of necessary maneuvering are thrown at them. Starting them out on a section of river too difficult for their level of training can be terrifying and ruin their chances at returning to the river.

## Switching Sides

Switching paddling sides (changing sides *and* hand grips) to resolve an immediate problem is not recommended in the action of whitewater. Why? Because in that instant when one hand lets go of the paddle (for a new grip) there is a momentary vulnerability, a split-second in which the paddler can be caught off guard by a sudden lurch of the boat. Furthermore, if one member of a team switches sides, he can no longer provide a low brace on his assigned side to prevent a capsize. Therefore, each team member of every tandem team should make a commitment to paddling one side for the day.

On another day, it would be an excellent idea for these same team members to switch assigned sides for the day. There is an enviable practicality in being an ambidextrous paddler. There are times when entering a rapid with the paddle committed to a particular side holds a definite advantage. A paddler equally adept at right- and left-side paddling will never find himself at a disadvantage.

Though *switching* sides is bad form, *crossing over* is not. A cross-stroke is often a necessity, especially for a bow paddler making an eddy turn to the off-side. The cross-eddy-turn-stroke "winds up" the torso like a spring for a very powerful maneuver.

## *The Eddy Turn Revisited*

The greatest safety factor you can give to your student paddlers is maneuverability. The more efficiently they can move their boats across the water, the more they will stay out of harm's way. Perhaps no maneuver is so important as being able to turn a boat into an eddy and "stick it." Catching an eddy has saved many a paddler from drifting into a problem for which he is not prepared.

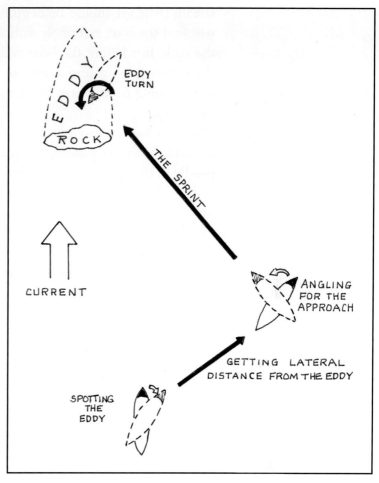

As a review from Chapter 19, listed below are the individual steps involved in an eddy turn.

1.  **Get to a starting position laterally distant from the eddy.** This lateral distance varies with current speed, but let's average it to three to ten yards for the initial lessons. Later, shorten that distance when students have learned to accelerate faster.

2.  **Set the angle for the sprint.** Positioning the boat for cross-current momentum should be performed well above the eddy (two to three boat-lengths as a minimum) so there is plenty of time to execute the approach to the eddy. The faster the current, the farther upstream the paddlers should initiate this angle. Set the angle at 45 degrees by a partial draw or pry spin.

3.  **Sprint for the eddy.** Establish a cross-current (diagonal) momentum and maintain the angle. At the beginning of the sprint the boat should be aimed at some point upstream of the rock, because the current is always pushing the boat downstream. The current itself will make the adjustment of finally having the boat enter the eddy and miss the rock. Time the maneuver so the canoe enters the eddy as high upstream in the eddy as possible.

The cross-current momentum that a team establishes is vital, because the canoe must aggressively leave the downstream current and penetrate the diametric eddy current. It won't happen on its own; the paddlers must make it happen. Besides the timing, the most problematic aspect of the sprint is that—as everyone learned on the lake—paddling very hard encourages the boat to veer off course. Therefore, much attention must be paid to keeping the boat on the 45-degree approach angle. Tandem teammates must constantly communicate as to which partial spin is needed to maintain the angle.

4. **Establish the turn just before entering the eddy.** If, at the end of the sprint, the canoe is losing its proper approach angle and just starting to turn downstream (when it should be beginning its turn upstream in the eddy) the team will find the boat extremely difficult—if not impossible—to turn back toward the rock. Just before the boat reaches the eddy, the stern paddler can initiate the turn by performing a draw or pry. For a stern-lefty turning left: pry. For a lefty turning right: draw. For a righty turning left: draw. For a righty turning right: pry.

5. **Make the turn.** As soon as the bow paddler can reach across the eddy line into the eddy with her paddle, she plants the proper turning stroke and holds the paddle in that position (statically). At the moment that the bow penetrates the eddy, both paddlers must lean and tilt the boat to the inside of the turn, just like on a bicycle, until the boat swings around to point upstream.

6. **Hold the boat in the eddy.** As soon as the boat has turned upstream, both paddlers may need to use forward strokes to hold the boat in place. Correction strokes may also be necessary to keep the boat pointed upstream.

## *Coaching the Eddy Turn*

As the teacher, you'll want to be able to tell your students exactly why they are failing to catch a given eddy. Use the same eddy over and over, so the students are not facing new variables with each try.

If the site you have chosen does not allow the students an easy way to paddle upstream for repetitive runs, instruct them to walk their boats in shallow water. To help you to pinpoint which part of their technique is causing them to fail, consider the suggestions on the opposite page.

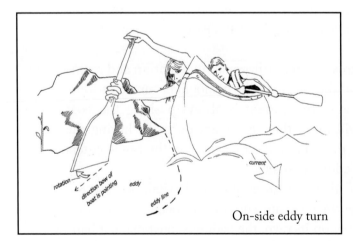

On-side eddy turn

Off-side eddy turn

---

**Common Errors in Attempting the Eddy Turn**

1. Starting too close (when well upstream) to the side of the river to which the turn will be made.
2. Starting the sprint too late. (Hitting the eddy too low or missing it entirely.)
3. Not aggressively sprinting . . . thinking that by pointing the boat at the eddy, it will magically get there.
4. Losing the 45-degree angle during the sprint.
5. Bow person rotating the paddle shaft the wrong way for the turning stroke.

---

### The Learning Eddy

Choose a large eddy with an unobstructed approach and a well-defined eddy line where students can practice eddy turns and then easily paddle or tow their boats back upstream for repetitive attempts. Coach them on each of the points in the previous two boxes. Practice until every team has demonstrated a tight turn close to the boulder or jut of land that forms the eddy.

Going back for another try

### A River of Endless Eddies

As you continue on your river journey, point out every feasible eddy (well downstream) and challenge your class to catch it one boat at a time. Those who wait their turn must hover in the current or park in another eddy.

### Eddy Turning without a Turning Stroke!

A paddle-less turn is an excellent practice for beginners, as long as the eddy being used is a wide one. Allow one canoe at a time to attempt this turn by having a perfect approach and then raising their paddles at the sound of your whistle. (Make this whistle blast occur in the instant before the boat enters the eddy.) Both paddlers should make the proper lean and boat-tilt as they hold their paddles horizontally before their bodies, prepared to execute a low brace should the canoe begin to capsize his or her way.

In this exercise it is important that the stern paddler's last stroke in the current (draw or pry) initiates the proper turn of the boat. If the sprint leads the team too high or low in the current (toward the rock or below the eddy), abort the attempt by three sharp whistle blasts. That team should return upstream to get in line for another attempt.

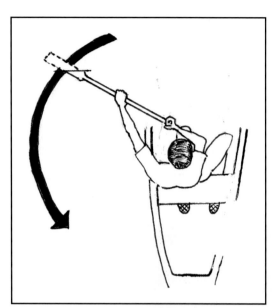

Path of the forward sweep stroke

# The Sweep Stroke

Now it is time to add a new stroke to the paddlers' repertoire. We will first consider an eddy turn in a direction that is an on-side turn for the bow paddler. Just before the boat reaches the eddy, the stern person—who is paddling on the side away from the eddy—has been initiating the turning of the boat by a draw stroke. There is another stroke that will help him turn the boat and at the same time thrust the boat forward into the eddy. This is a modified forward stroke called a *"forward sweep."*

In this stroke the blade pushes water to the rear while following the path of a large letter C—with the open side of the C toward the boat. The shaft of the paddle should be slanted (rather than vertical) for this stroke. The forward sweep maintains forward momentum while providing a turning force.

### Using the Forward Sweep (Stern Paddlers Only)

On the next attempt at an eddy turn to the stern paddler's off-side, inform each stern paddler that she will not use a draw to initiate the turn just before entering the eddy. Instead, she will employ a forward sweep in the main current. Then she will immediately lean inside the turn with her paddle held at the ready for a low brace (should the boat try to capsize to her on-side).

## A New Stroke for "Sticking" (Staying in the Eddy)

Because the sprint includes downstream momentum as well as toward-the-eddy momentum, a canoe that has just turned into an eddy might slide downstream out of the eddy if the paddlers do not make the turn "stick." Such an unintentional drift could become a predicament if some complication in the river awaits downstream. As mentioned earlier, a few forward strokes may be necessary. But for an off-side eddy turn the bow paddler might want to use a *cross-forward stroke*. (A stern paddler never uses this stroke.)

This stroke is made on the off-side, with the paddle crossed over and the paddler's body twisted at the waist. The power side of the blade pushes water to the rear. To recover the paddle for another stroke, rotate it 90 degrees so the blade's power side faces the boat and then quickly feather it out of the water toward the front. The cross-forward stroke provides an immediate thrust higher into the eddy without losing time in crossing the paddle back to the on-side. More power can be applied to the stroke by leaning body weight down onto the paddle as it pushes water toward the stern.

<u>Using the Cross-Forward Stroke (Bow Paddlers Only)</u>

On the next attempt at an eddy turn to the bow paddler's off-side, after the turn points the boat upriver at the boulder, ask each bow paddler to keep his paddle on the off-side and convert his turning stroke into a cross-forward stroke to help keep the canoe in the eddy.

# *Peeling Out from the Eddy*

Exiting the eddy is very much like a condensed version of entering it. First, the boat must be angled in the eddy toward the current. (This is nearly the same angle that was used for entry. The degree of angle is determined by current speed.) If not enough angle is used (pointed upstream too much), the boat will be pushed back into the eddy by the main current. If too much angle (say, perpendicular to the current) the chance for capsizing upstream is high!

Once angled in the eddy, the paddlers must sprint toward the main current using forward strokes. As soon as the bow paddler can reach the main current with her paddle blade, she performs the same stroke she had used to make the turn into the eddy . . . but this time to turn the boat downstream. Both paddlers lean and tilt their boat *downstream* just as they enter the main current. The arc of reentering the current can be wide or tight, all depending upon the angle of entry and the discretion of the bow paddler (how much muscle she uses in the turning stroke). This maneuver is called *"peeling out."*

**Information for advanced paddlers:** In river currents of great volume and velocity, peeling out of an eddy can be no mean task. Fast water rushes past boulders with such force that the level of the eddy (filling up the space behind the rock) can be from several inches to more than a foot lower than the main current. For a peel out this necessitates climbing up a sheer wall of water to return to the main current. It's like trying to mount a sidewalk curb while riding in a child's wagon. As if this were not vexing enough, the eddy level can fluctuate in surges. Look for miniature versions of this phenomenon where a partially submerged rock interrupts a fast flow of water.

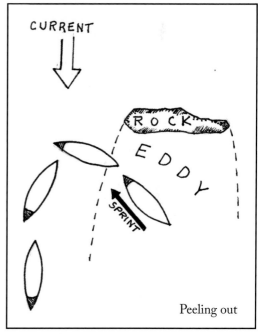

Peeling out

<u>Peeling Out</u>

A perfect site for peel out practice awaits where two boulders sit side by side in the river with a twenty-foot-wide tongue of current between them. First, challenge a team to catch one of the eddies and then ferry from that eddy to the other. Next, have them ferry back to the original eddy.

Once they have shown good control in the ferrying, have them peel out from one eddy without touching the other. Then they should paddle back upstream to perform a peel out from the other eddy.

 ### A Tighter Peel Out

Choose an eddy with a narrower current (say, ten feet wide) running past it. Here a peel out must be made in a tight arc. The bow paddler can speed up the turn by performing a strong draw stroke on the downstream side. If that bow person is paddling on the off-side of the turn, he can perform a *cross-draw*, a stroke made only from the bow. This stroke is not static like the eddy turning stroke. With the torso twisted, pull water straight in from beside the thigh toward the thigh. Before the paddle can contact the boat, feather it out the front. Repeat as needed.

*And the thunder rolls and the clouds portend, and the river knows we shall begin again.*

—from *Amicalola* by M. Warren

## CHAPTER 21

# Now Let There Be Otters—Advanced Maneuvers, at Play on the River

## *TROUT*

My paddling friends and I have enjoyed many hours of a game called "TROUT." It's basically like HORSE in basketball. TROUT improves any player's paddling skills. And it's a fish-barrel of fun. Like slalom racing, it asks you to try certain feats that would not ordinarily come up in the process of running of a river.

### Playing TROUT

On a river trip, paddlers take turns naming a challenge as they progress downstream through the rapids. The namer specifies the terms by which an invented maneuver must be carried out. Here's an example: As tandem teams sit in an eddy with a good view of the current, team #1 begins by explaining a challenge:

"See that rock across the current that is topped by a patch of moss? From this eddy you have to peel out wide enough to turn your boat downstream without touching the rock but close enough that one paddler in the boat can touch the moss with a paddle."

Team #1 goes first. The others watch to see if the challengers successfully touch the moss. If they do, they remain letter-less.

Team #2 takes a turn. After they peel out, if neither can reach the moss, they earn the letter "T" in the word "TROUT."

Team #3 peels out too wide and bumps the rock with the bow of their boat. This team also earns a "T."

All the other tandem teams take their turns, each trying not to earn a letter.

After all teams have had a try, it's team #2's turn to name a challenge. All beach their boats and stand on the riverbank to scout a rapid they are about to run. Team #2 offers this challenge:

"You have to enter the rapid backward on the left side of the big boulder, put your stern in the eddy behind the boulder, and spin 180 degrees. Then continue down the rest of the rapid forward, and catch the small eddy on river right."

And so it goes. Throughout the next hour or two, whichever team first spells out the word "TROUT" is the loser. The game is over.

### Reverse Hovering

Ask your class to hover without spinning their boats to face upstream. Not only is the feat more challenging to maintain the proper angle, but it is also more difficult to maintain position without drifting downstream. Lots of communication is needed between teammates. Point out an object on shore and let this serve as a landmark. A boat should remain lateral to its assigned marker throughout the exercise.

### Paddling with a Robot

Assign a maneuver to be carried out—such as catching a particular eddy that is within sight downstream. Instruct the bow paddler to do nothing at all unless commanded by the stern paddler. Each command given warrants only one stroke from the robot. If an incorrect stroke is ordered, so be it. It must be performed.

### Paddling with the Other Robot

Repeat the above exercise, but this time the stern paddler must be the mute robot who obeys commands from the bow paddler.

### Reverse Ferry

The principles are all the same as the forward ferry, in which paddlers face upstream; but this time paddlers face downstream. Most challenging is trying this from an eddy. Entering the current requires aggressive paddling and attention to boat angle. Most beginners who attempt this move are spun immediately by the main current as they exit the eddy (performing a backward peel out). With time they learn to pick up speed and use only a slight ferry angle when they enter the current from the eddy.

Here is the reason this last maneuver is difficult: The stern paddler is closer to her end of the boat than the bow paddler is to his; therefore, the stern lies deeper in the water and receives more push from the current at the moment the boat leaves the eddy.

### Dropping In to Visit a Hydraulic

For this exercise provide helmets for your advanced students. Choose a very small hole (hydraulic) for a team to drop into while their boat is broached. The hole should be about as long as the boat and the water should be deep enough to preclude injury from rocks should a boat capsize. The trick of remaining upright is to tilt the boat downstream immediately when entering the hole. Both paddlers must lean. The teammate whose paddle is on the downstream side has the responsibility of keeping the boat upright with defensive low braces. The other paddler remains prepared to use a low brace if the canoe begins to capsize upstream.

Repeat the exercise with the boat turned 180 degrees so the other partner is in charge of the downstream low brace.

### Self-Rescue

There comes a time when your whitewater students should become more autonomous. At that point, when a capsize occurs, there should be no personal, scattered items floating down the river. All gear should be fastened inside the canoe . . . **but not in such a way that ropes or webbing can create a trap for a body**. It is the capsized canoeists' job to hold on to their paddles. When a calm section of river provides the opportunity, all tandem teams should help with the monumental task of "tug-boating" a swamped canoe to shore.

As a practice, swamp a boat in a large, calm pool in the river and challenge your class to get the canoe to shore.

## *The Vacuum in a Capsized Boat*

If you rent canoes that are not outfitted with flotation bags, rescuing is more difficult but still manageable. A curious phenomenon of physics surprises students who try to lift a swamped canoe (without airbags) that is upside down in the water. If the boat is lifted straight up (hull toward the sky), a vacuum of air might remain inside the canoe. This bubble exerts a powerful sucking resistance against being lifted out of the water. Even though the canoe is upside down, the rescuers are having to lift the volume of water that is inside the boat. The pocket of air between the trapped water and the hull refuses to be expanded and so it sucks that enormous volume of water up with it as the boat is raised. All that is needed is a rotation of the boat as if to right it. The trapped air escapes and the pressure is released. Then as the tilted boat is easily lifted, the water trapped inside empties.

### The Invisible Giant Sucker

For an impressive exercise in physics, capsize an empty canoe in two feet of water, leaving a small pocket of air inside. Position every student in your class around the gunnels and have them lift straight up without tilting the boat. Watch them attempt to out-wrestle the suction of the air pocket. When the exercise has failed, tilt the boat enough to allow the air to escape and then all lift together. Easy!

### Limited Strokes

Choose a place on the river with a good eddy and an easy way to paddle back upstream above the eddy for multiple attempts. Begin with a number of strokes that you deem ample for catching the eddy from a starting point.

"You and your partner may use nine strokes (each) total to get into the eddy and stick. You must paddle in a synchronized fashion so that we can count out loud for you. If a stroke is made alone by a single paddler, it counts as one of the nine. The sustained turning stroke by the bow paddler counts only as one stroke, unless that turning stroke turns into a forward stroke. In that case, we add to the count each time a forward stroke is made."

Let everyone try it. You, the leader, should count the strokes loud enough to be heard by the team presently making an attempt. After several teams have accomplished the challenge, get all the boats back to the starting point again. Try the same goal again with eight strokes. And so on. See how low the count can go.

### Canoe Stalking

Paddle a calm section of river while making absolutely no sound. Learn to enter the blade into the water without a liquid disturbance. Do this by moving the blade as if for a stroke even as you enter it. Strokes should be made so slowly that water does not swirl noisily around the blade. The paddle shaft should never touch the gunnel. The blade should never touch the hull. Use the thumb (carefully) like a pad between shaft and boat. Exit the blade from the water and hold the blade low to the water's surface to allow silent dripping.

Make all movements fluid and extremely slow. While in this stalking mode, whenever you spot wildlife downstream, you'll want to have a silent and subtle signal that lets everyone know that a real-life stalking session is beginning. All paddlers should quietly lower themselves in their canoes so their boats look more like floating logs than human watercraft. (See *Volume 3* for canoe stalking stories.)

### No-Hands Ferry

Challenge your students to ferry from one eddy to another nearby eddy positioned laterally across the current . . . all without a stroke in the current. Start with a ten-foot-wide current between boulders. Paddlers start by picking up speed in an eddy, being attentive to the angle at which they will enter the current. At the instant that the bow touches the eddy line both team members must lean and lift their paddles out of the water.

No exercise teaches the ferry angle better than this one. On their first attempts, the chances are high that their boat will be turned quickly by the current as they peel out bow-first downstream. On a second try, when they try to counter that tendency, they might over-compensate with not enough angle. In such a case, they will stall for a moment and then be pushed back into the starting eddy. Eventually, they will adopt aggressive strokes for the precious few they are allowed in the eddy and learn the perfect angle for their boat.

You can increase the difficulty of this drill by choosing a site with a wider current between eddies—the target eddy a little downstream of the starting eddy.

When the students are allowed to use their paddles again for a ferry, they will feel more adept at the skill. Ferrying will become easy.

### No-Hands Peel Out

Repeat the above exercise, but now the goal is to peel out rather than ferry. This exercise will bring home the necessity for leaning downstream. If the exit strokes in the eddy are not powerful, the boat will end up back in that same eddy. To succeed with this exercise, the boat should completely exit the eddy and continue downstream with the bow leading.

### Switching Sides

After accomplishing any of the exercises in this chapter, ask the tandem teams to reverse their paddling sides and repeat the challenge. As you will see, in many cases it is like starting over with a brand new pair of students. But learning to be whitewater-ambidextrous is a great asset to any canoeist.

### Switching Places

Again, repeat any accomplished maneuver covered in previous exercises, but first have the paddlers trade places in the boat. Being skilled in either end of the boat and on either side of the boat is the ultimate versatility for a tandem canoeist.

### Slalom Course on the River

If you can obtain permission to string wires (about eight feet high) across a section of river, you can create one of the most exhilarating playgrounds known to river runners—a slalom course. Even if there are no rapids present, the introduction of current to the slalom concept is exciting and instructional.

The entire production makes a great class project. Each canoe team can make one or two slalom gates. Here's what's needed for a gate:

**1. Gate cross bar**—One three-inch by three-quarter-inch **board** that measures about five feet long. Drill a **hole** in each end to accommodate a **shower curtain hook**. These hooks attach the gate to and slide along the wires strung across the river. Another hole is drilled in each end for tying a string with which to hang a gate pole. These **pole holes** should be separated from one another by the width of your canoes at mid-ship plus fourteen inches.

**2. Two gate poles**—one-and-a-quarter-inch PVC **pipes** (or trimmed **bamboo** canes) that measure five feet long. Drill a **hole** completely through at the top end and insert and **glue** a six-inch-long **wood dowel** as a crosspiece. Tie one end of a four-foot length of nylon string to a pole under its crosspiece. Tie the other end to one of the cross bar's pole holes. By twirling the pole from the water (with the rope winding beneath the crosspiece), you can adjust the hang of the pole from a canoe.

**3. Spanning wires**—Purchase coils of multi-strand, three-sixteenths-of-an-inch-thick wire long enough to stretch across the river. When attaching to trees on the riverbank, use sections of scrap garden hose for padding to protect the trunks. If trees are not available, erect pressure-treated four-inch-by-four-inch posts on the banks.

By rearranging the positions of the gates as you slide them on the wires, you can create a great many courses on the same stretch of river. Adjust the pole heights so each pole hangs six inches above the water. Hold races, timing teams by stopwatch from an upstream starting place at the shoreline to a finish line well below the gates. A finish line judge can wave a flag at the moment a boat crosses, signaling the starting judge to stop her watch. Position judges for each gate to keep a tally of penalties for touched poles.

If a pole is touched by a boat, paddle, or body, add ten seconds. If the same pole is touched in the same negotiation of that gate, another penalty is not added. If the other pole is touched, another penalty of ten seconds is added. If one or both paddlers' bodies do not travel through the gate (between the poles), add fifty seconds for a missed gate.

Of course, beaver can maneuver through a whitewater slalom course without need of a boat, but they would have more fun in a canoe.

Racers are always seeking maneuvers and new horizons of strength to improve their time and reduce their penalties. Slalom boosts their skill levels probably faster than any other exercise on the water. This sport will perhaps hook at least a few students for life. Their exposure to slalom racing is a cornucopia of gifts: strength, ambition, grace, self-esteem, salubrious time spent in Nature, and the joy of knowing how to do something well. Starting them in their early years might be fortuitously life-changing. As we all know, many of the greatest athletes were inducted into their sports in their formative years. One of my young friends eventually paddled a decked boat in the Olympics representing the United States. He began slalom on a pond behind my cottage. Our course was comprised of two bamboo gates hanging above flatwater.

## Wildwater Racing

The other half of whitewater racing combines strength and endurance with paddling skills and an ability to read water. In the racing world this course might be four to eight miles, but the distance could be whatever you wish . . . even one hundred yards. From a starting point, give a countdown and send teams off in one-minute intervals. You'll need cellphones or synchronized watches to measure time elapsed for each boat. Judges at the end of the course mark the time at which a boat crosses the finish line.

Wildwater racers learn a great deal about how water flows. They find those paths where the water is swiftest and without obstacles. They learn to ride the fine line at the edge of eddies and standing waves. Few upper body activities are so beneficial to the cardiovascular system.

*"But how do you know which way to go?" said the beaver kit.*
*"You've got to read the water," replied old Gnaw Tooth.*
*"Read it?" asked the young one. "You mean like a story in a book?"*
*The aged beaver leaned in close. "Exactly like that . . . except that while you're reading, be sure to be looking a few paragraphs ahead."*

—Robert B. Beaver from *Conversations in the Upper Room*

## CHAPTER 22

# Reading the River— Pathfinding on Water

My dog Elly would not willingly jump into water if her life depended on it . . . or so I believed. But once at a canoe race, after I had left her high on the bank near the starter as the countdown began, all that changed. When I was given a "go" I put in three powerful strokes to get up to speed fast. By my fourth stroke I heard the spectators on the shore burst out in laughter. By reflex I looked back. Elly had made a spectacular dive off the steep bank and was heartily swimming after me like a hungry otter after a rainbow trout.

Elly had a thing about canoes—or more specifically . . . my canoe. Though she detested getting wet, anytime I knelt in a lake canoe in her presence, she jumped in and took a stalwart stance in the bow as if she was prepared to cross the Bering Strait with me in mid-winter.

And so I began taking her on some of my river trips—first on flatwater (without rapids), next graduating to class I and then class II whitewater. By the time she had developed her "river legs" and was braving class III rapids, I am dead-serious when I tell you this: She had learned to read water. (She drew a discretionary line at class IV rapids and walked around those.)

When we descended whitewater streams, her attention was riveted straight ahead at the oncoming rapids, her ears up, mouth closed. I never was able to see her eyes, but I'll bet they were sharp and bright as she inspected the route ahead.

When we approached an eddy her stance widened and she began the correct lean into the turn. If a diagonal wave loomed in our path, she braced for the lateral shift. When a drop was in store for us, she crouched. Short of calling out instructions, she did everything a captain could expect from a lookout in the crow's nest. She never even barked at me for hitting a splashy wave at a bad angle.

The point of this is not to say: If a dog can learn to read water, so can you. The point is this: Reading water is not mystical. It's visual. You just have to pay attention. With your ears up and mouth closed.

In the fourteen years we lived together, our boat never capsized—not while she was aboard. Much of this credit should go to Elly. She never leaned the wrong way. Nor did she scowl at me for choosing a bad route. In the calm stretches she enjoyed doing exactly what I enjoyed—admiring the scenery and watching for wildlife. So let's add another moral to her story—an aphorism that extends far beyond the banks of a river: Choose your partner carefully.

## *The Braille of Water*

The texture of a river's surface can deliver a wealth of information:

1. A section of myriad, very tiny waves or ripples that are cobbled closely together like pieces of a puzzle means very shallow water—a place where your canoe is likely to get stuck.
2. A V etched into the surface and pointing upstream denotes a shallow rock or other obstacle that is close enough to the surface to make its mark.
3. A larger V (with a vague V-point) pointed downstream marks a good passage between obstacles.
4. A steady "path of waves" (the waves being four inches tall or more) points out a deeper channel where one is less likely to get a canoe stuck. This route often has some whitewater as a part of its composition. In a shallow river, a canoeist is constantly looking for such a path.
5. When a ledge appears downstream as a horizon line in the water, two features can help locate the deeper passage when the river is shallow. A slight dip in the horizon line (a shallow depression) usually advertises a runnable channel. Whitewater below the drop denotes good water volume spilling over that spot in the ledge.
6. Diagonal waves can bump your bow to one side just as if you had run into a sidewalk curb from the street. If the wave is breaking and curling back to form a diagonal trough of whitewater (a long narrow hole), the bump to one side can slow your boat and cause it to enter the hole sideways. If the paddler does not lean downstream, there is a good chance he will capsize upstream.

7. Holes (almost always "boiling" with white foam, but not in every "silty" instance) are caused by water plunging downward into a lower level of water. Large holes are generally avoided by canoeists unless their holding power provides part of the strategy for running a rapid.

8. When no surface textures give a clue and the river appears homogenous and flat, the outside of a bend usually provides the deepest channel on low-water days. At very high levels, the safer routes are found on the inside of bends. In high water, it might be best to avoid the outside current, which might swing your boat into the entrapping foliage hanging out from the bank.

Learning to read the unabridged literature of rivers takes years, but the basic signs listed above provide what you need to get started.

## *Standing Waves*

A series of large waves spaced by deep troughs is famous for sloshing water into an open canoe. While kayakers and other decked boaters can bulldoze through such formations with no more consequence than a fresh wake-up of cold mountain water in the face, a canoeist suffers this approach with water splashing into the boat. The added weight and the resultant decrease in maneuverability are a liability. There is a trick to running waves in a dry fashion.

First and easiest, if possible, skirt the waves on one side, riding the differential line between currents. This is often an eddy line. If being out in the waves is a necessity, tandem paddlers simply perform reverse strokes until their boat speed matches the current speed. The canoe will ride up and over the multiple crests without knifing through the waves and without taking on water.

However, keeping the boat aligned (pointed downstream) requires constant attention. Whenever a craft slows to the water's speed, boat control is sacrificed and the river takes over. The current constantly tries to turn the boat sideways; therefore, paddlers employing this technique are not only busy reverse stroking but also drawing and prying to maintain a boat position parallel to the current.

### Staying Dry in the Waves

When you locate a section of standing waves—these waves being at least two feet high—gather your group upstream on shore and empty all the water from all the boats. Each team attempts to run its canoe through the middle of the waves without taking on any water. At the bottom of the rapid, gather everyone together and measure the water in each boat to find the high-and-dry winner.

### Abdicating the Throne

After you and your class have discussed and experienced a number of these river-reading phenomena, let your students take turns leading the trip. Scout each rapid from shore and allow the new leaders to make the suggestions for the most prudent route. If the chosen route contains a potential for hidden danger, ask the proper questions that will bring that to light. If your tacit suggestions are not heeded, and if a threatening scenario lurks ahead, re-take your throne and protect your subjects by a benevolent dictatorship.

### Scouting and Planning

One of the most gratifying moments for a teacher in the evolution of a canoe class is watching and hearing the students discuss from shore a rapid that has not yet been run by them. First, let them assess the rapid without your input. Give them time to make a plan. Then let each team declare its intended route through the rapid. Once this is done, share your own insights about the rapid—especially any inherent dangers or problems—and discuss the downsides to some routes and the upsides of others. Drawings in the sand are very helpful. Describe those misadventures that are most likely to happen to unwary canoeists and give a name to each rock and wave and hole and eddy. Here are some examples of those names (young paddlers love to name rapids and their components):

"Backboard Rock" (one you expect a boat to bounce off of)
"BP Wave" (where a boat can pull in and fill up)
"Hungry Beaver Hydraulic" (which eats boats)
"Measles Twice Eddy" (something you'll never catch)
"Blind Alley" (a dead-end route that leads to getting stuck on rocks)
"Car Wash" (the outside of a bend where shrubs and trees on the bank would rake the boat and occupants)
"New Hairdo Salon" (a low branch under which paddlers must duck)

"Olympus Eddy" (only the strongest of paddlers will get into it)
"Broken Nose" (an underwater rock at the bottom of a drop)
"Tsunami Ambush" (a wave sure to splash water into a boat)

### Advanced Planning

After a good plan for running a rapid has been settled on by your students, point out a challenge for those who might like to meet it—like an eddy turn in the middle of the rapid . . . or going to the left of a certain rock instead of to the right. Give them more time to adjust plans and re-declare their routes.

*The water is wide . . . I can't cross over . . . and neither have I wings to fly.*
*Give me a boat that can carry two, and both shall row . . . my love and I.*

—Traditional song, author anonymous

# Epilogue—Twice in a Lifetime

One winter I traveled to the lower piedmont of Georgia to present environmental programs at a conference. During these four days, an unexpected break opened up from my duties, and I took the time to visit a nearby river. It was a cold day in January, just the kind of day I favor for exploring a new river, but without my boat and paddling gear I contented myself by walking the banks for a few miles just to see what I could see.

The river was wide, perhaps fifty yards from shore to shore. Unlike most wide rivers of the area—which tend to be flat and featureless—this stream caught me off-guard with its unique beauty. Dotting its surface was a maze of grassy islands, each green in the dead of winter, each a variation on a teardrop shape and no larger than the deck of a large sailboat. Though the river was not in flood, the grassy islands were submerged under a couple inches of water. But the grass grew over a foot above the water's surface and swayed with the current. I stood still and admired the scene for a long time. The movement of the grasses was hypnotic.

In the mountains, I had known two other streams with islands like these and had enjoyed drifting through the grass-lined channels of my choice. It had been dreamlike. The islands of grass opening before me had been like verdant clouds. The long blades of the grasses waved in the current as though to point the way for me.

On this winter day I wished for a canoe. I was like a kid staring through a shop window at the toy I wanted so badly for my birthday.

## *An Angel with a Flattened Tail*

Feeling that riverine lure, which had become a central theme of my life, I walked downstream and continued to admire the islands from a distance. As was my habit, I walked quietly, following the ever-present fisherman's trail, taking my steps softly so as not to alert wildlife. In less than a minute a thick stand of dead horseweed and goldenrods rustled to my right. I stopped and waited. Ten feet in front of me the weeds parted, and a dark, wet head poked out onto the trail.

Standing perfectly still, I watched a beaver—fresh from the river—waddle across the path. Only three yards away, the beautiful, dripping creature never looked my way. The wind flowed upstream, taking my scent away from the beaver. It had come from the river side of the path and now it disappeared into a tall stand of desiccated weeds that spread deeper into the floodplain.

Naturally, I followed.

It's not difficult to trail a beaver. As our largest rodent it is a cumbersome walker, and its eyesight is poor. This fellow-paddler made a lot of noise in the dry stems and leaves. Its tail worked back and forth, like a lazy scythe too dull for cutting. I stayed a few yards behind it walking in the trail it had blazed. My new guide never looked back.

Ahead of us was a low swale of land with something brightly reflecting light back at us. At the lip of the swale the beaver turned back toward the water and completed the last leg of a strange horseshoe-shaped trek that seemed without purpose. I stopped next to the depression in the land with my attention divided between the beaver and the treasure to which it had led me. When my unexpected guide left me and slipped back into the river, I stared down into the depressed area at a perfectly water-worthy canoe. It was an old aluminum model painted on the outside to simulate birch bark. Taking in the surprise of an unexpected gift, I laughed out loud.

The boat was almost full of water and listed a few degrees to one side under its shiny, lopsided deck of ice. Beneath the ice and gelid water lay a blanket of dead leaves from seasons past. I broke up the ice with a stick and splashed water out until I could lift one side and dump the remaining water and scrape out two inches of slimy leaves. I couldn't believe my luck. All I had to do now was fashion a paddle.

I looked around for a splintered tree, from which I hoped to carve a usable tool—something broad enough to push water. That was when I found the paddle. It was the kind you might find in a bait shop for six dollars, but a genuine canoe paddle nevertheless.

Some things are meant to be, I guess. I spent the few hours left to me exploring the channels out in the river. I've spent the many years since wondering about riverine serendipity, furry angels, and beaver-ine intervention.

# Suggested Reading

*Cherokee Bows and Arrows* by Al Herrin, White Bear Publishing; Tahlequah, Oklahoma.

*Bulletin of Primitive Technology* by The Society of Primitive Technology; Rexburg, Idaho.

*American Indian Archery* by Reginald and Gladys Laubin, University of Oklahoma; Norman, Oklahoma.

*Primitive Wilderness Living & Survival Skills* by John and Geri McPherson, Prairie Wolf; Randolph, Kansas.

**with gratitude for our conversations in the upper room**

Dr. Robert B. Beaver

Professor Emeritus of all things riverine, arboreal,

dental, mythological, and philosophical

# Index

Numbers in bold indicate photographs/illustrations.